CERTAIN CONCEALMENTS

A VOLUME IN THE SERIES
Becoming Modern: Studies in the Long Nineteenth Century

EDITED BY
Elizabeth A. Fay

CERTAIN CONCEALMENTS

Poe, Hawthorne,
and Early
Nineteenth-Century
Abortion

DANA MEDORO

UNIVERSITY OF MASSACHUSETTS PRESS
Amherst and Boston

Copyright © 2022 by University of Massachusetts Press
All rights reserved
Printed in the United States of America

ISBN 978-1-62534-647-6 (paper); 648-3 (hardcover)

Designed by Deste Roosa
Set in Bulmer MT, Agenda, and Schmale Mediaeval
Printed and bound by Books International, Inc.

Cover design by Rebecca Neimark, Twenty-Six Letters
Cover art: Classified advertisements from *New York Daily Herald*, and the *New York Sun*, c. January 1841. Courtesy of Library Company of Philadelphia.

Library of Congress Cataloging-in-Publication Data
Names: Medoro, Dana, 1967– author.
Title: Certain concealments : Poe, Hawthorne, and early nineteenth-century abortion / Dana Elizabeth Medoro.
Description: Amherst : University of Massachusetts Press, 2022. | Series: Becoming modern: studies in the long nineteenth century | Includes bibliographical references and index.
Identifiers: LCCN 2021054601 (print) | LCCN 2021054602 (ebook) | ISBN 9781625346476 (paperback) | ISBN 9781625346483 (hardcover) | ISBN 9781613769256 (ebook) | ISBN 9781613769263 (ebook)
Subjects: LCSH: American fiction—19th century—History and criticism. | Abortion in literature. | Poe, Edgar Allan, 1809–1849—Criticism and interpretation. | Hawthorne, Nathaniel, 1804–1864—Criticism and interpretation. | LCGFT: Literary criticism.
Classification: LCC PS374.A24 M44 2022 (print) | LCC PS374.A24 (ebook) | DDC 813/.3093561—dc23/eng/20220316
LC record available at https://lccn.loc.gov/2021054601
LC ebook record available at https://lccn.loc.gov/2021054602

British Library Cataloguing-in-Publication Data
A catalog record for this book is available from the British Library.

Portions of chapter three were previously published as "So Very Self-Evident: Adultery and Abortion in 'The Purloined Letter,'" *Literature and Medicine* 26, no. 2 (Fall 2007): 342–63 and "This Rag of Scarlet Cloth: Nathaniel Hawthorne's Abortion," *Studies in the Novel* 49, no. 1 (Spring 2017): 24–48.

For Rilke Elizabeth Medoro Cuthbert

Contents

Preface ix

Acknowledgments xvii

INTRODUCTION 1

Part I: Detection, Confession, Termination: Three by Edgar Allan Poe 23

CHAPTER ONE
Stargazing on the Rue Morgue 29

CHAPTER TWO
Averse from Swerving in "The Mystery of Marie Rogêt" 57

CHAPTER THREE
An Unusual Gaping in the Joints
Delivering the Purloined Letter 74

Part II: Nation, Plantation, Annihilation: Three by Nathaniel Hawthorne 95

CHAPTER FOUR
Passwords and Countersigns
The Scarlet Letter 99

CHAPTER FIVE
Alleged Necromancies within a System
The House of the Seven Gables 126

CHAPTER SIX
The Blithedale Romance and Abortion's Conditional Perfect 150

CONCLUSION 178

Notes 183

Index 211

Preface

This book is admittedly idiosyncratic. Its exclusive pairing of Edgar Allan Poe (1809–1849) and Nathaniel Hawthorne (1804–1864) with the subject of abortion not only spotlights their approach to a corporeal experience that lay outside their immediate comprehension but also sees in their work a radical position on the right to terminate a pregnancy. As far as I can tell, no other writers contemporaneous with them explored abortion and its criminalization in their fiction, at least not to the extent that Poe and Hawthorne did. This is not to say that Poe and Hawthorne tackled an issue about which early nineteenth-century women were silent but rather to assert that they extended it into literary frameworks and in particularly distinctive ways. For while a number of women published sophisticated defenses of reproductive control—for instance, abortionist Madame Restell and reformers Mary Gove Nichols and Frances Wright—they did so via treatises, medical advice books, and advertisements, not fiction. Their ideas influenced Poe's and Hawthorne's work, either directly or as part of the wider culture to which feminists contributed, in challenges to legal and medical classifications of human lives.

Among the broadsides and short stories published in New England between 1830 and 1860, about a handful include references to abortion, designating it as a dangerous option for victims of seduction.[1] The narratives are brief and tend in the direction of moralizing, whereby the scandal of an unplanned pregnancy is intensified by some form of interchangeable, fatal violence. Tragic plotlines proceed through an inevitable sequence of unfortunate events: a young woman finds herself pursued by a rake or a rapist, is left "in that condition," and then dies by murder, suicide, or a botched procedure.[2] It is interesting to note that when the tragedy involves abortion, the substance of the scandal pertains less to an unmarried woman's desperate recourse to the procedure, and more to her death at the hands of an incompetent or murderous physician. This unfolding significantly departs from the message circulated by the medical and popular press, especially toward midcentury, that it was women abortionists who were dangerous, unqualified, and criminally connected. From one ballad and tale to the next, the real menace involves men who sham affection or expertise and then get away with it.

Preface

Taken together, these publications provide a distinct glimpse of the arrival or incursion of men into the business of women's medicine and form a backdrop for reading Poe's and Hawthorne's approaches to the subjects of reproduction and exploitation. By consigning them to context, I do not mean to downplay the narratives' importance to the study of American print culture but to clarify that their often-anonymous authors did not expand on abortion's meaning or practice, other than to align it with misconduct and misfortune. With Poe and Hawthorne, something shifted. Ambitious writers, they drew from narratives of scandal and seduction and reworked them, upending conventions of form and content. They saw in literature a uniquely imaginative way of exploring imaginative entities—namely, white America and the so-called unborn—and illuminated the fictional nature of human hierarchies from within fictional frameworks. Through their work, they asked how nonexistent or otherworldly entities could be narrated into reality with such force, in suspensions of disbelief regarding the personhood of those actually alive.

Both Poe and Hawthorne cut their teeth as writers in cities spilling over with scientific information and pseudoscientific opinions about birth and death, pregnancy and posterity, race and nation. In the chapters that follow, I demonstrate how they explored these subjects from intellectual and creative angles, positioning fetal personhood as an existential axis around which other issues turned in striking ways. But it is also possible to make a case for a more personal level of interest in abortion's criminalization—to consider the ways in which their insistent focus on concealed deeds transpires in relation to self-disclosure and retreat, under cover of gothic motifs, and to attend to the forms of "cross-gendered identification" that arise in their narratives, to borrow a compelling phrase from Eliza Richards's *Gender and the Poetics of Reception in Poe's Circle*.[3] This sense of identification or sympathy with those made vulnerable to sexual scrutiny and trespass is corroborated by biographical details and suppositions, four of which I think are especially persuasive.

First, the intellectual circles to which Poe and Hawthorne belonged consisted of men and women dedicated to understanding the world and to setting things right. It is highly unlikely that they viewed subjects such as abortion and infanticide with detached curiosity or worked through such issues solely on paper. To take health reform activist Mary Gove Nichols (1810–1884) as an example here: Poe knew her quite well, and she treated his wife Virginia when her tuberculosis took a turn for the worse. Nichols articulated her position on maternity in forceful terms, drawing from her own experience of a violent first marriage. In her words, "Marriage, with its almost invariable attendant, an involuntary, compulsory, often repugnant, and almost always, painful maternity, is the cause of disease, suffering, and premature death to both mother and offspring.... Freedom in love will put an end to all involuntary, compulsory, and repugnant maternity.... The hundreds of thousands of miserable beings that now perish in infancy *will not be born.* When women have children, it will be because they wish to have them" (Nichols's italics).[4] Although somewhat vague about the beings who "perish in infancy," Nichols's assertion reflects the concerns raised by countless reports of infants, to quote Friedrich Engels, "stuffed up chimneys or buried under floorboards" and of women who gave birth on factory floors.[5] Her position on suffering as worse than coming into existence at all is shared by Hawthorne and Poe, in the moments in their narratives when their villainous characters stand for the exact opposite point of view.

Poe and Hawthorne also knew Margaret Fuller (1810–1850) and were doubtless familiar with what she called her "dark epiphany" regarding marriage and maternity: her horror at witnessing the death of a woman by a botched abortion; her sudden insight into the fact that a "nightmarish destiny" awaited those trapped by untenable and unforeseen circumstances.[6] Fuller herself deeply feared the prospect of giving birth, and her own pregnancy was accidental. The equally renowned feminist Frances Wright (1795–1852) likewise experienced an unplanned pregnancy, and her career was halted by painful childbirth and the infant's death six months later. Although I am not sure if Poe or Hawthorne were personally acquainted with Wright, they must have heard or read about her. She lectured to thousands of people in New York and Boston in the three decades before her death, alarming conservatives with her eloquent defense of reproductive rights, atheism, and abolition. Her rhetorical skill was said to have been spell-binding. Attempting to shut her up, Wright's critics slandered her in the press as "the high priestess of infidelity" or as "the red harlot of infidelity" and argued in treatises that women should be precluded from public oration.[7]

What I wish to emphasize with these brief reflections on Nichols, Fuller, and Wright is the milieu within which Poe and Hawthorne were made familiar with women's voices and ideas, especially as those voices carried substantial weight on radical subjects. We might consider the representation of sound in their fiction from this perspective, such as when the screams and words of women surface with meaning and intensity, only to be distorted, redirected, or silenced by men. In *The Scarlet Letter*, for instance, Hester Prynne must compel Dimmesdale into speaking for her when the governor ignores her pleas and attempts to seize Pearl; in "The Mystery of Marie Rogêt," Marie's mother Estelle is dismissed by Dupin when she testifies to her brutalized daughter's identity. Such nightmarish scenes of stifled utterance and sexualized cruelty draw much of their power from the realities of pregnancy, maternity, and abortion about which feminists spoke and wrote. In self-conscious depictions of men pontificating in the place of women, both authors fold themselves into their characters, in turn producing tongue-in-cheek admissions of guilt or acknowledgement for what they purloin from women for their fiction.

This brings me to my second point. Even as both Poe's and Hawthorne's narratives open onto other voices, they seem also to inwardly constrict, moving in the direction of something hidden and otherwise unspeakable for the authors themselves. Their relentless accounts of psychic, lexical, corporeal, and architectural violations convey a visceral grasp on abuse and perhaps communicate a deeply felt need to disburden from a position of concealment. It is possible to consider that what each author attempted to convey—alongside their intricately formed standpoints on art and existence—was a private history of sexual abuse: in Hawthorne's case, at the hands of an uncle, following the death of his father; in Poe's case, at the hands of someone at boarding school, after which his good-natured disposition turned intensely angry, to the bewilderment of his foster parents. Such awful intimacy with oppression might have made them keenly aware of other forms of injustice and degradation. Their interest in the meaning and practice of abortion makes sense from this viewpoint, for if they were forced to bear in secret the memories of rape, then abortion's criminalization might have appeared particularly cruel to them—as forcing the additional, terrifying weight of a pregnancy on an already wounded and encumbered person.

According to Jordan Stein in "Rappaccini's Son," evidence of childhood sexual abuse in Hawthorne's life arises in the space between Hawthorne's fiction and biography. He contends, for example, that Julian Hawthorne's allusion to "some secret in my father's life, which had never been revealed," might be brought to bear on Hawthorne's insistent representation of encroachment, violation, and shame.[8] The absence of biographical evidence yields only conjecture, Stein notes, but conjecturing becomes a worthwhile task if it involves speaking truth to power. Refusing to do so, moreover, preserves the cultural silence that envelops survivors and protects abusers. Stein thus proposes a reading practice that treads carefully and attends to uncertainty. He starts with the fact that Hawthorne's family was forced to reside with his uncle for several years and that Hawthorne, as an adolescent, had to share a bed with him. We know nothing about what Hawthorne thought or said about this arrangement. Given the significant discrepancy in circumstance, authority, and age between uncle and nephew, however, this biographical omission does not imply that nothing happened. On the contrary, it infers the opposite, especially in light of Hawthorne's fiction.

Stein reminds us that Hawthorne's tales and novels repeatedly address sexualized abuse. Indeed, from one story to the next, devious men obtain access to the spaces, bodies, and minds of those made vulnerable to them. Chillingworth is an obvious example, as he gets past security and confronts Hester in jail before making his way into Dimmesdale's abode. Jaffrey Pyncheon is cast through insinuations of rape throughout *The House of the Seven Gables*, as is Beatrice Rappaccini's father, in "Rappaccini's Daughter," whose main preoccupation, apart from experimenting on his daughter's blood, involves probing into the depths of flowers." For Stein, interpreting these motifs in the shadow of Hawthorne's biography becomes a way of heeding how a survivor might disclose abuse and reach past shame.

Poe's biographical record and its missing pieces might similarly be read through the bleeding and buried entities that haunt his work. In letters to acquaintances, he referred to agonizing memories that only drinking alleviated and to moments of suicidal despair. According to biographer Kenneth Silverman, Poe recalled his time at boarding school "as lonely and unhappy," a period in his life followed by angry outbursts and what his foster father, John Allan, called "sulky & ill-tempered [behavior] to all the family."[9] In view of this information, the fury directed at a boarding school master in "William Wilson," which is followed by the narrator's harrowing self-division, perhaps divulges something about the author who pens the tale in tandem with William Wilson. Writing it down, Wilson says, becomes his way of "seeking relief."[10]

Leland Person makes a similar case in "Queer Poe: The Tell-Tale Heart of His Fiction," arguing that the sadistic boarding-school culture of the nineteenth century informs the panicked expressions and closeted spaces of "William Wilson."[11] Bringing historical accounts of sexual intimacy and abuse among the male students into comparison with "William Wilson," Person meticulously tracks the narrator's delineations of fear, anger, repression, and predation. He also reads the narrator's self-described "utter helplessness" through the homophobia particular to the 1840s, and argues that vulnerability and panic echo throughout Poe's oeuvre, beating like a tell-tale heart about relationships with men that are distorted by betrayal and ruthlessness. While the losses Poe repeatedly experienced in his life cannot be dismissed from his keen sense of haunting and despair, they do not align with the sexualized violence and repressed memories that repeatedly break his characters down the middle. Again, we cannot know for sure, but if an experience of sexual abuse underlined his recurring portrait of a cruel and shattering patriarchy, then it might also account for a sympathetic response to abortion. It is possible that he saw the act of terminating a pregnancy as the procedure by which a person salvages a sense of coherence from possession by another, one who is internal to that person's body, dividing it into two.

Some now-infamous statements by Hawthorne and Poe—regarding scribbling women and beautiful, dead ones—come into conflict with this impression of sympathetic identification with women. But it seems undeniable that they worked through their culture's oppressive structures and, to quote what Joel Pfister says about Hawthorne, "shook up [their] own ideological tendencies" in the narratives they created.[12] A rich tradition of scholarship elucidates the complicated queer and feminist undercurrents of their work and establishes the framework within which, as I argue, abortion becomes similarly legible. As a practice that disrupts reproduction and detaches women from maternity, abortion tends in the direction of queerness and liberation. It is countersigned, so to speak, by nonreproductive ways of being and thinking.[13]

A third route into Poe's and Hawthorne's personal interest in abortion thus follows. In a letter to Horatio Bridge in 1851, Hawthorne announced the birth of his second child: "Mrs. Hawthorne published a little work, two months ago, which still lies in sheets."[14] This convention of sexual/textual reproduction runs through both Poe's and Hawthorne's fiction and, as the scholarship also maintains, entwines with obsessive depictions of gestation and birth. By shifting this perspective slightly, we might see where abortion plays into this convention and overlaps with authorial rights in feasibly conscious ways. Allusions to Hester Prynne's pregnancy and Marie Rogêt's abortion, for example, take place in narratives that are as much about the prerogatives of writing, editing, and excising as they are about sexual scrutiny and reproductive secrets. Both Poe and Hawthorne represent the material of the text as subject to authorial decisions about what to see through and what to expunge; they draw attention to their narrators' oversight and sense of their own work as spaces of conceiving, brought into existence by ink and effort. Casting pregnancy as a form of creativity that a person might choose to eschew, they bring childbirth in line with copyright. Until the entity—fetal or textual—is finalized and named, it is not separate from the mind, body, or prerogatives of its creator.

As Meredith McGill demonstrates about nineteenth-century publishing, "texts were frequently subject to circulation without editorial or authorial control." Intentionally plagiarized and reprinted tales, Poe once asserted, constituted theft by "purloiners of his property" who left him to starve.[15] He agreed with Charles Dickens that pirated texts resembled counterfeit banknotes, aware that the absence of international copyright laws entailed a kind of extortion of work and payment from authors by unscrupulous publishers.[16] At the same time, he understood that ideas did not arrive ex nihilo but in forms of connection, in a kind of collective consciousness in speech and print. The problem pertained to the exploitation of an author's name or words in the deliberate redirection of remuneration.

McGill makes this point too, noting that Poe defined writing as something that shifted between forms of possession and dispossession, opening up to wayward lineages of thinking and its dissemination. Neither Poe's nor Hawthorne's fiction aligns writing with originality—but copyright perhaps clarifies reproductive rights, especially with regard to questions of corporeal and textual control. What also develops in their work is a fascinating approach to the matter of inspiration, in an undermining of the widely accepted notion that inspiration derives from a spiritual incursion into the human mind. As I argue, they configure inspiration in terms of matter and energy, not as a form of conception that mirrors insemination, itself understood in conservative thought as a divine route into the source of human existence.

Finally, the fourth point—the context of antebellum existence. Abortion's proponents advertised their remedies in appeals to people who could not afford another child or whose bodies could not survive another pregnancy. Abolitionists circulated reports of the forced reproduction of Black women and the sale of their children. It seems impossible for Poe and Hawthorne not to have understood their own families against the background of a deeply unjust world—for them not to have recognized that they were afforded prospects in the shadow of others' oppression. We know that Poe worked hard to support his wife and mother-in-law and that he experienced disinheritance firsthand. Often impoverished himself, he relocated his family almost yearly, residing among the "troubled minds and abused bodies," to quote Scott Peeples, "of the soldiers, slaves, and immigrants" in the cities where he pursued work.[17] Hawthorne had it easier, but as historian Shawn Johansen notes, his small family with Sophia was a product of a deep sense of responsibility to her and part of a demographic trend rooted in reproductive control.[18] Letters and journal entries refer to the intentionally spaced timing of Sophia's pregnancies, as well as to a miscarriage that coincided with Hawthorne's composition of "The Birth-Mark." While they may have timed menstrual cycles and practiced abstinence, it is also likely that Sophia turned to the most common method of contraception, ingesting an abortifacient following a missed period.

Perhaps it is not that odd to concentrate on Poe and Hawthorne through the abortion debates that gathered steam from the 1830s onward. Reproduction was a topic in which white, educated men were invested, and literally so when it came to the market in enslaved Africans and their descendants. The years in which Poe and Hawthorne published their work were also the same ones in which medical professionals established legislation against abortion, condemning its practice in newspapers, periodicals, textbooks, treatises, trial reports, health manuals, and marriage guides. As skilled writers genuinely interested in law and medicine, Poe and Hawthorne crafted subtle retorts identifying the existential panic attendant on redefinitions of conception and gestation. They composed stories in which women are strangled to death, reflecting assertions in the press that abortion constituted the "strangling [of] the unborn" or the "quenching" of the "immortal spark in thousands of the unborn," and traced this thinking into the ruthless reactionary politics, sexism, and white supremacy it generated and sustained.[19]

Acknowledgments

This book started out as a study of Nathaniel Hawthorne and nineteenth-century medicine (thank you to the Social Sciences and Humanities Research Council of Canada for the grant to do so, back in the day) and then widened to include Edgar Allan Poe. It also began with a particular framework in mind, involving the sharp decline in the birth rate of the white population in the 1800s and a sense of abortion as an urban phenomenon. But this framework never really held, not even for Hawthorne's white protagonists or the busy city featured in Poe's Dupin trilogy, because it rested on divisions that the narratives themselves defied. It wasn't until I researched the extent to which slavery functioned in the capitalist structures of the antebellum United States that I could comprehend abortion's criminalization and its connections to white supremacy and plantation ideology more clearly. I am thankful to Poe and Hawthorne for pushing me to think harder about everything and to all the scholars whose work I cite in the pages that follow. Thanks also to the anonymous reviewers of the manuscript and my editors at the University of Massachusetts Press for their hard work and for requesting that I write in more visible ink.

Shorter versions of the sections on "The Purloined Letter" and *The Scarlet Letter* were first published in *Literature and Medicine* and *Studies in the Novel*, respectively, and I am grateful for the generosity and expertise of their editors and readers too.

Thank you to the Faculty of Arts for different forms of funding over the years and for never once asking why my annual progress reports noted that I would finish the thing the year before, and the year before that, and so on. I am also very lucky to belong to a supportive department; thank you, everyone, especially my sixth-floor confidants. Thank you to the University of Manitoba for my interesting, brainy colleagues in the humanities and for my equally talented students. I wish I could thank every student I've taught over the years for their inquisitiveness, insights, and encouragement.

Many thanks to the Occupy Bartleby Collective for letting me think ahead and for their patience as I finished this project. And to my friends in the animal rescue world—your kindness keeps me afloat, as do your veterinarian services (Jonas) and inspiration (Twyla and Brittany and Jonas again). Thinking about pigs and chickens made me smarter; I wish I could do more for them.

Acknowledgments

Much love and gratitude to WnD (and extended families), PoB (Tim Riggins forever), Jenny (and boggle), Jila (and rooftop reveries), Tatiana and Phil (and hounds), Pam K (for meeting me at conferences all over the place), Karin (and Miami, Key West, New Orleans, and Savannah), Shelley (for taking me on a quest to find Madame Restell's place) and Marcel (for knowing exactly what pennyroyal tea was), Alyson (and *As I Lay Dying*), Jeremy (and carrot-suit), Laura (for everything, especially for taking me to the Sibyl's temple in Naples), Ken (for the memes), and my parents. I'm very thankful for Dr. Lori-Ann Lach and Dr. Teressa Grosko and for the Women's Health Clinic. If I've missed anyone, I'll make it up to you somehow.

Thank you also to Ann Lohman (Madame Restell) and all the fortune-tellers who helped nineteenth-century women find their way.

Endless gratitude and love to Caitlin McIntyre and Serenity Joo for listening to a million conference papers and conversations about this book, its various permutations, how long it was taking, and how painful it was to read about botched abortions and enslaved Black women and the American empire. Thank you to Sara Crosby for more than you know. And to Andrew Loman for all the reinforcements and shared excitement about the 1840s.

My dog Grip and cats Kenny, Busker, and Tim Riggins, who were here at the beginning, were sure to keep an eye on my progress, as Alexander Greyhound and Lafayette do now. I am so grateful for this four-legged family, past and present.

This book took a long time to write. My daughter Rilke grew up alongside the writing and research. I was pregnant with her when I sat down to tackle "The Purloined Letter" following my obsession with its references to sharp gynecological instruments. When Rilke started to read, I turned the books on my shelves around, hiding the titles on their spines. I did not want her first full question to be "Mother, what does 'infanticide' mean?" She is now a teenager, and I have never met anyone as open-minded and compassionate as she is. She is just like her generous and brilliant father, David. I cannot thank her and David enough for letting Edgar and Nathaniel basically move in and take over our house forever.

CERTAIN CONCEALMENTS

INTRODUCTION

I. Backward from the Death of Madame Restell

> What herbs, what medications did my nurse not bring to me and insert with bold hand, so that from deep within my viscera—this alone I concealed from you—the growing burden might be shaken out.
> —Ovid, *Heriodes* 11.41–44

> There is no haste as she disrobes. . . . She stands just as she entered the world, so is she going to leave it.
> —Bishop Huntington, *Restell's Secret Life* (1897)

On April 1, 1878, New England's legendary abortionist Madame Restell was scheduled to appear in court, having been charged with breaking a new federal law that forbade the trade in materials related to the practice of contraception and abortion. Two months earlier, the equally infamous Anthony Comstock (secretary of the New York Society for the Suppression of Vice) had disguised himself as a desperately poor man seeking advice about an unplanned pregnancy and tricked her into a transaction. Her arrest followed this interaction in a swift sequence of events: supplied with enough evidence, Comstock secured a search warrant for her mansion; Restell's instruments were discovered, confiscated, and displayed before a judge; and Restell was jailed, her bail set at $10,000 (over $255,000 in today's currency). Given her long-standing connections with New York bankers and lawyers, she was able to liquidate her assets and post bail with similar efficiency. Within twenty-four hours she returned home, there to await her trial. When April 1 arrived and she did not turn up at the courthouse, her absence made national and international headlines.

On April 2, Restell's lawyers and family members issued statements describing her state of mind after Comstock's entrapment of her, noting in particular the distress caused by the newspapers' two-month celebrations of her arrest and looming imprisonment. Instead of facing the possibility of another conviction (she had served a one-year sentence three decades earlier), she cut her own throat and bled to death in her bathtub. The record is unclear as to the weapon she used; some sources report a carving knife, others a straight-edged razor. The coroner called to Madame Restell's house documented only the fact of her death, its date, and the words "inquest to follow" on a small piece of paper, now in the holdings at the Arthur and Elizabeth Schlesinger Library at Harvard University. An inquest did not take place, and Restell was quickly buried next to her husband in Sleepy Hollow Cemetery.

In an editorial about Restell's suicide, the *New York Sun* condemned Comstock for his deceptive methods and hollow victory: "No matter what the wretched woman was who took her life with her own hand yesterday, her death has not freed the world from the last of detestable characters. Whatever she was, she had her rights and the man who cunningly led her into the commission of a misdemeanor acted an unmanly and ignoble part." Consisting of three paragraphs, the editorial is remarkable for its even-handedness. While it places Restell among the world's wretched characters, it also asserts her right to fair treatment and notes her crime as a misdemeanor, in a telling avoidance of the term "felony," the offense predominately attached to abortion by its nineteenth-century detractors. "There is a healthier sentiment afloat today," the editorial concludes, "concerning the policy of doing evil that good may come, which [Comstock] has seemed to be pursuing."[1] The nature of the debates surrounding excessive forms of punishment and public morality can be glimpsed here, as well as a sense of sympathy for Restell as a casualty of their enforcement. "Better that the infamous Madame Restell should be alive now than that she should have been ensnared and driven to suicide by a lie told by a Christian," reported the *Index* on September 19, 1878.[2]

Restell had lived in the center of public debates throughout her career, her character repeatedly assassinated in print and her mansion mobbed long before Comstock arrived on the scene. Undaunted, she steadily expanded her business and took out advertisements that not only promoted her skills but also asserted the right of individuals to decide their own reproductive futures. For over four decades she sold abortion powders and pills and offered procedures for women in Boston, Philadelphia, and New York. She also practiced midwifery, arranged adoptions, and provided sliding-scale fees. Poor women could pay as little as one dollar for her pills and five dollars for an abortion induced by instrument; rich women were charged up to one hundred dollars. That these services sustained women's freedom of choice and their liberation from poverty and suffering in childbirth mattered to her, the wealth she amassed evidence of a demand she met, even as she brilliantly marketed her talents and wares. In other words, she did not have to exaggerate the "heart-rending afflictions," as she repeatedly described them, of unwanted pregnancies and dangerous labor: their social, physiological, and psychological repercussions were well known.[3] Restell saw herself as an advocate of betrayed, abandoned women in particular, and was willing to help them escape ruin and poverty. Comstock played right into her sympathy for people in trouble.

Rumors followed her death on April 1, speculation in the press that Restell had staged an April Fool's Day hoax. Another woman had died in her mansion, the newspapers suggested, and Restell had slipped her rings on the body's fingers and fled New York. A headline in the *Boston Daily Globe* inquired, "Madame Restell Dead: Or Was Her Reported Suicide All a Sham and a Pauper's Body Buried for Hers?."[4] Such intimations may seem outrageous, but they followed a particular logic. Restell's enemies had persistently described her work as a trade in deception and concealment, through which a woman could pretend to be other than who she was. According to the antiabortion narratives that surrounded her, Restell specialized in corporeal counterfeiting: with her abortifacients and instruments, she worked to erase the evidence of sexual encounters in women, allowing them to reinvent themselves as chaste for unsuspecting suitors. Thus, along this line of misogynistic reasoning, a faked suicide was par for the course, as an analogous evasion of consequence and judgment.

At the same time, the rumors point to Restell's doggedness and belief in her work. The official statements about her despair jar with the history of Restell as a self-possessed woman who had read about herself as a baby-killer and monster for years. She knew what was said and published about her, and she shot back with rejoinders, aiming specifically at the sexist nature of her culture. "It may be that sticklers for morality will still demur to the positions I defend," she asserted in 1846. "They will perhaps tell me, as the committee of a certain society in this city lately did, that the power of preventing conception holds out inducements and facilities for the prostitution of their daughters, their sisters, and their wives. Truly but they pay their wives, their sisters, and their daughters a poor compliment! Is then this vaunted chastity a mere thing of circumstance and occasion? Is there but the difference of opportunity between it and prostitution?"[5] This was someone who had taken her business from Greenwich Street to Fifth Avenue in 1865, in a spectacular move that not only flaunted her wealth but also prevented New York's archbishop from purchasing the plot of land next to his church. Decisively outbidding him, in a purposeful settling of scores for denouncing her from his pulpit, she secured the plot and built a mansion on it.[6] For her to have conceded defeat to someone like Comstock seems implausible.

In addition, a month before her trial, she had published a newspaper column in self-defense, announcing that the "number of little doctors who are in the same business think if they can get me in trouble and out of the way, they can make a fortune."[7] It looks as though she was prepared to name names in court, including releasing a list of high-profile male clients. Once again, Restell did not have to exaggerate her claims. Male physicians had pushed for licensing laws throughout the first half of the nineteenth century as a way of making inroads into the world of reproductive medicine by moving unlicensed women out of it. She lived in the "abortion capital" of the United States, according to sensationalist-press headlines, and had witnessed the ways in which licensed physicians established themselves as experts in gynecology and as the moral arbiters of the city's public health.[8] The first volume of *The New York Medical and Surgical Reporter*, for example, carried a multipage exposé of Madame Restell in 1846, its editor outraged by the fact that university-trained professionals had to contend with her and in the name of life's ostensible sanctity. And yet, their consolidation of control over women's medicine hardly made a dent in her income, nor did it alter her commitment to reproductive rights.

In her fictionalized autobiography of Restell, titled *My Notorious Life* (2010), Kate Manning casts her as a woman who saved other women's lives and who practiced careful reproductive control herself. Manning also imagines an afterlife for Restell, in which she does not commit suicide but makes it to Boston, proving the late nineteenth-century rumors right. "I put my rings on her.... All my jewelry," Manning's protagonist recounts, as she urges her husband to tell everyone that "it's me. She is me. Will you do it?"[9] The novel ends with her in London, alive and well, and thinking about love. A few years ago, I asked Manning if she thought that Madame Restell had, in reality, cut her own throat, or if someone had murdered her, or if she had staged the whole thing and escaped to Massachusetts. She replied that she believed Restell had killed herself.

Restell had once publicly declaimed the "immense and crushing engine of power" that men wielded against women and to which women like her had no access.[10] Cutting her own throat, she set the terms of her defeat. "The aborters' cry is 'Liberty or Death,'" wrote a woman under the name "conspirator" in an 1868 issue of the *Revolution*. "The only thing that would solve the abortion problem in America," she exclaimed, "would be 'liberty to women, freedom entire.'"[11] According to historian James Mohr, Restell made an intentionally symbolic statement with her suicide. She knew that it would be widely publicized and that Comstock and her prosecutors would be reproached for it.[12] Dying by her own hand, she left blood on theirs.

I return to fill out the biographical details surrounding Madame Restell in the following chapters, working from the position that Poe certainly knew of her, and that Hawthorne must have too, given the extent to which she shades into Hester Prynne's characterization. As early as 1839, New York's *Sunday Morning News* was already announcing that Restell "perseveres in her nefarious traffic," despite the statutes against it, and that her "daily practices [were] not to be borne by this community."[13] My argument proceeds from the premise that it would have been next to impossible for her notoriety and the abortion debates that preceded and swirled around her to have escaped their notice. As one Gustav Lening remarked in 1873 about Restell in the 1840s, "She was the sensation of the day and the name Restell as well as her business was spoken of by everybody. The [1841] trial had been for her an immense advertisement. The result of this was that her business assumed large proportions. That it paid well was seen a few years after when she bought some real estate on Fifth Avenue near the park and there built a palace which may be regarded as one of the finest buildings in the street."[14] We know that Poe followed the newspaper reports as they twisted Mary Rogers's murder into the lie of a botched abortion (one connected with Madame Restell) and that he responded with "The Mystery of Marie Rogêt," pointing a finger at men's lethal violence against women. It is a subject that he addressed in 1841 with "The Murders in the Rue Morgue" and to which he returned with "The Purloined Letter" in 1845, sustaining what I see as an intricate three-part meditation on the meaning of reproduction in relation to obdurate, patriarchal ideas about life and the living.

We know too that Hawthorne published "The Birth-Mark" and "Rappaccini's Daughter" contemporaneously with Poe, in 1843 and 1844, in which an "abortive experiment" (Hawthorne's phrase) twice unfolds, first alongside a fantasy of whiteness, and second inside a guarded genealogical scheme. Where Beatrice Rappaccini ingests an herbal concoction, taking herself out of her father's uterine enclosure, thwarting his plan to breed her,[15] Georgiana shrieks, "Remove it, remove it, whatever be the cost!," in an echo of an entreaty ("Get rid of it!") already familiar in the nineteenth century.[16] Even "The Artist of the Beautiful" (1844) tackles the meaning of gestation, weaving it together with artistry and slavery through pointed allusions to the cotton gin.[17] The scene in which a sewing needle is leveled at the mechanical-butterfly-in-progress—crushing its vitality and reversing all of the artist's work—reads like an abortion by metal instrument, and it is no simple coincident that Hawthorne pairs a woman's pregnancy with the butterfly's arduous story of coming into being. In retrospect from the novels published between 1850 and 1852, these stories appear as components of an obsessive working-through—centered on conceiving, misconceiving, reconceiving—of a problem taken up by *The Scarlet Letter*, *The House of the Seven Gables*, and *The Blithedale Romance*. For, in one novel after another, Hawthorne intricately arranges the subjects of existence and nonexistence, reproduction and termination, around three representations of America itself as an abortive experiment.

What I demonstrate with this book is the significant extent to which Poe's and Hawthorne's narratives represent the incompatibility of abortion and nationalism—how they illuminate the violent entanglements of race, reproduction, and American exceptionalism—and that they do so by means of shared devices and methods of syntactical and semantic unraveling or undermining. Stories unfold through thwarted plotlines, genealogical interruptions, and terminated ideas; sentences and scenarios get underway only to change course or close without warning. As miscarriages of justice are mirrored in miscarriages of meaning, modes of narrative experimentation become newly legible in relation to the abortion debates before the Civil War. And these debates, along with abortion's commercial availability, streamed through every feature of the print culture, itself accelerated by the new steam-powered printing presses of 1820s.[18]

As James Mohr asserts, Madame Restell may have been the "most flamboyant and the most publicized of the abortionists who began to appear during the 1840s[, but she] was no isolated aberration."[19] She was part of a world in which individuals increasingly chose to forestall or eschew childbearing, both in cities and on plantations. Looking back from 1858, for instance, William Sanger remarked, "Were it possible to form any definite idea of the abortions actually procured . . . the amount would be startling."[20] The extensive practice and business of abortion raised existential questions about the origin and value of human life (at conception? invested with a soul?) and made their ways into Poe's and Hawthorne's thinking about reproduction in the race-based capitalism of the antebellum decades.

In the 1840s, as Mohr describes it, a "great upsurge" in both the practice of abortion and its cultural visibility took place. "To document fully the pervasiveness of those open and obvious advertisements," he explains, "would probably require the citation of a substantial portion of the mass audience publications circulated in the United States around midcentury." Addressing the effect of the advertising on women's sense of independence from men and maternity, he notes, "One indication that abortion rates probably jumped in the United States during the 1840s and remained high for some thirty years thereafter was the increased visibility of the practice. It is not unreasonable to assume that abortion become more visible at least in part because it was becoming more frequent. And as it became more visible, more and more women would be reminded that it existed as a possible course of action to be considered."[21] In *Revolutionary Conceptions,* Susan Klepp adds to this intersection of supply and demand by charting the declining white birth rate after the Revolutionary War. Taking the women's rights movement in New York as a case in point, she writes, "That region [New York state] shows a particularly steep decline in fertility levels between 1830 and 1850—another indication of the dethroning of patriarchal 'lords of creation' by self-assured wives who wanted to place reasonable limits on their marital commitments. Women's rights, women's opportunities, and fertility decline were linked."[22] The upsurge identified by Mohr and the downturn traced by Klepp looped together with noticeable effects on Anglo-American nationalism, specifically on the nativism in the imperial self-fashioning coined as Manifest Destiny, all channeled by Poe and Hawthorne into the anxious, conservative voices of their unreliable narrators.

Historians of abortion concur that the shift from the fairly private practice of family limitation in the eighteenth century—communicated primarily through recipe books, word of mouth, and instructions for domestic herbariums—into public debates about abortion followed developments in the speed and expansion of early nineteenth-century print technologies. Before the turn of the nineteenth century, women kept small gardens for growing the herbs that restarted menstruation, should their cycles become "obstructed" or should the desire to terminate a pregnancy arise. The language surrounding this world of herbal lore remained veiled, as did the ethical connotations of terminating a pregnancy. Menstruation and health remained in focus, not fetal viability, itself a topic of concern only once fetal movement could be ascertained around the sixteenth week of pregnancy and by the person bearing the fetus. The practice of abortion stayed mostly inside domestic networks of knowledge, even as Indigenous and African traditions crossed into those of the white colonists.[23] Once that network opened up and commercialized, the practice of menstrual regulation or early pregnancy termination became subject to medical and legal redefinition.

Janet Farrell Brodie stresses in *Contraception and Abortion in 19th-Century America* that the migration of women to cities also shifted forms of communication into print, and that the proliferation of books and pamphlets on reproductive control followed this demographic change, as did the market in abortifacients.[24] This market was also significantly driven by the rise of the international pharmaceutical industry, the agents of which not only prepared and sold abortifacients (using the familiar emmenagogic ingredients of pennyroyal, rue, and savin) in urban pharmacies but also advertised their willingness to deliver these preparations to rural areas.[25] According to Klepp, by the turn of the nineteenth century, a lucrative pharmaceutical enterprise had built up around first-trimester abortifacients, with newspaper announcements as an established component of it. And by the middle of the century, as Brodie puts it, "Products purporting to affect menstruation flourished in ever greater quantity in an escalating commercial trade. Americans ... had access to scores of commercial pills, fluids, and extracts marketed innocuously as Woman's Friend, Female Regulator, Menstrual Regulator, and Periodical Drops."[26] Between 1800 and 1900 the white birth rate accordingly fell—and by 49 percent. The data gathered by Brodie, Klepp, and Mohr show that its most precipitous decline took place toward the midcentury, when Poe and Hawthorne were publishing their tales about decaying houses and expiring family trees.

The expansion of obstetrics and gynecology into powerful areas of male medical specialization occurred alongside these developments, as the medical schools of the early 1800s took notice of the commerce surrounding women's medicine and as their physicians pursued surgical treatments for gynecologic diseases. For physician-historian James Ricci, whose study

One Hundred Years of Gynaecology, 1800–1900 attempts a comprehensive overview of the field, the escalation in number of practitioners, publications, and clinical developments is astonishing. He puzzles repeatedly over what he calls the crazes in gynecological remedies, from the invention specialized leech-forceps to the overuse of uterine probes, describing procedures that appear to involve abortion but about which nineteenth-century physicians were vague in their reporting. (This postscript, for example, printed in a minute font, is appended by one "J. H. Ross, Cupper and Leecher" to the end of his advertisement in the January 7, 1841, edition of the *New York Lancet*: "P.S. Mrs R. applies leeches to the Os Uteri," along with instructions to go around to the backdoor.) It is interesting to see how Ricci overlooks the role of abortion in the escalation of the field, especially when some of the examples he cites appear to point directly at it. What was it, for instance, about the use of the curette—the instrument used to excise intrauterine growths—that caused such a conflagration at an 1846 medical conference in Paris?[27] Why would someone consent to the vaginal insertion of leeches, especially when reports existed of gynecologists failing to match the number inserted with the number removed?[28] Retaining an indistinct lexicon about certain procedures, the publications that most perplex Ricci document the inventiveness and urgency surrounding women's pursuit of reproductive health. As James Mohr demonstrates, although it is challenging to trace the number of abortions by instrument, sometimes called mechanical or instrumental abortions, that were performed in the first half of the nineteenth century, it is nonetheless clear that the rate increased in the 1840s.[29]

According to Ricci, the study of embryology played a key role in gynecology's developing power and sophistication, as new questions about fertilization, cellular development, and the origins of species came into focus and shifted research in interesting new directions, particularly following the discovery of the mammalian ovum in 1827.[30] Treatises and journals spilled onto the market, circulating intricate charts and theories about racial pedigree and extinction in relation to rates of pregnancy, abortion, and infanticide. As different medical and evolutionary sciences overlapped with one another in definitions of human life, their concepts tended to remain rooted in hierarchies of being, even as feminists, materialist philosophers, and abolitionists pushed back against them. University-trained physicians spoke of the uterus as uncharted territory, opened up by the speculum. They retained the belief that the human entity acquired a soul at conception, in a

INTRODUCTION

kind of commitment to what Joseph Needham calls "theological embryology."[31] Devising different kinds of stethoscopes to ascertain the fetal heartbeat, they validated the importance of the physician's sensorium over that of the pregnant individual's. They also warned each other in print about both free and enslaved women tricking them into terminating pregnancies.

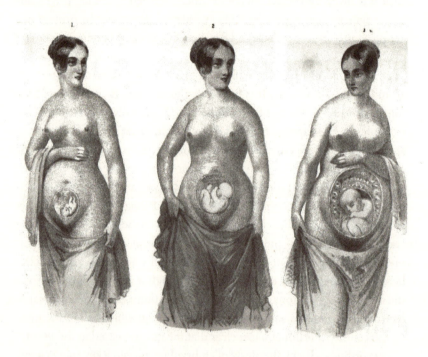

FIGURE 1. From Wooster Beach, *An Improved System of Midwifery* (New York: Baker & Scribner, 1850). The visibility of the fetus and the sequence through which it moves seem self-evident in such a compelling illustration of a white woman's pregnancy. Courtesy of HathiTrust, https://babel.hathitrust.org/cgi/pt?id=ien.35558002592349&view=1up&seq=90&skin=2021.

In *Abortion and the Politics of Motherhood,* Kristin Luker in fact highlights the study of embryology in the antiabortion position of conservative physicians, for it renewed the focus on conception or fertilization and served the position that the quickening could be discounted as the temporal line at which fetal viability was traditionally acknowledged. Luker demonstrates that physicians strategically popularized the notion of pregnancy as a biologically continuous process, from conception through to birth, showing that as early as 1817 they circulated illustrated embryological sequences designed to visualize an embryo and full-term fetus as the same entity. Embryo sequences were designed to appear as if predestined and not in fact subject to time and interruption, not successive but rather somehow instantaneous. Wielding stethoscopes and specula ("the technological tools of modern medicine"), university-trained physicians claimed their status as scientists who protected an embryo's life in exaggerated "differences between themselves and the lay public."[32] Ricci's inclusion of an 1848 lecture by gynecologist Charles Meigs provides an interesting example of the exaggerations of which Luker writes. Here is an excerpt of Meigs's lecture as quoted in Ricci's book:

> It is perhaps best, upon the whole, that this great degree of modesty should exist even to the extent of putting a bar to researches, without which no very clear and understandable notions can be obtained of the sexual disorders. I confess I am proud to say that in this country generally, certainly in many parts of it, there are women who prefer to suffer the extremity of danger and pain rather than waive those scruples of delicacy which prevent their maladies from being explored. I say it is evidence of the dominion of a fine morality in our society . . .
>
> You who know the skeleton human and the attitude of the uterus within the pelvis, do you think that Mrs. A. to X. would, out of missionary zeal, suffer her name to appear as one of the wonder-worked cures of a shameless procidentia, by what is, at our daily breakfast table, brought up in the morning paper to stare the ladies out of countenance under the modest title of a utero-abdominal supporter? Who wants to know or ought to know that the ladies have abdomens and wombs but us doctors? When I was young, a woman had no legs even, but only feet and possibly ankles; now, forsooth, they have utero-abdominal supporters, not in fact only, but in the very newspapers! They are surely not fit subjects for newspaper advertisements, nor would they be advertised but out of our own stupidity or remission.[33]

When the American Medical Association (AMA) formed in 1847, it did so in the name of male medical expertise and as officially opposed to the unregulated trade in abortion procedures and products. Its position rested not only on poison control and the protection of pregnant individuals from quackery but also on the averred personhood of the fetus.[34]

For example, in *Foeticide, Or Criminal Abortion*, the publication of his often-cited 1839 obstetrics lectures, physician Hugh Hodge defined abortion at any stage as the "destruction by parents of their own offspring before birth" in a forceful statement about the practice of birth control as a felony-level crime.[35] It was in this lecture that he asserted intelligence in embryos, claiming that they could think.[36] Hodge's work paved the way for Horatio Storer, who headed the AMA's antiabortion committee in the 1850s and dedicated himself to documenting the extent of the practice. Rummaging in morgue records for numbers of stillbirths and calculating what he saw as a population crisis, he produced *On Criminal Abortion in America* (1860). By means of a complicated lexical choreography, Storer argued that terminated pregnancies at any stage constituted murder. "If the foetus be already, and from the outset, a human being," he wrote, "alive, however early its stage of development, and existing independently of its mother, though drawing its sustenance from her, the offence becomes, in every stage of pregnancy, MURDER" (Storer's emphasis).[37] What I want to point out here is the sentence's contortion through contradictions—from "*however* early" to "*though* drawing sustenance"—in order to indicate the entanglements of life and not-life, human and not-human, fetus and mother with which such antiabortion rhetoric contended. As much as physicians like Hodge and Storer tried, the fetus remained indeterminate, difficult to define for medical jurisprudence. Neither a separate entity nor one merged with the person carrying it, fetal existence remained at the limits and "undecidability" of language, to quote Barbara Johnson, and thus eluded capture by words such as "life" or "murder," no matter how forcefully printed and pronounced.[38]

Of the thirty-one abortion trials brought to the Massachusetts courts in the 1850s, Storer recorded, none resulted in conviction, a testament to the ambiguities encircling embryonic and fetal existence. What practitioners like Hodge and Storer aimed to accomplish was a clear line, an indelible categorization: if something was not alive, then it was dead.[39] A blunt instrument, this logic also worked in reverse: if something was not dead, then it was alive, from the first moment onward. Even if many physicians found themselves compelled to acknowledge "the conditional" status and rights of the embryo, thereby leaving the question open in cases of hazardous pregnancies, their antiabortion rhetoric circulated widely in the print culture of the nineteenth century.[40] As contemporary philosopher of abortion Barbara Duden stresses, the notion of fetal life came into being in what she calls the fetus's technogenesis, its perceived existence inseparable from the microscopes and scalpels of modernity's science. This technogenesis conferred on the fetus "a destiny of its own," in an ideological loading of life, a word she describes as not only meaningless in itself but also used against living women.[41]

"The substantive *life* appears in the natural sciences," Duden asserts, "only in the second and third decades of the nineteenth century." It arrived with all "the factualness characteristic of modernity" and as something distinct from the contingencies of "aliveness." In an outpouring of pamphlets and treatises, life was hashed out by vitalists, materialists, and mechanists, and took hold as a reality. As an abstraction made into a public object, it carried metaphysical clout.[42] Life became distinct from death in the same way as eternity departed from time. It was against the background of life's timelessness that pregnancy could thus be described in terms of the "antenatal history of the human being," the title of Henry Clarke Wright's popular lecture series of the 1850s, and infanticide widened to include "the destruction of the foetus in utero, or of the child after it is born," to quote John Beck's 1817 *Inaugural Dissertation on Infanticide*.[43] In this temporal dimension, the "not-yet" of a nonexistent child acquired legal contours.[44]

Its visualization in illustrated manuals and anatomical models rendered the fetus "seemingly transcendent and autonomous," to quote Karen Newman.[45] Thus represented, it also appeared as if an individual were stilled in bounded, exposed permutations, even as scientific modernity established its cellular proliferation and material composition.[46] Like other objects of clinical observation, it was ideologically concealed or framed as such: that is, as awaiting discovery, its existence preceding and understood in terms of an "apparatus of Revelation."[47] Despite the impact of epigenesis following the 1759 publication of Kaspar Friedrich Wolff's *Theoria Generationis*, in which the notion of embryonic transformation overtook that of a preformed unfolding, obstetrical manuals persisted in representing the "unborn," in Karen Newman's words, as "whole and undivided, always male, and virtually never dissected, opened wounded, or permeable." This figure's representation required the breached borders of a woman's body, its singularity determined as bounded and protected, and hers as relinquished or failed.[48]

"Why has the practice of midwifery been snatched from the hands of women," asked Morris Mattson in his popular botanical health guide in 1841, and "why should a medical man wish to intrude himself into the chamber of parturition?"[49] In a similar publication, a Mrs. Benjamin Thurlow asserted to women midwives that it was under "the great and powerful Dollar [that] Truth has been veiled" and, here quoting Mattson, that "women's rights [were] usurped by the medical profession." Perceiving an "odious monopoly" at work, she advised her readers to resist it.[50] Such expressions of distrust notwithstanding, the influence of obstetrician-gynecologists increased and the number of practitioners expanded. They did so as confederates in public health initiatives, particularly in the areas of infant mortality and predictable birth rates among the white, Black, and immigrant populations. The scientific, statistical expertise they asserted in the early nineteenth century combined with what Dana Nelson calls "the purview of national manhood and professional masculinity" and conferred on gynecologists a recognizable civic identity, productive of wealth and conservative values.[51] As advocates of the application of vital statistics to the foundation of healthy cities, they aimed to calculate, understand, and eradicate the illnesses and unsanitary practices associated with high mortality rates. But as a consequence of this documentation and medical reform, stillbirths came under new scrutiny, increasingly registered in a category separate from those for births and deaths, and increasingly perceived as suspicious. From within the paradigm of vital statistics and the concept of preventable deaths, pregnancy and abortion became matters of the states' bookkeeping, their records being administered by licensed physicians.

Such forms of accounting, in which population growth was measured against national productivity, framed the institution of slavery. An enslaved woman's reproductive potential, according to Thomas Jefferson, consisted of a "silent profit" that could be calculated alongside a plantation's projected agricultural yields.[52] The irony of a slave-owning nation's investment in the life and personhood of the so-called unborn thus turned on the brutal reality of enslaved women's forced reproduction, even if that violence went under cover of preventable deaths and economic growth. The lexicon of "breeding" that accompanied that of slavery's perpetuation did not shift into arguments pertaining to white women, that is, but criminalizing abortion in the name of a white future echoed it. Assertions of white supremacy, understood in this case as reactionary from within the falling white birth rate, entwined with perceived crises surrounding failures or refusals to reproduce and subordinated sex to race. In other words, although antebellum natalism implicitly framed white women as breeders, it sustained a racialized hierarchy in which white women could profit from Black women's enslavement. Incursions into women's medicine were claimed for the advancement of civilization, on the one side, and for this civilization's slave market, on the other.

As Leslie Reagan demonstrates in *When Abortion Was a Crime,* nineteenth-century antiabortion activists engendered anxiety in white American men by linking the birth rate to their diminishing power in the direction of the country's political and economic future. Referring to the westward invasion of Indigenous territories, she quotes Horatio Storer on the patriotic duty of white women to reproduce: "Shall these regions be filled by our own children or by those of aliens? This is a question our women must answer; upon their loins depends the future destiny of the nation."[53] In this retrospective excerpted from the 1867 edition of the *Boston Medical and Surgical Journal,* a similar view arises on the connection between reproduction and white supremacy. Asserting that "the best stock the Puritan world ever saw [was] running out" because of women's "settled determination . . . to have no children or a very limited number," the editorial not only described the practices of these "degenerate females" as consisting of a "positive violation of the great laws of life and health," but also noted that the crisis had been several decades in the making.[54]

For the Black women enslaved throughout those decades, their childbearing potential represented capital, and their offspring interest on the investment.[55] *Partus sequitur ventrem,* the practice of enslavement through the maternal line (drawn from the Roman maxim "the issue follow the womb") made slavery inseparable from what Jennifer Morgan calls the "explanatory power of race" in legal notions of hereditary.[56] Hawthorne's novels about property and inheritance, which his narrators pretend have nothing to do with "realities of the moment," make latent the story of the ideological and physiological reproduction of slavery, in explorations of violent acts overwritten by legal deeds that turn generations of bodies into an estate, bequeathed as such. Saidiya Hartman describes the system as the mechanism by which maternity conferred the death of personhood on the offspring of enslaved women, quoting Christina Sharpe's chilling comparison of childbirth under slavery with the Middle Passage:

> The sexuality and reproductive capacities of enslaved women were central to understanding the expanding legal conception of slavery

and its inheritability. Slavery conscripted the womb, deciding the fate of the unborn and reproducing slave property by making the mark of the mother a death sentence for her child. The negation or disfigurement of maternity, writes Christina Sharpe, "turns the womb into a factory reproducing blackness as abjection and turning the birth canal into another domestic middle passage." *Partus sequitur ventrem*—replicates the fate of the slave across generations. The belly is made a factory of production incommensurate with notions of the maternal, the conjugal or the domestic. In short, the slave exists out of the world and outside the house."[57]

As Diane Klein shows, *partus sequitur ventrem* existed in English law to clarify disputes surrounding ownership of livestock and where they were born. It was then "repurposed," as Virginia expanded as a slave-holding state: "Virginia law blurred the distinction between the status of the mother and ownership of the offspring, as dual aspects of her 'condition,' lending a patina of age and legitimacy to a particularly inhuman aspect of the emerging Virginia law of chattel slavery (a word aptly sharing its etymological origins with 'cattle'): the treatment of the enslaved as human livestock, rather than (at worst) persons bound in a contractual and terminable relation of servitude."[58] For Klein, the "foundational status question" that secured humans as a form of livestock also secured the meaning of race, pairing whiteness and humanity on the other side of slavery, inside American citizenship.

To quote Jennifer Morgan again, a "commodified maternity" was crucial to the development of the Atlantic slave states in the early 1800s: "In 1819, while considering the role of enslaved women on plantations, Thomas Jefferson wrote, 'It is not their labor, but their increase which is the first consideration.' Jefferson's words articulated a crucial expression of racial capitalism in a time and place that predate the rise of the antebellum plantation economy on which much of our critical attention to the links between slavery and capitalism attends. His nineteenth-century ruminations, much like the *partus* act, thus reflect a much older set of practices and calculations."[59] From the beginning, however, enslaved women often terminated the pregnancies forced on them, in assertions of ownership over themselves, and with the botanical knowledge they carried with them, across the Middle Passage, or which they learned from Indigenous women's traditions. By the seventeenth century, displaced Africans had learned from Indigenous peoples which plants produced miscarriages, and it is clear, explains Londa Schiebinger, that Africans arrived with similar knowledge, if not with the actual seeds from plants too.[60]

The effective nature of the abortifacients, along with the circulation of knowledge about them, can be ascertained in the plantation records' notes on the increased numbers of miscarriages and stillbirths among enslaved women. Assessing the problem of barrenness in a chapter titled "On the Breeding of Negroes," plantation physician Dr. Collins wrote in 1803 that difficult work and poor nutrition accounted for "accidental abortions" but that "the art of the negro herself" must also be considered, especially if she perceived her "pregnancy an evil."[61] An 1833 edition of the *Anti-Slavery Reporter* noted, for instance, that the "perpetuation of abortion" among the "breeding women" was a "striking" fact of the institution.[62] In 1839, the American Anti-Slavery Society documented the forced reproduction of enslaved people "like other livestock" in concerted attempts to reverse the birth rate, in the multi-million-dollar slave trade that operated throughout the South.[63]

"*Partus sequitur ventrem*," declared a planter in the Virginia Legislature in 1831, was "coeval with the existence of the rights of property itself, and founded in wisdom and justice. . . . *In its increase consists much of our wealth*" (italics in original).[64] In Deirdre Cooper Owens's words, "White southerners knew black women literally carried the race and extended the existence of slavery in their wombs." For Cooper Owens, the history of American gynecology must be traced to such powerful investments in the reproductive health of enslaved women—to the maintenance and continuation of slavery in the face of women's undermining of it. Its expansion in the early nineteenth century interconnected with the abolition of the transatlantic trade and the increasing sense among planters that enslaved women were more valuable as "breeders" than as workers. In 1843, for example, Virginia clarified its law on the administering of abortifacients by "any slave, free negro or mulatto" to a pregnant woman, stipulating imprisonment, the lash, and the death penalty (for second offenses) "without benefit of clergy."[65]

It was in this context that the rise of plantation obstetrics also took place, as licensed physicians cooperated with plantation owners to establish their authority in relation to the Black midwives and healers trusted by enslaved women. In *Birthing a Slave: Motherhood and Medicine in the Antebellum South,* Marie Jenkins Schwartz explains the different ways in which obstetricians convinced enslaved women to carry to term and give birth, ideally with their assistance, and not with a midwife's.[66] They set up plantation hospitals and expanded their lying-in rooms in order to curb declines in fertility rates. And yet, as Schwartz also shows, despite their condemnation of abortion as immoral and criminal, physicians agreed to terminate pregnancies deemed life-threatening. In other words, they claimed for themselves an ostensibly moral flexibility when it came to defining abortion as murder, a point that Kristin Luker also makes, even as they promulgated the notion that life began at conception, sparked into being by a divine principle.

Despite the licensed physicians' authority and influence—Marion Sims, for instance, brought his forceps to difficult deliveries on Alabama plantations and then stitched up postpartum injuries—most enslaved women sought out African and Indigenous healers, in covert routes around the physicians and planters and before their pregnancies advanced or to contravene the chance of pregnancy entirely. As antebellum physician J. H. Morgan's multiply republished 1860 report notes, "Abortion [was] frequently accomplished among the blacks," despite interventions by southern physicians.[67] "They take it [camphor] just before or after menstruation," Morgan explains, "in quantities sufficient to produce a little nervousness for two or three days [and] they consider themselves safe."[68] Plantation owners and their wives often knew who the healers were and how to contact them for medical assistance. They also suspected that the healers were skilled abortionists who circulated their recipes and knowledge to enslaved women who, in turn, concealed what they knew and what they did with that knowledge.

II. Forward into the Fiction of Poe and Hawthorne

> There is one secret—I have concealed it all along, and never meant to let the least whisper of it escape.
> —Nathaniel Hawthorne, *The Blithedale Romance*, 1852

> You have nothing to conceal. You have no reason for concealment.
> —Edgar Allan Poe, "The Murders in the Rue Morgue," 1845

The above overview provides only a glimpse of the meticulous scholarship by some of the historians of abortion and cannot do it justice. In each of the following chapters, I return to this work, both to further establish the framework it provides and to widen it, particularly into the existential questions that surrounded abortion and its criminalization. For what Edgar Allan Poe and Nathaniel Hawthorne comprehended with particular acumen was the materialist philosophy within which the problem of abortion surfaced: the popularized, scientific theories that atoms and cells comprised existence and that there was nothing spiritual about it. Materialist thinking was radical, a tribute to scattering or distribution over a celestial chain of command. (Hawthorne's self-described conservative, Miles Coverdale, loathes materialism and everything affiliated with it; Poe's C. Auguste Dupin is utterly unnerved by things of "inconsequence and incoherence".[69]) In the fiction I discuss here, abortion and materialism entwine in representations of restructured worlds, in fascinating propositions that humans are also animals, destined for dirt and not an afterlife. Nobody's birth matters more than another's; nothing exceptional about America exists for its white citizens. Both Poe and Hawthorne move these ideas into gothic tropes, through which the horrifying tenacity of the race-based system of slavery involves submission to a patriarchal god—or, at the very least, to configurations of birthright informed by this submission.

Wary of the purposes for which life's legibility and reproduction could be claimed in the name of American citizenship, Poe's and Hawthorne's fiction undermines the existence of the human soul, defying further the belief that the soul arrives at conception to secure human immortality. What I trace in their narratives is a shared sense of the perniciousness of this belief, not only as it asserts human supremacy over animals but also as it underwrites the existence of white supremacy. Because, while enslaved men and women were permitted to possess and believe in their own souls, the hierarchy still held; white-embodied souls manifested and replicated God's presence more clearly, and arguments could be made for different lines of racial descent from biblical fathers. Cutting God entirely from the picture entailed something different, a leveling that pulled power and meaning from such organizing concepts as eternity, destiny, purity, and whiteness. Materialist principles summoned the opposing ideas of contingency, accident, decay, and nothingness. Responding to the revival of Epicurean thought in the late eighteenth century, for example, one Reverend Shepherd insisted in 1826 that "man [is] a compound being consisting of spirit and matter.... This is that principle which distinguishes him from the brute creation and thus he stands in the chain of nature."⁷⁰ Along the same lines, the strategic denouncement of abortion in the early 1800s buttressed the foundation on which white humanity steadied itself, as a form of life spiritualized in ways that in turn recognized white men as life's natural superintendents.

Throughout their work, Poe and Hawthorne make knowing allusions to Epicurus, to atoms and molecules, and to things smashing into nothingness. The strange, experimental style that characterizes their writing—the abstruseness of form, allusion, and syntax governing Poe's "The Murders in the Rue Morgue" (1841), "The Mystery of Marie Rogêt" (1842), and "The Purloined Letter" (1844) and Hawthorne's *The Scarlet Letter* (1850), *The House of the Seven Gables* (1851), and *The Blithedale Romance* (1852)— fold definitions of human life and birth into ambiguity and retain for them the obscurity that reactionary forces try to straighten out and make clear, particularly when it comes to reproducing hierarchies of the living. The allegorical devices and covert styles of narration, for which both writers are especially renowned, reflect the secrecy and visibility surrounding the practice of abortion, the coded advertisements that made its availability at once obvious and covert. Their work engages with the debates that surfaced with new intensity in the 1830s, the one side maintaining humanity's divine origin and obligation to the future; the other side indifferent to that entwined position. Because it is on this other side where Poe and Hawthorne's fiction falls, with a paradoxical clarity achieved by the circumlocutions of their prose. Imitating the secrecy and savvy surrounding the market in abortion remedies, procedures, and advice in New England cities, their words reflect the abortionist's disinterest in preserving what fetal life symbolizes on the outside of a pregnant person's body. To read their stories for the secrets of abortion enclosed within them, one must be initiated into the coded communication on which their fiction draws and through which abortionists advertised themselves as "clairvoyant physicians for women" and their remedies as "purifying" or "emetic."

As their narrators harness the energy of puns, riddles, and typographic disruptions, they break with the conventions of storytelling and disrupt plotlines with patterns of allusion. Arrangements and developments come undone, departing from an origin's foreseeable becoming, rejecting the pull of sequential ordering. Instead, they cut into their stories with enigmatic prefaces, mangle the logic of conclusions, and split open their sentences with brackets and double dashes, all in the name of holding something in suspension and conceptualized separately from its successive disclosure. Whatever is conceived, in both senses of the word, may not come to pass. It may be put off, terminated, or diverted. Periods of confinement in their fiction layer the terminology surrounding pregnancy into the notion of a sentence served. And in one way or another, each tale and novel revels in the echo of womb and tomb. It is thus through the realm of the literary—with its wealth of devices and syntactical tricks, its boundlessness and daydreams— that their words confront the limitations and half-truths of the medicolegal language surrounding abortion. Alert to the ways in which an imagined entity (a fetus, an orangutan, a nation) can become more real than what is actual or living, their fiction opens up the questions that closed down abortion's practitioners and procedures: what is and is not murder; what constitutes a sign of life; who gets to draw the line between human and not-human.

With this book, I argue that Poe and Hawthorne thus attend to what is secret and indeterminate about pregnancy and existence in contradistinction to the fetus's technogenesis, as alive or already human in the expanding print culture or their time. In the name of opacity, their tales and novels take what I think are ironically clear positions against the processes of female disembodiment required to confer legal rights on fetal entities. The meaning of existence from one story to the next becomes nothing but an accident of birth. The goal of existence entails shattering hierarchies of the living. Through moody celebrations of genealogical nonreproduction and patriarchal decay, their narrators convey the sense that only a cosmic joke could sanction juridical protections for embryonic humans at the same time as it classified Black humanity along with objects and livestock.

The state-by-state criminalization of abortion that began in the 1820s entwines with the origins of detective fiction in Poe's three tales featuring C. Auguste Dupin. As nineteenth-century physicians redefined abortion as murder, they set the stage for a genre that performed something, as Poe once put it, "in a new key." Theodric Beck's *Elements of Medical Jurisprudence* reiterates, for example, the word "detect," insisting that forensic practitioners detect the ways in which a terminated pregnancy revealed itself on a woman's living or dead body. Poe's trilogy takes its details from Beck and construes a faux Parisian setting—where Paris is and is not New York; and where a fetus is and is not human—to explore the problem of translating life and death into the language of criminality and calculation. Its three tales come together around Detective Dupin, who appears only in them and who, as I argue, kills the women in the first two tales and threatens the woman in the last with death. Each of the women characters is affiliated with abortion, either as practitioners or procurers of it. The trilogy then comprises the confession of the unnamed narrator for his own connection with the killer. Working in the shadows of Dupin's lies, Poe's narrator tells a story of the extortion of meaning and money from the reproductive labor of others.

I then argue that Hawthorne follows Poe's lead and likewise crafts an abortion trilogy through *The Scarlet Letter, The House of the Seven Gables,* and *The Blithedale Romance.* Published one after the other in rapid succession, each novel not only centers on the sexual secrets of women but also unfolds according to the interplay between concealment and detection. Each goes over the same ground, its narrators obsessively questioning what it means to be born into white America, let alone being born at all. Composing a kind of extended anti-epic with three spines, Hawthorne turns abortion into a trope that subtly and steadily cuts through the patriotic lexicon of a national birth brought into being by its white citizens. Hawthorne makes repeated allusions to the second story in the structures of his fictional houses, accomplishing the same feat as Poe does before him, to represent abortion by obscuring it, so that its legibility remains connected to the privacy of its practice.

Both writers move the Aristotelian maxim—that anything capable of being is capable of nonbeing—into the landscape of their tales, holding actuality apart from potentiality, and potentiality apart from probability. Carefully thinking about nonexistence becomes a route out of the shocking forms of violence that overwhelm the spaces and worlds within which their stories take place; it demands the nonreproduction of the institutions built on that violence. If the word "nation" derives from the Italian *nascere* (to be born) and arrives in modernity as what Giorgio Agamben calls an "integration of medicine and politics," then abortion perhaps points toward its disintegration and makes possible the separation of the living from the state's classification of and capitalization on life.[71]

PART I

DETECTION, CONFESSION, TERMINATION
Three by Edgar Allan Poe

Preamble: An Air of Method

This section proceeds from a distinct standpoint on Poe's clever detective, C. Auguste Dupin, tying him directly to the murders he ostensibly solves and interpreting the trilogy as an extended confession on the narrator's part. I argue that Dupin's counterfeit, bombastic expressions of expertise signpost his murderous motives, particularly when he expounds on motiveless crimes and chance opportunities. Everything is staged or inverted, including his rivalry with the Prefect and the Minister D——. His allusions to antagonism, in other words, mask collusion; his insistence on happenstance conceals intent. Dupin is as cunning and sadistic a figure as any of Poe's villains, and he not only gets away with murder but also profits from it. The facts included about the different crime scenes, and which are corroborated by different figures, get lost in Dupin's devious, excessive redirection of information. It is up to the reader to heed Poe's carefully formed distinctions between fraudulence and fiction, deception and representation, against the grain of their semantic correspondences.

Poe also draws a line between the concept of life and that of the living, casting Dupin as someone driven to obscure it. On the trilogy's allegorical level, this obscurity serves the contradictions of the nation-state well. It licenses military massacres and prohibits abortion in the name of a population's life, configuring maternity as something abstract or oriented toward policed and rewritten borders. Poe locates this dangerous, contradictory configuration not only in the murders at the center of the trilogy but also in the presence of the naval officers to whom Dupin repeatedly alludes. Military figures appear in association with the dead women and alongside echoes of "naval" and "navel," "seamen" and "semen." While his references rely on historical links between sailors and sex workers, and between sex workers and abortionists, they also introduce into the textual landscape the officially sanctioned violence represented by men in military garb. From the perspective of the conservative Dupin, the borders that should be secured by the navy are breached by the presence of immigrants. Their movement into the city's center does not constitute a healthy sign of growth but rather of the white population's adulteration.

In each of the tales, abortion arises in opposition to the state's guarded shorelines and its reproductive imperatives. Dupin murders the L'Espanaye women and Marie Rogêt in the time before the trilogy opens because he knows that the former practiced abortion and that the latter procured one. When the tales begin, their corpses are covered in readable signs of his motive. In "The Purloined Letter," the last of the three tales, this trail of blood arrives at the door of the terrified, unnamed woman who wants her letter back. As I argue, the letter links her to the abortionists on the Rue Morgue. She knows the gruesome manner in which they died and that the rummaged paperwork in their safe connects her to them. Dupin, letter in hand, knows that she knows, biding his time until the reward she offers for its return is large enough.

Dupin covertly articulates his darkly ironic pro-life position by means of allusion to the structure of rivalry and payback in which he exists. Although he coolly says that he desires to outdo, take vengeance upon, or settle debts with the Prefect, the bank clerk, and the Minister D——, he in fact combines these motives into a concentrated fury and unleashes it on the L'Espanayes and Marie Rogêt. The tales may involve revenge, but men are not its target. Dupin's insistence on payback stages a cover under which he hides his real contempt for women who withdraw from the patriarchal order of things. The subject of rivalry functions in the same structure of doubles and echoes that marks the trilogy and subtly establishes the dead and terrified women as Dupin's adversaries.

The tendency among Poe scholars, however, is to back away from concluding that Dupin is a sham and a killer, in part because they perceive the tales in which he is featured as departures from Poe's standard practice, rather than grouping them together with, say, "The Black Cat" or "The Tell-Tale Heart." For while the unnamed narrator who tells Dupin's story may not rip up the floorboards or bang on the wall, he points in the same direction of guilt, shame, and concealment. He repeatedly hints that we should back up through the tales and read for patterns, more so than for progression through a sequence. To read as carefully as possible is to be remunerated with a second story—in this trilogy about multiplying rewards—and to resist being hoaxed, not only by Dupin but also by the cultural assumptions behind which he hides. At every turn, Poe indicates that the intelligence and refinement exuded by Dupin are altogether compatible with the violence he commits. This is not to say that Poe scholars have failed to call attention to Dupin's unnerving, misogynistic arrogance or to sound the alarm about his suspect expertise, but that one step further is required to dismantle Dupin's insistence on motiveless crimes.[1]

Dupin appears with one foot in the criminal underworld and one in the French establishment, deviously balanced between them and working both angles. The first detective to appear in American fiction, he is modeled after Eugène-François Vidocq, who not only established the French Bureau of Investigation in 1833 but also specialized in committing crimes as much as he did in solving them. It seems clear that Poe extensively drew on Vidocq's widely published exploits for Dupin's characterization. An internationally renowned cad with a wide circle of criminal associates, Vidocq was a master of disguise, double-dealings, and forgery.[2] He was also notorious for cooperating with the police and turning against them, a detail that informs the rivalry and collusion that take place between Dupin and the Prefect.

In "The Murders in the Rue Morgue," Dupin mentions Vidocq and his methods, condescendingly suggesting that Vidocq loses sight of the facts because he pays too much attention to details, when skimming the surface is a far superior route to the truth. "Vidocq," he says, "was a good guesser, and a persevering man. But, without educated thought, he erred continually by the very intensity of his investigations. He impaired his vision by holding the object too close." None of this is correct. Vidocq was a skilled investigator, and Dupin's statement runs counter to what the narrator carefully advises in his preamble, regarding "the more concentrative player ... who conquers."[3] Here, Poe drops the first of many hints regarding the fraudulent nature of his detective. It is Vidocq's criminality that corresponds with Dupin's, not his renowned expertise.

Dupin is, however, far worse than his real-life double. Poe takes elements of Vidocq's biography and stretches them into the characterization of a vicious misogynist. Through Dupin, he explores the ways in which forensic detection and the antiabortion rhetoric of the early 1800s combined to legitimize surveillance of pregnancy and reproductive control. The brutalized women in the Dupin trilogy are recipients of the violence this rhetoric makes possible or authorizes, especially when it functions as a call to protect the unborn from murderous abortionists. While Vidocq's exploits do not include a trail of mutilated female bodies, they do provide Dupin with a bag of tricks, including an aptitude for assumed identities, costumes, and allegiances. Thus, the epigraph that opens "The Murders in the Rue Morgue" regarding Achilles hiding among women carries the solution to the locked-door puzzle that follows; it combines with the allusion to Vidocq to indicate that Dupin disguises himself in women's clothing in order to obtain access to the inner sanctum of the L'Espanaye residence. There, he simply knocks on their door and they open it for him.

The conversation about acting and actors in which Dupin and the narrator engage in "Rue Morgue" before they discuss the murders gestures backward to the epigraph and forward to the orangutan who mimics the sailor. In other words, it raises the subject of a man acting like a woman, and an ape acting like a man, and invites us to consider the extent to which everything is theater when it comes to Dupin. From this line of approach, the actor whom he mentions at the beginning of the tale reappears in the role of the naval officer seeking a renegade orangutan. He plays his part well, except for the beard he sports while describing the repeated act of shaving. Dupin is also a performer—of intelligence and exile—and the narrator's story involves gradually realizing his own role as Dupin's alibi and bootlicker. He sees behind the mask and seems trapped with his terrifying friend, and yet he seems to shift into more knowing forms of involvement in Dupin's world. Inside this network of white men, where the last of their backroom deals with the Prefect literally takes place in Dupin's "little back library," pipe smoking and intrigue are financed by crimes committed against women.

In his often-quoted letter to Phillip Cook, Poe remarked, "You are right about the hair-splitting of my French friend: that is all done for effect." He adds, "These tales of ratiocination owe most of their popularity to being something in a new key. I do not mean to say that they are not ingenious—but people think them more ingenious than they are—on account of their *air* of method. In the 'Murders in the Rue Morgue,' for instance, where is the ingenuity of unravelling a web which you yourself (the author) have woven for the express purpose of unravelling? The reader is made to confound the ingenuity of the supposititious Dupin with that of the writer of the story."[4] There is only an "*air* of method" and therefore nothing substantial or true about a murderous orangutan, a botched abortion, or a seemingly opportunistic purloining of a letter. It all comes back to Dupin and his scheming, and it begins with the safe filled with letters in the bedroom on the Rue Morgue. The French settings, moreover, permit all manner of puns and duplications to take place, including the word "rue" that opens the trilogy, the echo of "Restell" in "Estelle," Marie Rogêt's mother; and the question of being (*l'être*) in "The Purloined Letter."

CHAPTER ONE

Stargazing on the Rue Morgue

> The botanical, Latin name [of rue] "Ruta" comes from Greek, translated as "to set free."
> —Jim Long, "Rue: The Forgotten Herb," 2013

> Rue has repeatedly induced abortion.
> —John Burns, *The Principles of Midwifery*, 1843

"The Murders in the Rue Morgue" is a tale flooded with forms of manipulation and coercion—linguistic, ideological, biopolitical—each running alongside astonishing shows of physical strength, each associated with brutal attempts to force open locked doors and get inside our heads. The violence takes insidious and outright forms, as Poe merges human bodies and architectural structures into a shared lexicon of details and features. Locks denote both hair and bolts; nails secure window frames and fingertips; a house's passageways contain "no secret issues" even as its inhabitants heave with mystery.[1] At the center of this world of echoes and homonyms lie the mutilated bodies of two women, arranged in such a way that their lying tells the truth about their deaths. Their corpses bear a message about life, from the murderer to the city, in a deliberate display of blood and bruising. As I argue in this chapter, a seemingly passing reference to the L'Espanayes as fortune-tellers introduces the cover under which nineteenth-century abortionists advertised their services. It combines with the messages conveyed by the objects and architecture to establish their deaths as executions. Particularly gruesome, these executions produce mutilated bodies that are meant to double what the killer believes abortion entails for embryos and fetuses.

A story about a motivated killing, "The Murders in the Rue Morgue" is deceptively spun through the fiction of motivation's exact opposite: as accident, misfortune; the rampaging of a primate who unexpectedly crashes into the spaces of human existence. Together, the opposing concepts of premeditation and happenstance bookend Poe's philosophical inquiry into precisely the meaning of that existence. As "mind struggles with mind" in his narrator's seemingly random preamble about parlor games, we are cautioned about the intellectual coercion that lies ahead and thus works in tandem with material force. Poe's narrator wants us to know from the very beginning that his way with words implicates him in the violence surrounding the dead women and that he fell for a terrifying "young gentleman ... of an illustrious family" who moved him like a chess piece into defeating a police officer in "his own castle." When he drops the hint about being unintentionally knocked over by a fruit-seller on his way to work, he indicates its counterpart in the very methodical, purposeful pressure that the leisured, aristocratic Dupin enacted on him, until he discarded "from [his] thoughts the blundering idea of *motive*" in the murder of two women.[2] He thus sets up the accidental, physical force of the fruit-seller as the counterpart to his seemingly fortunate meeting of Dupin at a library where they searched for the same rare book, as if in a fated meeting of the minds.

The substance of the nameless narrator's disclosure or confession involves his subjugation to Dupin, horrifically recognized in retrospect. It follows from his realization that he bore a ferocious man's scheme to the police station and there delivered the tall tale of a berserk orangutan. His narrative comprises a confession for having embraced the image of Dupin's aristocratic birthright, just as he miscarried his incipient awareness of the truth. "A vague and half-formed conception of the meaning of Dupin flitted over my mind," Poe's narrator confesses about a conception that did not come to fruition. "I seemed to be upon the verge of comprehension, without the power to comprehend—as men, at times, find themselves upon the brink of remembrance, without being able, in the end, to remember." When he looks back, he sees how Dupin "seduces [him] into error," something he cautions us to avoid. The sexualized language of seduction is deliberate, indicating a sense of violation that mirrors what happens to the women on the Rue Morgue. A word interchangeable with "rape" in the medical jurisprudence of his time, the seduction of the narrator by Dupin plays out again when Dupin backs the sailor into a corner at gunpoint and forces him to birth an invented backstory about the orangutan's arrival in the city.[3] Or rather pays him to invent it, as I suggest in the preamble regarding the presence of a stage actor in the tale

This cornering includes the tale's readers, who capitulate to what Dupin demands of us. In spite of all the evidence to the contrary, the tendency is to buy Dupin's confident, aggressive performance of expertise on questions of life and death. But if we attend to the narrator's hint that a "true state of affairs" exists, then the literally reclined corpses communicate Dupin's profoundly vicious mockery of what the women metaphorically stood for. Throughout this chapter, I demonstrate that such doubles and reversals structure the ways in which Dupin twists what he does into not-murder. He seizes this definitional complexity of murder from the work of abortion in his tale about an orangutan, a nonhuman creature exempted from the notion of murder's premeditation. If the women whom Dupin kills defined pregnancy along the lines of accident and misfortune, then he uses the same paradigm against them by invoking an unfortunate, random encounter with an ape to close the case. Avenging fetal life (as if every fetus were a rare book, authorized by God), his motives also arise in the narrator's carefully distributed allusions to hierarchies of being and to souls, especially when it comes to "men of the highest order of intellect" who descend from God, not from apes.[4] Thus, with "The Murders in the Rue Morgue," Poe sets up the first of his three explorations of abortion as a practice involving philosophical questions irreconcilable with conservative positions on human existence and destiny.

The laundress in the lineup of witnesses says she "believed that Madame L. told fortunes for a living" and comes up from the bottom of Dupin's social structure to overturn his alibi. He cuts her from consideration, and she slides from view, as if her words are worthless. But Poe plays her from his hand and she is the first to testify.[5] Her statement about the L'Espanaye women imparts the code by which abortionists advertised their services throughout the nineteenth century, as clairvoyant physicians or fortune-tellers. ("Let them be aware of the danger, and pay no attention to the nostrums of fortune-tellers," the editor of *The Medical Adviser* noted in 1824, especially their "decoctions of *savine*").[6] I return to this subject toward the end of this chapter and trace the connecting lines among the laundress, the Sabine deity with whom the narrator opens his tale, and the goddess Laverna with whom Dupin closes it. What I wish to emphasize first is that Dupin knows of the furtive lexicon surrounding abortion and that he observes the women's work as a profound form of insubordination, as noncompliance with the spiritual hierarchy that accords him rank and significance. From this position, abortion means far more than a disburdening for women, becomes far more complex than a procedure that frees someone from an unwanted pregnancy. It becomes a battle between the abortionists' safekeeping of living women, on the one side, and the wardens of spiritual embodiment, on the other.

CHAPTER ONE

Composing a tale that breaks into newspaper extracts and terminates suddenly, Poe's narrator arranges pieces of information as if they were cards on a table, some faceup, some facedown. "A casual or inadvertent word; the accidental dropping or turning of a card," he notes in his preface, "afford... indications of the true state of affairs."[7] With this hint about his method, he breaks from plot and works with patterns of correspondence. This fragmentation of form in turn reflects a key point about the tale's content, together illuminating that existence itself is a matter of composition, recomposition, and luck. Nothing is destined by god to unfold, and everything is subject to shuffling and chance. Dupin's motive arrives from the opposite direction, as a meting out of divine punishment against the women for the atheistic materialism that he associates with the work of abortion. He also wants their money, as if making them pay on a literal level for his sense of dispossession.

It is no coincidence that Madame L'Espanaye withdraws her savings from the bank before she dies. Dupin may say that the money left behind at the crime scene underscores the disconnection between the two events, but he lies. The fact that the two bags of money remain behind introduces mishap and accident into the scheme of things, not coincidence. A well-planned heist, orchestrated along with the bank clerk whom Dupin later establishes as an old pal, is fumbled, even if the murder is accomplished. As Poe develops his allegory of abortion, the image of the money bags folds castration into the meaning of Dupin's vengeance. From his reactionary perspective, a terminated pregnancy severs insemination from mattering and implicitly disavows the soul's arrival at conception. It withdraws a pregnant person from the fiction of eternity that develops inside a uterus, denying god's role in human procreation.

Dupin's crime thus surfaces from within the narrator's translucent concealment of it as a reactionary attack on a world conceptualized as accidental, not foreordained, and into which women and immigrants make their ways, tripping up the white men whose footing is no longer secure. Everything is crumbling, foreign languages proliferate, and modernity parts ways with the nobility with which Dupin identifies. As Dupin and the narrator move through this world, Poe surrounds them in allusions to atoms and particles in an advancing materialism indifferent to their self-perception. It is for this reason that Dupin can read the narrator's mind when he stumbles, because he remembers discussing Epicurean philosophy with him: "As we crossed into this street, a fruiterer, with a large basket upon his head, brushing quickly past us, thrust you upon a pile of paving stones collected at a spot where the causeway is undergoing repair. You stepped upon one of the loose fragments, slipped, slightly strained your ankle, appeared vexed or sulky.... You kept your eyes upon the ground—glancing, with a petulant expression, at the holes and ruts in the pavement, (so that I saw you were still thinking of the stones,) until we reached the little alley." This detailed description of the narrator's tumble serves as an allusion to the threat represented by these "loose fragments" everywhere. "I saw you were thinking of the stones," Dupin remarks; "I knew you could not say to yourself 'stereotomy' without being brought to think of atomies, and thus the theories of Epicurus."[8] Their own dislodging from relevance (the narrator's and Dupin's) is insinuated by these scenes, with the nineteenth-century's understanding of Epicurean materialism as involving theories of atoms in corrosions of human exceptionalism. In W. J. Watts's words, "The Epicurean belief that the soul was purely physical and resolved into scattered atoms after an inevitable death ... made abortion morally irrelevant.... It required a Christian belief in an indestructible soul *and* one which needed to be saved, for abortion ... to be widely considered an inconceivably evil practice" (Watts's italics).[9] The fear raised by Epicurean thought, that it extinguishes human hope for immortality, arises in Dupin's violence, propelled by his sense of birthright.

Poe, however, works materialism into his narrative in order to rethink being human from the ground up. As John Tresch demonstrates, it is through matter that Poe prepares "new envelopes of thought and being" and conceptualizes existence through nonexistence, reordering bodies into affinities with objects.[10] Matthew Taylor makes a similar case, arguing that Poe's materialism "accords objects existence and agency beyond our use of them."[11] These objects indeed assert themselves in "The Murders in the Rue Morgue," demanding to be read alongside the living characters: the cobblestones, the room full of beds in on the top floor of the L'Espanaye's house, the safe in the L'Espanayes's room, the laundry that comes and goes. This list significantly extends to the six spoons mentioned by the narrator because when translated back into French (the original language of the tale, according to Poe's narrator) from English, "spoons" become *les cuillères,* which is another term for "forceps" or *les mains d'obstétrique.* As much as Dupin wishes to relegate these things to the background of the crime scene he pretends to interpret, he is only partly successful because they seem kinetic. The cobblestones come loose and the safe seems to swing open

CHAPTER ONE

and spill its contents, imitating the volition involved when English turns into French and back again.

Such an ontological reshuffling of animate and inanimate things into shared properties of energy and matter undoes the dominion of mind over matter, along with the entire chain of being into which it extends. Paying close attention to what is mistranslated, overlooked, downgraded, and taken for real, becomes for Poe a way of seeing the lies that might be cut from textual reproduction. In this trilogy, he aligns the work of abortion with atheism to take aim at the soul as the thing at stake in so much violence. By forcing the human and its prized possessions of soul and consciousness onto the same existential plane as other creatures and things in his fiction, he imagines another story for the land of the living. The world as it is consists of watched-over and brutal enclosures, evident in the narrator's allusions to the safe, the zoo, the jail, the sailor's closet, locks, and keys.

Throughout "The Murders in the Rue Morgue," Poe repeatedly puns on the words "sole" and "soul," insinuating that the conservative Dupin clutches a spiritual essence at the foundation of his being. He places this foundation beneath Dupin's feet as the superiority on which he stands, bipedal, erect, and gazing heavenward. Why else turn a cobbler into a figure of obsession as the story opens, so that a "mender of soles" accompanies Dupin's ability to "fathom [the narrator's] soul"? Shoe and street repair pervade the section in the tale that precedes the newspaper announcement of the murders of the two women. The cobblestones are coming apart as Dupin and the narrator walk, subjecting the soles of their feet to an uneasy form of contact and their minds to fragmentary thoughts. The narrator warns us of the "sole methods (sometimes indeed absurdly simple ones)" that direct interpretation, foreshadowing the "wound in the foot" experienced by the orangutan. In other words, a shoeless ape suffers from "a splinter on board the ship" because, as someone like Dupin would believe, solely those with souls put soles between their feet and the ground. As the story unfolds, the narrator learns to see in Dupin's "rich ideality" a terrible kind of cruelty.[12]

By pairing an ape with a woman beaten beyond any "semblance to humanity," Poe asks what this humanity is that standardizes the semblance. The narrator's sudden voicing of the word "mammalia" intensifies the query. He says aloud, "The gigantic stature, the prodigious strength and activity, the wild ferocity, and the imitative propensities of these mammalia are sufficiently known to all."[13] He introduces the term that categorized humans and apes together with other placental creatures, all linked by live births, and thus runs a maternal and primate genealogy into the very notion or symbol of humanity that Dupin guards. An emblem of the contestation surrounding human origins and forms of racialized classification, the ape on whom Dupin projects his horror also comes into focus as suffering (captive, injured, beaten) and thus alive in a way that a human fetus is not and subjected to harm in the same way as the women are.

Killing the L'Espanaye women, Dupin attacks the notion that the human is simply another kind of primate, purely material and borne into the world by accidents of fate. His alibi in the orangutan signals this motive as much as it obscures it. While there may indeed be an orangutan squirreled away at the Jardin des Plantes by the end of the story, this creature does not storm the L'Espanaye residence, was nowhere near it. The scene is all made up. Poe takes the orangutan as symbolic of the kind of bodies over which white men lose control: female, racialized, fetal, and mammalian. He then explores the means by which they recover that control in fictions of souls as housed in ascending levels of finer corporeality and spirituality.[14] In fact, taking back the house in which Dupin kills them ("a good house—not very old"; the "sole occupancy" of the women) before the story begins, the women initiate the allegory of ownership over structures and bodies that prevails in the tale. The house, we are told, was always the women's own property, in a reconceptualization of self and possession that gives the slip to god and living under his tenancy.[15]

Nineteenth-century midwifery guides and abortion advertisements make consistent references to women's bodies as physiological edifices within which fetal forms reside. Wooster Beach's popular and beautifully illustrated *Improved System of Midwifery* consistently names the "Divine Architect" as the figure who created the "mechanical contrivance of the pelvis" as a wondrous passageway through a pregnant woman's body. "The Great Architect of animate frames," Beach asserts, secures the development of new forms deep inside eggs and uteri.[16] Using the same terms, Madame Restell advertised her abortifacients in the antebellum press, announcing her willingness to consult women at her "office and residence [at] 148 Greenwich street . . . with the strictest confidence on all complaints incident to the female frame."[17] (In 1844, Poe moved to 130 Greenwich, where he lived for a year and during a high point of hostility against Madame Restell). As the authors of *Medicine Unbound* demonstrate, the long-standing image in

CHAPTER ONE

medical literature of the fetus as "housed" inside a woman gave rise to the antiabortion rhetoric describing its entrapment. Perceived as trapped and subject to its jailor's whims, the fetus came to be seen in terms of its legal and ideological independence from gestation, as a form of public property requiring protection from possible life-threatening harm.[18]

In "The Inversion of Exceptionality: Foucault, Agamben and 'Reproductive Rights,'" Penelope Deutscher takes a close look at this corporeal architecture as a component of modern biopower. What this image of the female frame accomplishes, she says, is a thoroughgoing "reducibility to reproductive life" of a woman's existence, a transformation of her body into a dangerous zone of suspended legal rights for a potential fetus. As such, it calls to mind the space of the internment camp in Giorgio Agamben's formulation of it, in which the fetus is perceived as caged and vulnerable to execution. Tracing the criminalization of abortion in the United States, Deutscher argues that the legislation proliferated into concepts involving "freedom, life, fetal life, personhood, potential personhood, right to life, rights over one's body," at the same time as it detached "life" from the biological, material structures of its realities. A woman thus simultaneously holds in place *and* disappears from the framework of fetal development. In this legal and ideological world, a strange prenatal temporality unfolds, in which woman and fetus effectively engage in a "battle of sovereignty" in a time discerned as "prior to" birth. Here, the fetus transforms into a pseudo *homo sacer*, the Roman figure whom Agamben describes in terms of the legal distinction between who can be murdered and who sacrificed. "Neither zoe, bios, bare life, nor *homo sacer*," Deutscher writes, the fetus is also "all of these" once configured as a form of "rights-bearing life."[19]

With "The Murders in the Rue Morgue," Poe thinks through what it means to see a woman's reproductive body in terms of legal tenancy. He establishes Dupin as a renter who takes up with the narrator before he introduces the L'Espanayes as homeowners. In the background of the plot, the women lay claim to the house they previously leased, clearing out and replacing the men who lived there. The narrator underscores the fact that the women refuse "to let any portion" of their house to any tenant.[20] On the metaphoric level of meaning, this terminated tenancy includes a fetus's claim to symbolically returned property—to a woman's body confirmed as proper to her. Poe sees this claim in terms of an epic battle waged by men against women. Achilles is, after all, introduced in the tale's epigraph. By taking back their house, the women become subject to a distorted form of vigilante justice that at once suspends and serves the law against murder. Killing the women, from within this ideological architecture, becomes a form of fetal liberation. And self-preservation is the other side of this liberation's coin, connoted in the mirroring between Dupin and the fetus, both subject to dispossession and eviction from significance.

The women's prerogative to evict the boarders for "abuse of the premises" carries the drift of abortion and the right to expel from within a body that which threatens or exploits it. The architectural metaphor permits a crossover between eviction and abortion to arise, conceptualizing a casting off that is essential to the preservation of structural integrity, as opposed to the other way around, wherein the structure lovingly houses its tenants. Dupin enters the scene shredded of "patrimony," reduced to a "small remnant" of its former power, and perhaps holding an actual key to the room on the top floor of the L'Espanaye house. On the literal level of the tale, in the time before the L'Espanayes return, a jeweler once "under-let the upper rooms to various persons," a detail about locks and keys that the narrator slips in among his descriptions of who rises and who falls in Paris, just before the press announces the murders on the Rue Morgue.[21]

He describes Dupin as "succumb[ing] beneath" his misfortunes, stressing the downward movement of a man whom he perceives to be superior by birthright. In the retrospective current of the narrative (the backward glance to "Paris during the spring and part of the summer of 18—"), he understands more clearly that he let Dupin talk his way into taking up residence with him, moved by "the wild fervor and the vivid freshness of his imagination." He remembers liking the fact that Dupin took "mere self" as his favorite theme. "Had the routine of our life at this place been known to the world," he states, "we should have been regarded as madmen—although, perhaps, as madmen of a harmless nature." The metaphoric key to this phrase, added on as if an afterthought, lies with the word "perhaps," itself set off by commas and breaking into the phrase in order to qualify the word "harmless." What he actually recounts is a memory of pistols, cudgels, bayonets, crowbars, whips, and razors—instruments that appear not only excessively phallic and dangerous but also as if magically conjured by Dupin throughout the tale. "Here is a billet of wood," Dupin casually informs him, "the circumference of which is about that of the throat," he says as he wraps a sheet of paper around it. "Here are pistols."[22] His hands are repeatedly in contact with things of a harmful nature. The realm of the "perhaps" is not the same as the realm of the actual.

"The suspicion is sufficiently forcible to give a definite form ... to my inquiries into the chamber." Dupin asks about the "impressions" he makes "upon [the narrator's] fancy," in a conceptual pairing with the bruises and wounds he leaves on the women's bodies. Attentive to such processes of impressing and marking, the narrator follows suit, guiding the story of Dupin's culpability through strategic uses of punctuation, spacing, and typography. Bracketed sides carry information that goes under cover of offhandedness. Even an entire paragraph is made to seem incidental when it in fact illuminates Dupin's terrifying nature and voice: "I have already spoken of his abstract manner at such times, [notes the narrator]. His discourse was addressed to myself; but his voice, although by no means loud, had that intonation which is commonly employed in speaking to some one at a great distance. His eyes, vacant in expression, regarded only the wall." These remarks read as a digression even as they underscore Dupin's propensity for self-division—his weird way of seeming to vacate his body to become only a voice and turn the strength of both against the L'Espanaye women. Italics, in addition, capture on the page what Dupin emphasizes in speech, setting off the exaggerations through which Dupin builds his alibi about the nonhuman nature of the killer, the "very *extraordinary ... unequal* voice," the "*excessively outré*" nature of the crime, a "*grotesquerie* in horror."[23] In John Tresch's words, "Poe was obsessed with the material technologies of printing and its ability or failure to produce the mental or spiritual transformation known as meaning."[24] Poe shifts into italics in order to convey the pressure of emphasis as a form of vocal coercion designed to attach an ape's hand to the excoriated bodies.

The asterisk that follows the tale's conclusion to introduce a footnote functions with similar significance. Part of a pair, it simply signals attribution, noting that the closing line in French and in italics ("*de nier ce qui est, et d'expliquer ce qui n'est pas*") derives from Rousseau's *Nouvelle Heloise*. Here, the narrator remains at two removes, as he quotes Dupin who quotes Rousseau, so that his final paragraph ends with a single quotation mark, followed by a double quotation mark, followed by an asterisk. Not only do all of these references expand the frame of the enclosed narrative, but they also function to credit authorship or copyright. Extending the notion of reproductive rights through them, Poe invites us to translate Rousseau's words and contemplate what exists and what does not, *de nier ce qui est*, and to remember that there is a distinction between what can be imagined as existing and what actually comes into existence. This invitation generates rich conceptualizations about material and bodily interconnections, as everything begins and ends inside something else, marked in asterisks. Between the epigraph and the final footnote, Poe's story comes into being, along with the notion that the stars reside beneath our feet as much as they shimmer above us.[25]

In Poe's time, Madame Restell ran ads in the newspapers that used asterisks in place of particular words, productively calling attention to the coded information in the stars. Her pills, she advertised, "are an infallible regulator of ******. They must not be taken when ********."[26] In Marvin Olasky's words, "Anyone could see, even in those days before Wheel of Fortune, that the asterisks stood for "menses" and "pregnant." In an 1839 edition of the New York *Sun* an advertiser described pills for women that could "produce a******n" if taken while pregnant. The stars, perfectly numbered, permit "abortion" to spell itself out inside a sequence in which the word concurrently disappears.

Poe draws us into such stargazing, the asterisks in his tale returning us to a moment when Dupin and the narrator look "upward to the great *nebula* in Orion" just before they look "over an evening edition" of a newspaper. Poe stages the reading of stars again when he has Dupin advise that one look "at a star by glances" and avoid a "scrutiny too sustained, too concentrated, or too direct." Through Poe, stargazing demands a level of close reading that Dupin advises *against:* "Vidocq, [he says of the historical French detective], impaired his vision by holding the object too close.... By undue profundity we perplex and enfeeble thought; and it is possible to make even Venus herself vanish from the firmament by a scrutiny too sustained, too concentrated, or too direct." Here, Dupin subtly redirects the angle of approach, throwing out of focus what the narrator hints must then be pulled back into view. To look directly on the night sky is not at all to "enfeeble thought": it is to see constellations turn into maps and figures.[27]

In order to perceive the stars as nebulae and constellations, one must know in advance what to look for. To a person unacquainted with the nebulae and the myths through which the constellations become vivid, the stars simply scatter in regular formations across a dark sky. Once initiated, an entire story unfolds into a readable map. As a result, the sky reveals to different

CHAPTER ONE

onlookers nothing and everything at the same time. Orion can therefore hide in plain sight. This sense of initiation is what I think Poe draws on for "The Murders in the Rue Morgue" by retaining for the abortionists their cover. He conceals them only so far, suspending them between legibility and illegibility, mirroring the function of the asterisks and euphemisms in their advertisements. The abortionists remain hidden but not all the way out of sight, so that those who comprehend their world can find it. In this way, a map of invisible lines exists from the L'Espanaye house to the morgue, from the beds on the top floor of the house to the woman who picks up the laundry. Against the plot that Dupin attempts to force into being, these lines crisscross into the epigraph, footnotes, and typographic marks to disclose what happens to the women and why.

Although primarily visual, this pattern involves ways of hearing too. It is reported, for instance, that Camille's screams are "long and loud—very awful and distressing"; they last "several minutes—probably ten"; and they express a "great agony ... long and drawn out." Nothing here indicates a swift execution by a frenzied ape. Instead, the "drawn-out" screaming records the fact of rape in sound, just as the coroner records it on paper, as the violation of Camille that we "need not mention," according to Dupin. This is the crux of Dupin's orangutan alibi or fabrication—the transformation of rape into ape. "Perdidit antiquum litera prima sonum," Dupin says in Latin as he looks up at Orion, the violent mythic stalker who flickers into existence at night.[28] Translated as "the first letter lost its ancient sound," the Latin words recall us to the aural world lost in Dupin's account of the murders and reconnect the *r* sound to the word "ape." Aural and visual records of rape exist in "The Murders in the Rue Morgue," documented by voices and accounts other than Dupin's. Nothing at all accounts for an orangutan on the loose, except for a bearded seaman who arrives out of nowhere too, in another of Dupin's conjured demonstrations.

Severing is Dupin's specialty. The misogyny that echoes in his reference to Madame L'Espanaye as "the old lady," for instance, functions to cut off her distinctiveness and render her as inconsequential. A decapitated "old lady" leaves no trail of information to the bright young detective, except in the hints that he drops. A particularly telling one surfaces in his description of the nail in the window, itself decapitated in his description of it. What he notes about this nail is its illusion of integrity—how it only appears to be unbroken, like a hymen, until he discovers its truth. As he builds his case, he notes how easily it splits apart with just a touch, allowing the window to swing open for any random primate.[29] It is his way of sneering at the work of the abortionist from his reactionary perspective, as the procedure that returns fallen women to the appearance of virtuous inaccessibility.[30]

Dupin only partially conceals his motives because he effectively signs his name at the murder scenes. All of the major characters are associated with writing in Poe's trilogy, including the L'Espanaye women, who own a safe filled with letters; Marie Rogêt, who signs her name in chalk; and the woman who authors the purloined letter. Writing is one means by which the living mark their presence in the world.[31] By killing in such ritualistic ways, Dupin authorizes his own significance, using the dead women's blood and bodies as writing instruments. He wants to leave a mark, underscore his motive, and disappear from view. For instance, his response to the Prefect's "sarcasm or two about the propriety of every person minding his own business" is to invoke "pictures of the Goddess Laverna," thus leaving another clue about his motive or dropping a card face-up for us to ponder.[32] What tends to be known about Laverna is that she presided over ancient Rome's scoundrels and thieves, as Poe scholars have discussed, but what tends to be forgotten is that she was also the goddess who presided over unwanted pregnancies.

A "bloody transaction," Dupin calls the murders, belying the extent to which he considers the crime a payback and indicating that a loss of economic control permeates an otherwise spiritual crisis.[33] Dupin surfaces as heroic, in a cunning display of his mind over matter, and he accords no space in the tale to mourning the women. Instead, he insinuates that they sell their souls for two bags of money. It is a spectacle of cruelty toward which Poe scholars remain drawn, anxious about the bodies that simply drop out of the narrative toward its conclusion. The two victims never speak for themselves, and their screams are likewise obscured inside Dupin's racist interchangeability of Asians, Africans, and apes.

Everything that Dupin says and does aims to accomplish a complicated double move that at once obscures and signs his message of white, patriarchal supremacy. As his deliberate crime is reversed into a framework of frenzy, a peaceful herbivore is made out to be a carnivorous nightmare.[34] He concocts a tale of a soulless beast who kills the women, as if to say, *This is the animal body you destroy, come back for revenge.* And he blames the Prefect for being clueless, because "in his wisdom is no *stamen*, ... like a codfish."[35] In the same way that his coercive lexical strategies function throughout the tale,

CHAPTER ONE

Dupin's mixed metaphors aim to impress, mystify, insult, and shut down the questions that Poe generates inside of them.

One of the newspapers quoted by the narrator raises an odd hypothesis with the words "if indeed a murder has been committed at all." In order to work with conjecture, Dupin pursues this strange possibility into the "question [of] whether the old lady could have first destroyed the daughter, and afterward have committed suicide." He does so for two reasons: to expound on suicide, as if it matters, and muddy the waters; and to reflect on the vilification implied by the newspaper, particularly as it informs Dupin's use of the terms "butchery" and "bloody transaction" in place of the word "murder."[36] The rest of the newspaper account is held outside of the frame but its excerpted hypothesis may be read inside the snide and sarcastic tones that sometimes arise in the tale. In other words, the excerpt indicates that it belongs to the same kind of newspapers that described, in Poe's time, abortionists as subhuman and nonhuman creatures—the kind of creatures to whom the word "murder" would not apply.

Madame Restell, for instance, was described in Poe's time as a devil, bat, female hyena, she-wolf, strangler, and vampire.[37] "This creature's advertisements are to be seen in our daily papers," the *New York Medical and Surgical Reporter* announced in 1846.[38] Two years earlier, an 1844 edition of the *Boston Medical and Surgical Journal* called abortion a "dealing in blood" and its practitioners unprepared for "God's avenging arm." Their clinics were described as slaughterhouses where blood was spilled and babies were butchered.[39] The editors and reporters at the *National Police Gazette* made it their mission to turn the public against abortion, especially throughout 1846. Although this postdates Poe's tale, it is well known that the *National Police Gazette* followed and intensified the gathering storm against abortionists, including Madame Restell. On February 28, 1846, they reported the following: "Murderess—The wickedness of the woman Restell, and the increasing developments of the atrocities daily practiced in her den in Greenwich Street, have at length aroused the indignation of the community to a pitch that defies restraint.... In calling attention last week to the outrages perpetrated by this wholesome female strangler, this modern Thug of civilized society, we impressed upon the attention of the public, the fact that her crimes are not confined alone to stifling the vital spark in the unborn, but that the adult mother also frequently falls a victim to her savage practices."[40] What can be gleaned from Poe's inclusion of fictional newspaper accounts is a sense of the actual ones he read and his understanding of what the rhetoric accomplished and the violence it made possible. If abortionists were not human, then they could only be killed, slaughtered, or butchered, in the same way as livestock.

Poe lays out the information about the women in a series of witness testimonies, each of which Dupin sifts into a problem of immigration and away from what the lively market implies about the L'Espanaye's lucrative work as fortune-tellers. Here, we get another glimpse of the Dupin to whom Poe returns in "The Mystery of Marie Rogêt," as a figure who despises not only the open borders of his city but also the women who purport to tell and direct its future. Through him, an allegory of nineteenth-century nationalism comes into view, with its calculations of a white birth rate and its adherence to a sacred national past and future. It is therefore highly significant that the L'Espanayes withdraw their money from the bank in a figurative cutting off of participation in the centralization of a male-dominated system. As abortionists, they become wealthy by rejecting the symbolic stuff of lineage, inheritance, and capital investment that configure women's bodies as the safety deposit boxes of the patronymic. They also spend their money, in another symbolic act of subtraction and divestment.

It is for this reason that Chillingworth's bequeathing of his wealth to Pearl at the end of Hawthorne's *The Scarlet Letter* reads as a creepy combination of claiming her, investing in her, and ejaculating on her, as much as it does a sign of generosity. The issues of inheritance and divestment also anticipate Hawthorne's *The House of the Seven Gables*, marked as it is by the consciously nonreproductive figure of Hepzibah and the decaying value of her real estate. Even as she opens it up to the commerce of the vibrant streets around the house, Hepzibah guards its interior as vehemently as Poe's women do theirs, refusing to exchange access to it for Jaffrey Pyncheon's money. For both Poe and Hawthorne, non-normative and rebellious figures draw and redraw the lines between the public and private obligations of their bodies and spaces, the prerogatives of which are perceived by conservatives as threatening on an existential scale. Just as the L'Espanaye room includes a small safe, once concealed beneath the women's bed and central to the scene of the crime, so too does Hepzibah's house, its walls hiding a vaginal recess that itself ostensibly hides the future wealth of the family name.[41] In secret places deep inside national structures, narratives, and bodies, the American myth

CHAPTER ONE

of founding and futurity empties out, undone by those who declare their independence from it.

In "The Murders in the Rue Morgue," Dupin works to draw attention away from the wider architecture of the house and collapse the contexts surrounding the L'Espanaye women. He closes in on one sound and one room; and then on one window and one rusty nail, in order to throw out of focus what I think matters the most, apart from the women themselves, their small iron safe. This safe is discovered, the narrator says, "under the *bed* (not under the bedstead). It was open, with the key still in the door. It had no contents beyond a few old letters, and other papers of little consequence."[42] This ostensibly locked-door mystery opens onto an unlocked and open safe. The incongruity between a heavily guarded safe and things of "little consequence" sheds light on Dupin's modus operandi, which is to detach the victims from time and place, specifically from the dates, return addresses, and signatories on those letters. His aim is to produce the notion of a senseless kind of attack, arriving like lightening, and not at all in response to a network of correspondences, in which the voices of actual correspondents might be heard in those letters.

Forcing us to see and hear what he wants us to, Dupin replaces Ockham's razor with an orangutan's, as an outrageous improbability replaces what the evidence plainly indicates.[43] It is so shocking, this account of a sudden strike through a window, that it almost entirely layers over the sound that puts the lie to it: the horrendous, ten-minute long scream, "long and loud, very awful and distressing," that emanates from the house as the women die.[44] A rapid assault with a razor blade does not produce ten minutes of protracted screaming. Over and over again Dupin insists on deciphering the voices surrounding the L'Espanaye house in order to drown out what this screaming implies about the nature of the crime against at least one of them.

"No woman could have inflicted the blows with any weapon," a physician testifies, in a moment that again calls attention to violence that is then corroborated by the "testimony and the opinions of M. Dumas," just before the self-styled detective Dupin sets out to obfuscate it.[45] For, by conceiving the lie of a murderous ape, Dupin throws out the fact that it is men who beat women to death inside urban dwellings, not wild animals, themselves held captive or beaten into submission for display.[46] Indeed, the brief allusion to the Jardin des Plantes, where a blameless orangutan ends up, brings the latter brutality into focus as a component of the violent spectacles paid for in Poe's world.

The representation of the fetus as an entity trapped within the potentially dangerous cage of pregnancy reflects this zoological entertainment, and Poe subtly sets these interconnections into motion with a newspaper's attention-grabbing headline: "EXTRAORDINARY MURDERS." The report opens a window into the scene of the crime, displaying a dead and bloodied mother and a daughter stuck upside down within the still-warm chimney of her mother's house.[47] If we can conjure up the image of an orangutan brandishing a razor, we can imagine Madame L'Espanaye crying from her broken body as Dupin throttles and rapes her daughter. As Gillian Brown puts it, "In keeping with Poe's anthropological project of discovering and preserving human consciousness, the murders in the Rue Morgue produce an anthropomorphic narrative. The tale presents a thoroughly legible world in which every event and its effects fit into a human grid."[48] Dupin, against Poe and his narrator, manipulates the grid, distorting the legibility of human violence into that of a scapegoated ape's.

"The Murders in the Rue Morgue" is taken to be detective fiction's inaugural story, "the birth of the genre."[49] It is "the foundation stone of mystery writing," a poster at the British Library proclaimed several years ago, along with the explanation that "the word 'detective' itself was not recorded by the OED before 1843."[50] Yet, the tale's own coded suspicion of detection or of the detective himself comprises a kind of turning-back on what it seems to birth, undercutting at every turn Dupin's procedures and his ostensibly rational, superior mind. The first story in American literature to feature a detective and a murder mystery is in fact the sidekick's confession, whose narrative bears a meditation on the problem of abortion as murder. It is rendered as a kind of abortion itself, of something he tires of carrying and fears to deliver. Like the sailor who draws a "long breath, with the air of a man relieved of some intolerable burden," the narrator reproduces what Dupin wants him to say and breaks it into contradictory fragments.[51]

We can see the genre's ironic birth in terms of the medicolegal developments of the first half of the nineteenth century.[52] Moving abortion into the category of murder, physicians cast themselves as detectives, trained to read criminality in and around a woman's body. For example, Theodric Beck's enormously popular *Elements of Medical Jurisprudence,* first published in 1825 and reissued ten more times before midcentury, devotes its largest chapters to the subjects of abortion and pregnancy and frames them within the problem of concealment. Establishing "five general rules for the detection of feigned diseases," from the "moral habits of the suspected person" to the falsely aggravated symptoms of "an actually present disease," he aims to make bruises, cuts, contusions, missing teeth, and so on into signs that either verify or disprove a woman's words about states of gestation. A physician, he explains, must then be able to deduce "the signs of abortion . . . from an examination of the female." Aware, though, that embryos sometimes die on their own, Beck devotes another ten pages to the complex matter of ascertaining this possibility, before he turns to the subsection on the "murder of the child after it is born."[53]

In 1867, physician Edwin Hale declared abortion the "great crime of the nineteenth century," the title of his book, and underscored it as problem of detection, which his book's subtitle raised as a series of questions: "Why it is committed? Who are the criminals? How shall they be detected? How shall they be punished?" Terminated pregnancies, under such rhetorical urgency, turned women into both criminals and crime scenes. As an "offence of a national character," abortion reduced the population "*in an appalling degree*" (Hale's italics). While difficult to detect, Hale noted, it nonetheless left a trail in the "fortune-tellers" and "lecturers on physiology," who advertised in the daily newspapers, as well as in the number of stillbirths that hid in the morgues under a "veil of secrecy." A secret disseminated in euphemisms and codes so obvious once cracked, Hale points out, abortion obliterated souls, often leaving "no chance of detection thereof."[54] For Hale, statistics, licensing, laws, and arrests against the practice could prevent the Anglo-American birth rate from further decline.

Hale's words not only underscore the association between abortion and detection but also return me to my earlier point regarding the laundress's remark about the L'Espanayes as fortune-tellers. So much significance is carried by the laundress's words and by her implicit connections with the goddess Laverna whom Dupin mentions toward the end of Poe's tale.[55] James Mohr notes that in response to abortion's criminalization, abortionists began calling themselves astrologists and fortune-tellers as early as 1840 and continued to do so throughout the century.[56] The language in which they advertised and described their services often combined allusions to celestial predictions and physiological remedies. For instance, in a book titled *The Mysteries of Astrology and the Wonders of Magic* (1854) one Dr. C. W. Roback discusses at length the value of fortune-telling in "consultations" regarding "nativities," and contends that celestial signs may be calculated for answers involving the fates of "the human frame." He contends, "If I can see and foretell dangers, why cannot I also teach the parties imperiled how to avert them?"⁵⁷ Providing a fascinating compendium of geomancy, divination, and astrology, Roback repeatedly insists that foreshadowing the future means intervening in it and "favorably" modifying its consequences.

While Roback's diction may point only vaguely toward intervening in a pregnancy, his charts and illustrations address it directly. His nativity charts in particular promise to ascertain the precise hour of conception (through moon cycles and angles) as well as that of birth, and he follows them up with a chapter on medicinal herbs known to midwives, those "certain plants having a semblance of the womb." Question six of his divining charts asks about pregnancy, with its corresponding answer as "abortion" in cases of "negative sentences." Other questions include life, illness, marriage, and things lost. The popularity of Roback's work, evident in the "thirty-eight thousand nativities [he] cast" over nine years in New England, indicates the success he experienced in "foretelling peril, and discovering the means of escaping it."⁵⁸ The book of fate could be edited; biology need not be destiny.

Even more significant to this connection between abortion and fortune-telling is Charles Leland's *Aradia* (1899), which includes a lengthy chapter on Laverna, the details of whom he obtained from an Italian fortune-teller about a decade earlier. The Laverniones, as the fortune-teller describes them, followed strict codes of silence and prayer, uttering invocations as silently as possible. They used herbs in their rituals—rue and concordia, two abortifacients, as well as poppy, a known analgesic—and asked to be relieved from pregnancies or painful births. According to the fortune-teller, a terminated pregnancy took place as the supplicant fell into a deep sleep, dreaming that Laverna whisked away the fetus and kept it until the woman changed her mind. The lengthy excerpt below includes her account, as Leland transcribes it in *Aradia:*

> And if a man had got any woman with child or any maid found herself *enceinte,* and would hide it from the world and escape scandal, they would go every day to invoke *Laverna.*
> Then when the time came for the supplicant to be delivered, *Laverna* would bear her in sleep during the night to her temple, and after the birth cast her into slumber again, and bear her back to her bed at home, and when she awoke in the morning,

> she was ever in vigorous health and felt no weariness, and all seemed to her as a dream.
> But to those who desired in time to reclaim their children, *Laverna* was indulgent if they led such lives as pleased her and faithfully worshiped her.
> And this is the ceremony to be performed and the incantation to be offered every night to *Laverna*.
> There must be a set place devoted to the goddess, be it a room, a cellar, or a grove, but ever a solitary place.
>
> ...
>
> Take of the herbs *Paura* and *concordia,* and boil the two together, repeating meanwhile the following:
>
> ...
>
> *Incantation.*
> I boil the cluster of concordia
> To keep in concord and at peace with me
> *Laverna*, that she may restore to me
> My child, and that she by her favouring care
> May guard me well from danger all my life!,
> I boil this herb, yet 'tis not it which boils;
> I boil the *fear,* that it may keep afar
> Any intruder, and if such should come
> (To spy upon my rite), may he be struck
> With fear and in his terror haste away![59]

The same fetus, it seems, could be asked to come back, in a ritual that imitated and reversed the earlier one. Terminating a pregnancy meant delaying the birth of a wanted child, a whisking-away to another realm where it awaited reconceiving.

Drawing on works by Horace, Virgil, and Ovid, and combining their words about Laverna with the fortune-teller, Charles Leland describes a forgiving deity who preferred to be on earth rather than in heaven among the gods. Her most loyal and clever followers could glimpse her whole and beautiful. Those whom she mistrusted were permitted to see only a headless body or a bodiless head. Her votaries also associated her with the poppy and the oblivion it could provide. Herbalists have explained throughout the centuries that keeping the beautiful head of the poppy together with its stem produces the best analgesic results. It is possible that the notion of seeing Laverna whole resided in this rule for plucking and preparing the poppy. Contractions induced by Laverna's rue might have necessitated poppy, and the oblivious woman awoke to know nothing of the agony of the night before.

Associated more with dishonesty than with wickedness, Laverna cleared a space for deeds performed in darkness, out of reach of violent punishment. In Horace's words, "If a man had got any woman with child, or any maid found herself *enceinte,* and would hide it from the world and escape scandal, they would go every day to invoke *Laverna.*"[60] Laverna's votaries performed left-handed libations, the kind associated with access to the underworld, and they worshipped her at an altar just outside of the Roman city gates. There, women also concealed their "faults," especially before marriage and in order to appear spotless.[61] Laverna's prayers and rituals were performed in secrecy and darkness, in a grove or temple dedicated to her, but a gate through the Roman wall bore her name and showed the way out—and it still does, the *Porta Lavernalis,* as does a roadway, the Viale Lavernalis. By virtue of this system, the Romans allowed a space for activities that followed a logic of their own, one incompatible with the laws of the city. Just as they included gods of the underworld and death in their sense of the sacred, so too did they include abortion and counterfeit within it, reflected against the city's world. Abortion, nighttime, secrecy, rascality, counterfeit, and wilderness formed an underworld against which childbirth, daylight, display, legitimacy, finance, and governance could take place aboveground, in the daytime.

This is not to compress the variations of laws and customs surrounding childbirth across the centuries of the Roman Empire into one practice but rather to contend that at a certain point in its pantheon, a goddess oversaw the difficult rituals surrounding unwanted pregnancies. Laverna's name is preserved in the Latin classics that Poe read, clearly tied to the concealment of pregnancy and abortion. I think that Poe ascertained how the left-handed rituals surrounding pregnancy accommodated its termination in a separately defined system of exchange in time and space: at night and on the outside of the walled city.

One of the problems that Poe appears to pinpoint about abortion in "The Murders in the Rue Morgue" involves its shift into the lucrative financial world on the inside of the nineteenth-century city, attracting the attention of those who do not understand it and who see it as a process of hollowing out the value of human life. As Barry Stephenson illustrates in his introduction to the study of ritual, ritualized practices address the demarcations of the human. These practices do not rest on an ontological given but rather comprehend the human as a disharmonious entity, pulled across parallel realities with other animals and sacred figures, between cognition and hallucination, and through cultural ceremonies of biological births and deaths. Ritual arises, in Stephenson's words, "at the troublesome zones" where ambivalence about external boundaries and internal hierarchies unfold. The violence that might otherwise resolve ambivalence or ambiguous borderlines is worked out in ceremonies that release tension and counter violence via dance, song, prayer, and stories. For Stephenson, ritual is heuristically effective and momentary, performed as an acknowledgment of discord and not as a permanent way out of it.[62] Neither does it follow social organization. Linked to the mysteries of being, its enactment as a temporary, active passageway through something potentially uncontrollable *precedes* culture—becomes something cultural because of repetition and out of the need to lift the psychological burdens involved in sacrifice, fear of pain and death, and grief, for example.

I take this theory of ritual into the reference to Laverna, in order to see "The Murders in the Rue Morgue" as a way of defining abortion in terms of a custom practiced apart from particular jurisdictions and ways of seeing. Abortion borders on those jurisdictions but cannot be translated into them, because its crossover entails violating the obscurity that the ritual sustains for it. Once translated across the boundary from ritual into forensics, abortion loses its legibility as a rite that assuages existential, psychological, and legal entanglements and becomes legible as a right inside legal visualizations of life and death. To draw a parallel with the facsimile of a hand that Dupin rolls around a wooden cylinder and presents to the narrator: while ink on paper may relay to the reader a corporeal experience (in this case, the sensation of strangling the life out of someone), it is not the same thing. The same may be said for the representation of a fetus, especially given that it cannot be seen outside of its translation into words or in the absence of medical technology.

It is for this reason that Poe also alludes to but does not display the letters in the L'Espanaye safe; they consist metaphorically of left-handed libations to Laverna, and Poe keeps their contents out of sight. With "The Purloined Letter," he returns to this issue, sustaining focus on what it means for a person to be trapped inside a reproductive ideology as a guarantee of lineage and life. A dark rite, painful and bloody, abortion releases a woman from this fate, permitting a cultural, opted-for body to exist apart from, or in conjunction with, a reproductive, mammalian one. But this form of self-conceiving threatens the structure of women's subordination to those who classify life in the name of god or human nature. In "The Murders in the Rue Morgue," Dupin vengefully separates the mother's head from her body and shoves her child back into a space described as "too narrow to admit the passage of a human being."[63] Drawing on obstetrical illustrations of impacted fetuses and instruments designed for their decapitation, he superimposes the image of late-term procedures in harrowing conditions onto early pregnancy abortions. The symbolic intricacy of the chimney opens onto questions regarding what comes out of that narrow passageway: a human being or its impossibility? Camille L'Espanaye is borne from it, but she is dead; therefore, the canal is and is not too narrow for a human being. In this site of indeterminacy, categorical divisions do not hold.

Before they died, the women's work announced itself in their relationships, including interactions with a "physician [who visited them] some eight or ten" times, and with "Alfonzo Garcio, undertaker" who lives nearby. It seems the Rue Morgue is a nickname as a result of his work or the L'Espanaye's, or both. A "nervous, . . . apprehensive" figure, the undertaker seems to be hiding something behind his testimony.[64] Together with the physician and the women, he forms a constellation of figures who attend to the bodies of the living and the dead. His nervousness indicates self-protection, a response to feeling threatened, and overshadows an expression of grief for the women. To a significant degree, this agitation underlies the tenor of the entire tale, with the narrator and undertaker sharing a partially concealed knowledge about the meaning of the murders. Noting, for instance, that his skin creeps in response to the unnerving nature of Dupin's investigation and frightening mind reading, the narrator indicates that he is pulled in different directions by his strange acquaintance.[65] He thus tells two stories with "The Murders in the Rue Morgue," composing them with both his right and left hands, so to speak. The two levels include the "vague and half-formed conception" that moves across his mind at one point—a conception that tellingly forms at "the verge of comprehension" and then fails to cross the threshold into being.[66]

Through such admissions, the narrator produces something of a "master stroke of cant," a phrase that Dupin utters but that becomes the narrator's own signature move.[67] Although the first definition of "cant" involves sanctimonious talk (the kind of which Dupin accuses the Prefect), the second

CHAPTER ONE

denotes the private language of an underworld. As he delivers and stifles his strangely discontinuous and abruptly discontinued tale, Poe's narrator moves into an underworld he shares with the L'Espanayes and about which he feels the need to confess. The substance of his confession involves falling for Dupin's aggressive rhetorical moves, all of which press on his consciousness the image of an orangutan.

The narrator lays out Dupin's tactics, one after another, to show himself a victim of seduction by hyperbole, appeals to authority, implicit ridicule ("the blundering idea of *motive*," Dupin sneers), invocations of scientific probability, shared maleness ("be ready . . . with your pistols"), and shared humanness ("this is no *human* hair"). "Two or three" locks of hair pulled out by the roots become in Dupin's rendition "half a million of hairs" and "(a hideous sight!) clotted with fragments of the flesh of the scalp." "Of the bruises upon the body of Madame L'Espanaye I do not speak," Dupin announces (even though he just did), before he replaces the existence of their malleable flesh with "a facsimile" of paper and unyielding wood.[68] All of these moments combine to reveal Dupin's underhanded process of layering near-imitations and harrowing images over actual objects, in an act of distortion that the narrator pushes us to see without saying outright. Again and again, Dupin produces something visually compelling and then lures the narrator into believing that he arrives at his own independent interpretation. Carried along by what he thinks he sees, the narrator becomes incrementally bound to Dupin's account, and can comprehend it only in retrospect.

In his prologue, the narrator urges us heed the imperatives he conceals inside his declaratives. "To observe attentively is to remember distinctly," he says, ostensibly about parlor games. *Observe attentively, remember distinctly,* he whispers. "Embarrassment, hesitation, eagerness or trepidation—all afford . . . indications of the true state of affairs," he offers, again about card playing but only if we read it as such.[69] Although the narrator tells a tale in a linear fashion, in which he meets Dupin and solves a crime, he carefully arranges words, statements, and inflections in patterns of correspondence and pairs.

To return to the epigraph is to see it, perhaps, as the first placement of a strong suit of cards. "What song the Syrens sang," it reads, "or what name Achilles assumed when he hid himself among women, although puzzling questions, are not beyond *all* conjecture."[70] Thus opening with a reference to women's voices, the imperative is to heed what they say ("not beyond *all* conjecture") as powerful men make incursions into their world. The reference to Achilles in disguise indicates how Dupin gains access to the top floor, slipping past the concierge, the "glazed watch box" of whom now stands suspiciously empty of its inhabitant. Costume and disguise are also encoded in the "changes of habiliment" noted in the women's room. If Achilles the great warrior himself could don women's clothing, his masculinity secured beneath the dresses and woman's name, then so could Dupin. The Homeric myth seems almost to license Dupin as he obtains entry, by subterfuge, into a world he thinks he knows and from which he profits.[71]

"It might have been a woman's voice," we are told twice, as Poe hints that two crime scenes exist: one outside, where Madame L'Espanaye is discovered; the other inside, where her daughter's body hides. Given that Madame L'Espanaye's severed head and body appear together in a semblance of a whole, it is impossible that she was "hurled headlong" through a window from the inside. She is cut down where she confronts her murderer, on the borders of her property. The duplication of the crime scene takes its place within the tale's obsessive series of paired figures and concepts, and it functions to align the L'Espanaye mother with the outside structure of the house in order to establish her daughter with its deep interior, upside down inside the warm channel of her "chimney." Outside of the house, the voices sound "—unequal—" one witness recounts. Inside of the house, the daughter's cries catch a passerby's attention. It is all we hear, as a kind of fading away before Dupin's voice takes over.[72]

We know that the room next to the L'Espanayes' contains eight beds, in a powerful evocation of a lying-in hospital. The L'Espanaye women may have led an "exceedingly retired life," but business came to them and they worked from home. What kind of work and how they summoned it is made more clear through the demonstrated ability of an advertisement to draw the desired readers to one's dwelling, when Dupin says, "This advertisement . . . will bring [the sailor] to our residence." The representation of this note, set off and printed in italics, encapsulates a world of correspondence and underscores the significance of the letters in the women's safe. Rectangular and carefully placed, the advertisement looks like a card adrift on the surface of the page and returns us to the moments when Poe's narrator asks us to recognize not only "what is played through feint" but also the "carelessness in regard to . . . concealment."[73] The presence of the laundress Pauline Dubourg and her brief, apparently inconsequential testimony arrive in this context.

CHAPTER ONE

Intimate with the women's dirty laundry in more ways than one, Pauline says that she "could not speak in regard to their mode or means of living," before noting them as fortune-tellers. In other words, through her, the French proverb "*Il faut laver son linge sale en famille*" ("we should wash our dirty linen in private") frames the translation of her words. The sole woman among all of the men who speak in this tale, Pauline describes the women as "affectionate towards each other" and willing to proffer "excellent pay."[74] Hers is a fleeting account of gestures and generosity—a way of keeping the women alive and configured within a relationship not only between a wanted, adored daughter and a mother but also between those women and herself.

In addition, Pauline makes a pair with Laverna, the "sable divinity" of the narrator's opening invocation.[75] The washer-woman performs a variation on Laverna's work, keeping secret and rinsing clean what the L'Espanayes hand over to her.[76] The beds that fill up the room next to the women's come with sheets, the stories of which Pauline refuses to disclose. That Pauline says she picked up the laundry is also a significant detail, because it involves a summoning to take something away. The sequence of her labor imitates the ritual of abortion over which Laverna presided, involving an invocation, the disburdening of something in her care, and the cleansing she accomplishes, before returning to the start over the entire cycle. If we call up the iconography of both figures, they appear with cauldrons, boiling, stirring, and washing away the secrets of a woman's bed.

As Barbara Johnson notes in "Apostrophe, Animation, and Abortion," figurative language accomplishes the feat of making something absent present, summoned in the mind's eye as congruent with what is materially perceived. Entities materialize in words that describe them, Johnson maintains, and particularly so when those words take the form of an apostrophe: "The fact that apostrophe allows one to animate the inanimate, the dead, or the absent implies that whenever a being is apostrophized, it is thereby automatically animated, anthropomorphized, 'person-ified.' . . . Because of the ineradicable tendency of language to animate whatever it addresses, rhetoric itself can always have already answered 'yes' to the question of whether a fetus is a human being."[77] This power underscores the "deviousness of language," in Johnson's words, through which personhood can be denied to nonhuman animals and enslaved human beings but extended to a white woman's fetus.

"How have I struck your fancy?" Dupin asks the narrator, invoking the printing metaphor of striking a page and leading him towards the image of

FIGURE 2. Image of a washerwoman, possibly Fanny McFarland. Clifton Johnson, *The washerwoman,* ca. 1902. Courtesy of The Jones Library, Inc., Amherst, Massachusetts.

an ape. "What impression have I made upon your fancy?" Dupin asks again. Manipulating the narrator into disbelieving what he sees with his own eyes, Dupin gets him to conceive his fiction. The result is also a kind of live birth, involving the delivery of Le Bon from his confinement in jail. "Le Bon was instantly released," he notes, "upon our narration of the circumstances (with some comments from Dupin) at the *bureau* of the Prefect of Police."[78] And yet the narrator carries another story, dispersing its fragments throughout the body of his text, in intimations of stained sheets, dropped cards, and detailed letters. In turn, the possibility arises that the "old letters of little consequence" left behind with the safe contain requests for abortifacients and procedures, along with payments and thank-you notes. The silence of the dead L'Espanaye women becomes sound, in the mysterious way that Laverna is said to have spoken from her headless neck or from her bodiless head.

With "The Purloined Letter," Poe keeps the L'Espanayes in mind, inviting us to see that two stolen letters (one from their safe, the other from the unnamed woman) produce the structure of blackmail that encloses the woman and threatens her existence. In between "The Murders in the Rue Morgue" and "The Purloined Letter," Marie Rogêt's mother switches places with "the old letters," as the "the old lady" whose words do not mean much. Poe, however, names her Estelle—the star or asterisk who extends the text's meanings outside of Dupin's control.

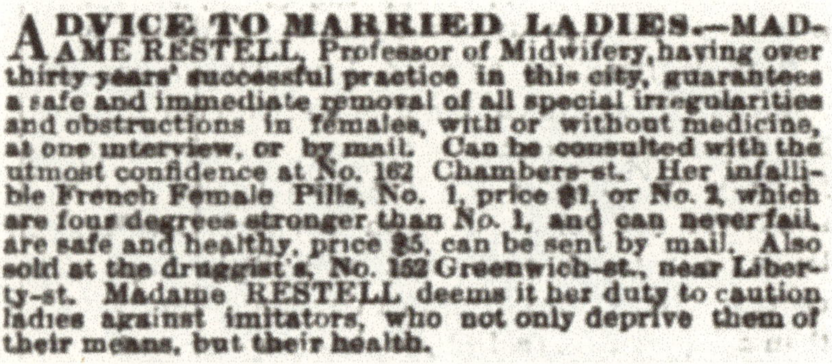

ADVICE TO MARRIED LADIES.—MADAME RESTELL, Professor of Midwifery, having over thirty years' successful practice in this city, guarantees a safe and immediate removal of all special irregularities and obstructions in females, with or without medicine, at one interview, or by mail. Can be consulted with the utmost confidence at No. 162 Chambers-st. Her infallible French Female Pills, No. 1, price $1, or No. 2, which are four degrees stronger than No. 1, and can never fail, are safe and healthy, price $5, can be sent by mail. Also sold at the druggist's, No. 152 Greenwich-st., near Liberty-st. Madame RESTELL deems it her duty to caution ladies against imitators, who not only deprive them of their means, but their health.

FIGURE 3. Restell's ad, *New York Times,* November 9, 1845.

CHAPTER TWO

Averse from Swerving in "The Mystery of Marie Rogêt"

> The fair Marie in his perfumery, . . . the charms of the sprightly *grisette*.
> —E. A. Poe, "The Mystery of Marie Rogêt" (1843)

> *Grisette:* a mushroom of the *Amanita vaginata* species; tends to grow in places where the earth has been recently disturbed.
> —Michael Kuo, mushroomexpert.com

"The Mystery of Marie Rogêt" announces itself, in its subheading, as "a sequel to 'The Murders in the Rue Morgue'" and follows up by reintroducing Dupin and the nameless narrator, paired once again with a mother and daughter. There is no trace of a father in either story. He is cut from the picture in the first and introduced as long deceased in the second. Although Dupin's target shifts from women who perform abortions to women who procure them, with the latter represented by Marie, in both cases a mother is forced to observe or bear witness to the mutilation of her daughter. In both, the figure of the daughter materializes in the recollections of others as the living product of a protective, adoring parent, and as a cadaver in the meticulous notes of a coroner who documents the signs of strangulation. If respiration constitutes a sign of life, then its deprivation by choking is particularly apt, as an act that reverses what breath means at birth. It communicates Dupin's motive as a symbolic form of infanticide, antenatal or otherwise, in the parlance of nineteenth-century forensics. As Theodric Beck asserted in 1825, "in the whole range of forensic medicine, there is not a question more important, and at the same time more difficult, than the one which relates *to the floating of the lungs as a proof of the child's having been born alive*" (Beck's italics).[1] Dupin strangles Marie Rogêt in violent retribution for her freedom not to confer breath and being on another and for effecting what he calls "certain concealments."[2]

These concealments arise again in innuendos and euphemisms for rape, menstruation, and pregnancy, encircling Marie's body in the newspapers and in Dupin's account of the crime. Nothing is directly named and yet everything appears in ascertainable outlines from within the veiled language about her brutalized virtue and her possible abortion. Where the furniture and architecture of the L'Espanaye residence silently collaborate with the dead women to convey Dupin's motive, the clothing and accessories on and surrounding Marie retain what happens to her. They double the details of her violation and decomposition, such as when her folded parasol tears "upon being opened" and her dress is discovered in "fragments . . . on the bushes." Dupin's descriptions of Marie's garters (how does he know about them with such specificity—how tightly she tied them and what kind she purchased?) and ready-made shoes, along with the bandages beneath her skirts, contribute to the picture of her as a figure wrapped in clandestine, enticing things. It is a picture designed to detract from the fabric so tightly wound around her neck that her once-living tissue swelled up around it, as if engaging in concealment itself. Dupin weaves his detractions into an insistence that Marie's disappearance followed her "accompanying [an] individual (*for whatever purpose—to her mother known or unknown*)" to frame her as cheap, just like her purchases, and her mother as secretive too.[3]

Dupin's gambit is the same as the one he develops in "Murders in the Rue Morgue": to suggest that the women die because they attract the violence to themselves. The story he concocts about the orangutan essentially rests on the premise that if the L'Espanaye women were not up at night, brushing their hair and counting their money like Judas figures, then no primate would have glimpsed the light in their room. It is likewise for Marie, whose dining at the boardinghouse of a known abortionist gets her killed on a Sunday, when she should have been at church, the paternal house with which Dupin is obsessed. "On Sunday," he says," the populace are chiefly within doors *preparing for church*."[4] He communicates his insinuations about Marie in a beguiling sotto voce made recognizable by the narrator's typographical shift into italics and brackets. His intonation is theatrical, belying his feigned equanimity. Poe calls attention to what Dupin's voice gives away when the narrator is thoroughly unnerved by it in "The Murders in the Rue Morgue," particularly when its pitch rises into "a treble" and his eyes go vacant.[5] Dupin modulates his tone to disarm the narrator and manipulate him into buying what he is selling: that "an accident at Madame Deluc's" killed Marie, and this is the story he plans to exchange for the reward money.[6]

To this end, Dupin also speaks in Marie's voice, again to insinuate that a devious quest for an abortion is the thing that kills her. "'We may imagine her thinking thus,'" he says by way of introducing his ventriloquist act, "'I am to meet a certain person for the purposes of elopement, or for certain other purposes known only to myself.'" The phrase regarding what is "known only" to Marie connotes something withheld from others and the key to the mystery of her murder, when it is neither. What is known only to Marie is just a private and inviolate conception, regarding the content of her own thoughts and the material of her own body. By stressing and repeating the word "certain," Dupin draws on an argot of the otherwise unsayable and redirects the fact of her murder to the prospect of her abortion. This redirection then effects an elision of the two. Abortion becomes murder and murdering the murderer a form of restitution. Poe flags Dupin's ventriloquism of Marie by setting his words inside double and single sets of quotation marks, which he then frames inside the pages of a story that is edited and enclosed in numerous footnotes. In a tale that often makes it difficult for us to ascertain who speaks when, these enclosures signpost the fact that Dupin concocts Marie's internal voice. Between the quotation marks, Marie arises in convolutions of text and fabrication. They wrap around her like the fabric that kills her, from the "strong band [of cloth] attached to her neck," to the "bandage about the loins ... its volution about the corpse, the *hitch* which embarrassed it."[7] And if her body likewise envelops an embryo, then this entity retreats farther inward from the story's frame, nonexistent apart from what is said about it: quotation marks within quotation marks within quotation marks.

Because Dupin's voice and turns of phrase sound more staged than astute, the sexual secrets of women become audible or apparent as tropes in narratives of detection or discovery.[8] The narrator notes here and in "The Murders in the Rue Morgue" that talking about them gives Dupin far too much pleasure and that mysteries are generated where there are none. The repeated unearthing of Marie Rogêt from her grave (where nothing new contradicts the coroner's report) underscores the trope on the literal level of the tale. Digging up dirt around women is all distraction, particularly from the "momentous political topics of the day," which the narrator admits to ignoring. In these moments, Poe informs us that we are being thrown off track. The message magnifies in repetition: "deflect from the line of ordinary inquiry," "divert inquiry," "divert... attention from the real scene of the outrage," "diverting thoroughly the two courses of events," "redivert this attention," the "diversity" of walking, the "frustrated design." The opposite also arises in the phrase "averse from swerving."[9] "Diversion" means entertainment, the disturbing word Dupin uses to describe the L'Espanaye murders, and intrigue about a young woman's abortion eclipses inquiry into slavery, genocide, and territorial annexation, the momentous horrors or topics of Poe's time and place.

The frightening scale of such violence is displaced onto or telescoped into the more focused issue of abortion, Poe's narrator suggests, redirecting the kidnapping, exploitation, and forced migrations of Black and Indigenous peoples. Poe underscores this redirection in his representation of Dupin's disgust at Paris's immigrants and of his misogyny, the counterparts of which lie in the white supremacy and murders on the other side of the Atlantic, as Poe holds New York and Mary Rogers in focus alongside Paris and Marie Rogêt. To quote Zoë Sofia on the "protecting superwomb of patriarchal culture," abortion and annihilation arise as two sides of the same biopolitical coin, for the same power that aims to guarantee fetal existence has "the capacity to exterminate whole populations and species." The military escalation of the modern nation-state—captured by Poe in references to guns, naval officers, and Dupin's implicitly sanctioned violence—accompanies pro-life rhetoric, both centering on what Sofia terms "articulations of a collapsed future." The "always already" of the unborn, she demonstrates, is temporally conceptualized along the same lines as the "bound to be" of invasion or occupation.[10] The murder of Marie Rogêt is configured in similar terms, as a mode of guarding the populace on the inside of racialized walls and of speaking for the white fetal life she presumably threatens.

Through Dupin, Poe represents the contours of nativist ideology, particularly in Dupin's insistent statistics, whereby "chances are ten to one" that Marie runs off with a dark-skinned officer from a warship, or that "in ninety-nine cases from the hundred [a] gang of blackguards" commits crimes, not "the individual man of genius."[11] In other words, Dupin's "Calculus of Probability" reflects particular developments in the formalization of population statistics in the early 1800s, whereby the registration of races and immigration rates was legislated and rates of productivity and fertility calculated in the interests of national power.[12] When the American Statistical Society organized itself and Massachusetts initiated the statewide documentation of births and deaths (in 1839 and 1842, respectively), they set into motion new standards for what Elizabeth Fee calls the "political arithmetic" of the state.[13] The concept of vital statistics assumed increasing significance, bringing childbirth and stillbirths into new focus. The sanitary conditions of cities were evaluated in relation to numbers of premature deaths, and the notion of preventable deaths followed. While many public health initiatives arose in response to the suffering of women and children, they also intensified demands for the criminalization of abortion, prostitution, and interracial marriage. The American Medical Association's formation in 1847 and its antiabortion position reflect these developments, especially in their collection and documentation of stillbirths and pregnancy rates.[14]

Poe incorporates Dupin's statistical lexicon into a framework of conservative thinking, in which recognizable assertions of power take place as numerical evaluations of social predictability and uniformity. Dupin's numbers and calculations give him a decided air of modern analytical thinking but they are hyperbolic and inaccurate, and they accompany his descriptions of a city desecrated by "desperate adventurers." Repeating the word "probability" and "wager[ing] one thousand to one," he winds around Marie some kind of mathematical possibility that a botched abortion killed her. That is, he subtly moves between probability and possibility, until Marie herself is cast as the criminal, an "unfortunate, led ... into crime."[15] I want to note in this context that Poe's characterization of Dupin brings the concept of probability to light as a feature of modernity that supplants the concept of potentiality in interpretations of life and death. A potential existence is not the same as a probable one. Probability pertains to biopolitical predictions and investments, and potentiality to the "not-yet" of something, to the enigmatic and not to the actual.

To quote Giorgio Agamben on the Aristotelian distinction between the potential and the actual: "All potential to be or do something is always also potential not to be or do, ... without which potentiality would always already have passed into actuality and would be indistinguishable from it." Where Agamben takes Melville's Bartleby's "I prefer not to" as the "formula of potentiality," in which Bartleby stands in indifference between Being and Nothingness, I take Marie Rogêt's possible pregnancy as Poe's exploration of the "de-creation" this indifference enacts. "In first philosophy," Agamben explains of Bartleby, "a being that can both be and not be is said to be contingent." This contingency applies to fetal existence, particularly in relation to time, given Agamben's clarification that a contingent entity is "something whose opposite could have happened in the very moment in which it happened."[16] What is potential consigns what is actual to chance, not to probability.

Through the narrator, Poe undermines everything that Dupin tries to secure in place. He may flatter Dupin's intelligence in order to maintain his own position of concealment, but the narrator also works with numbers and establishes Dupin at the scene and time of the crime. He explains, "Strange as it may appear, *the third week* from the discovery of the body had passed without any light being thrown on the subject, before even a rumor of the events which had so agitated the public mind, reached the ears of Dupin and myself. Engaged in researches which had absorbed our whole attention, it had been *nearly a month* since either of us had *gone abroad, or received a visitor,* or more than glanced at the leading political articles in one of the daily papers. The first intelligence of the murder was brought us by G——, in person" (italics mine).[17] *Three weeks* and *nearly a month* are two ways of saying the same thing. The passage can be translated or paraphrased like this: Marie is killed just before Dupin and the narrator leave town and go into seclusion; they permit a visit from the Prefect once the reward reaches thirty thousand francs. Or, to avoid the narrator's strategically passive grammar regarding Marie's murder, we can put it this way: Dupin rapes and murders Marie, "goes abroad" with the narrator, and waits for the Prefect to break under the pressure of his humiliation in the press for failing to solve the crime.

As readers, we are asked to track what permutations of time and existence hold Marie inside Dupin's fabrications and which ones clear a path outside of them. Thus, when Dupin argues that "'soon after dark' is, at least, *dark*; and *'about dusk'* is as certainly daylight,'" in an attempt to discredit Madame Deluc's testimony regarding the time of Marie's screams, he carves the day into imprecise halves. Poe's narrator, however, asserts specific moments against that imprecision. He says, "Marie Rogêt left the residence of her mother, in the Rue Pavée St. Andrée, about nine o'clock in the morning of Sunday, June the twenty-second, 18—— . . . to spend the day with an aunt who resided in the Rue des Drômes." Time's unfolding matters to Marie's disappearance and decomposition in contradistinction to Dupin's sneering that "mere *duration*" cannot account for anything. Even the plants that grow where she dies record duration. "The things had all evidently been there at least three or four weeks," a newspaper excerpt explains; "they were all mildewed down hard with the action of the rain, and stuck together from mildew. The grass had grown around and over some of them." The chalk that Marie uses to sign her name on a lover's slate likewise belongs to time's passage, as a substance associated with the impermanence of its form. Like the mildew, the grass, and the perfume for which she is known, it marks her in place as fleeting but also as real, in material that contrasts the composition of the tale "at a distance from the scene of the atrocity."[18]

These substances thread timelines of existence, duration, and decay into what Poe calls "the land of the living" and locate Marie in sensory corroborations with others. They establish her presence in discrete moments when she leaves signs of herself for others to read, hear, smell, and see. As a result, Poe imbues her with a vitality that not only contrasts her role as a corpse but also departs from the cheapness in which Dupin frames her, scheming as Dupin does to reduce her to the status of commercialized trash and therefore as expendable as the ready-made shoes she buys. Where Poe separates abstractions and calculations of life from the qualities of the living, Dupin works from the opposite direction. He argues that one must "go behind the mere words for an idea" to the "spirit of [the] principle." Gesturing toward the metaphysical realm which he believes superior to the material one, and asserting conceptions and principles against the statements of those who view her corpse, he sidetracks the physical evidence and duration of Marie's living and dying. From here, he introduces God into the picture. "The horrors of this dark deed," he says, "are known only to *one*, or two, living human beings, and to God."[19] When the narrator comes in toward the end with the statement that "with God all is *Now*," he reminds us that Dupin tries to make eternity override time. It is the same mode of thinking or belief that the divine and the eternal bisect in a person's uterus at the moment of human conception.

Dupin describes the torn-away fabric that is used to strangle Marie through this paradigm, working hard to render the material in terms of the spiritual, and as subject to uncanny forces and miracles. He announces, "To tear a piece off from such fabric, two distinct forces, in different directions, will be, in almost every case, required.... To tear a piece from the interior, where no edge is presented, could only be effected by a miracle, through the agency of thorns." He then repeats the words, but with new emphasis: "torn completely out, through the agency of thorns, from the unedged interior of the dress!" The Christian iconography of miracles and thorns makes it seem as if God arrives in the thicket to stop time and collaborate in Marie's death. Stressing the day of disappearance, Sunday, he renames it the Sabbath. "That fatal Sunday" in turn becomes "that fatal Sabbath." If we missed his theological lexicon the first time, he says, "I repeat that the circumstance . . . is to be looked upon as little less than miraculous."[20] It follows that the horrifying image of Marie's brutalized and decaying corpse, which is forced on those who identify her and her injuries, moves into a different light, as if a miracle of death takes place, in an inversion of the so-called miracle of birth. His version reproduces the body and its history as products of his superior conceiving.

In "The Murders in the Rue Morgue," Dupin pins the murders on a primate. In "Marie Rogêt," he moves up the Chain of Being and invokes the concept of God's handiwork. The accidental outcome of an orangutan's fury is now the miraculous event of a Sunday. In either direction, the category of the human retains its supremacy, positioned just above primates and just below God, uniquely combining the qualities of both. The ritualistic nature of the violence communicates Dupin's commitment to this categorization and vertical scale, in which the human is itself vertically organized into soul and body and characterized definitively by sex, race, and virility. It is his scale to protect, especially against those who challenge it at the source, and he spells it out: first, in his twisted propitiation to the hearth in the house on the Rue Morgue, in the "thick tresses of grey hair . . . dabbled in blood" he places there, so that the daughter's body must pass through the mother's blood and hair, in a spectacle of stillbirth and gore; and second, in a thicket, out of which he drags a daughter, head first with a piece of cloth tied into a hitch, as if performing a fetal extraction.[21]

With her arms "bent over on the chest . . . rigid," Marie is locked into the fetal position, delivered by Dupin to Nature and his God. The uterine thicket is a young man's "natural throne," Dupin says, made "highly artificial" by the things associated with Marie. Over and over he repeats the words "natural" and "naturally" in order to present her as unnatural. Here, murder is reconceived as an act of purification of a space turned into an "incongruous sink of pollution" by foreigners and by women who fail to perpetuate their "Christian and family name."[22] This nature/artifice lexicon subtly introduces the medical terminology surrounding abortion in Poe's time, as a criminal activity practiced against nature and accomplished by means of an infernal art. To quote physician J. H. Kellogg's observation from his perspective toward the end of the century, "The professional abortionist is skilled in the art of concealment and evasion of justice."[23]

The strange imperative in "The Murders in the Rue Morgue" regarding the "moral activity which *disentangles*" thus extends into this sequel. It involves working in the opposite direction of what entwines around Marie Rogêt, freeing her, at least from the metaphoric strangulation effected by Dupin's lies. Hinting at the ways in which belief systems split and twist together, both in the tale's epigraph and in its second paragraph, Poe's narrator quotes Novalis on the "ideal series of events [that runs] parallel with the real ones" and then explains that his tale forms into "two branches," one primary and the other secondary.[24] As I argue above, the conceptualization of an ideal realm or route into the world does not find Poe's validation in the pages he spreads before us. It may be imagined but it does not exist. Because Poe establishes Dupin's violence in "Rue Morgue" as a product of his mirroring with the fetus, the entity who materializes with a soul, it follows that his narrator's reference to an "ideal series" here pertains to Dupin's anxiety about its undoing in utero.

Ideally, fetal development is destined to follow a series of events, whereby an invisible embryonic origin is traceable back to the fertilized ovum from a visible birth. In reality, however, this development takes place as a duration, subject to accident and deviation, and inextricable from the concomitant growth of the placenta, the organ that tends to get left out of idealized depictions of fetuses. The ideal's bearing on the real is, in the narrator's words, "redolent with mischief."[25] It turns what is real into something derivative and the gestating body into a conduit, and these old viewpoints maintain their stranglehold on the living, informing the criminalization of abortion for which Dupin stands.

When the narrator shifts from the image of a series to that of a secondary branch, he establishes a route along the distaff line and slyly raises the issue of inheritance, the treasure stripped from Dupin and that he tries to divert back to himself. The distaff line denotes both a spinning stick for fabric and a line of descent traced through women. As a result of these allusions, the lineage Dupin retains (as the Chevalier, with ties to royalty) filters into the story as a facet of his motive or as his justification for murder. Marie represents a swerving from the birthright that he believes precedes conception and passes through women in a decidedly male chain of command. It is not something for women to break and redirect.

In his strange closing remarks, the narrator returns to the theological thinking that frames Dupin's crime and ascertains in it an excuse superior to the reward money. He says: "That Nature and its God are two, no man who thinks, will deny. That the latter, creating the former, can, at will, control or modify it, is also unquestionable.... It is not that the Deity *cannot* modify his laws, but that we insult him in imagining a possible necessity for modification. In their origin these laws were fashioned to embrace *all* contingencies which *could* lie in the Future."[26] The repetition of "modify" and "modification" stresses the insult intolerable to God. Having steadily represented Dupin as a man easily offended, especially when Dupin rants about "the unwashed" who desecrate his city and insult him by their very presence, the narrator implicitly brings Dupin and this Deity together on one side, and Marie Rogêt and Nature on the other. The offence to God that she commits inheres in her correlation with modification, particularly as she modifies her natural scent and reproductive potential. The narrator's words perform interesting acrobatics in order to separate himself from what Dupin believes and to stress the problem of contingency to theology. He does not want to be found out for his exposure and contradiction of Dupin.

Thus, intertwined with his theological lexicon is his distaste for it. Motivated by his own self-preservation and yet aching to confess, Poe's narrator attempts to get out from under Dupin's influence and excuses. The import of what he says in the above paragraph rests on the pronouns that stress the maleness of Dupin's deity and on the subject of modification, understood in relation to abortion as an alteration of god's plans and as unnatural.[27] Nature and God, he sneaks into his pronouncements, are products of men's thinking, not women's.

"Here is a tale of modernity and modernization," writes Amy Srebnick, "a story about the loss of patriarchal authority."[28] In the telltale signs of a nationalism erected on nostalgia, Dupin speaks for a Paris that seemingly existed before its "infesting" by immigrants and working women. Recalling "scenes of natural loveliness," he rationalizes murder as a form of purification. The women he murders own their own houses and make decisions about them, either opening them up to boarders or closing them down for solitude. In both "Rue Morgue" and "Marie Rogêt," paved roads replace cobblestone streets and make smooth the access to the city, its parks, and its inhabitants. Participation in the commerce includes working in the shops that take over the basement of the royal palace, altering its foundations.

Perfume, affairs, abortion, the purchasing power for handkerchiefs, garters, and shoes ("sold in packages," even) all surround Marie as she comes and goes.[29] When she leaves a rose in a keyhole for a man, she reverses the rules of pursuit. She consorts with a "man of dark complexion" identified as a naval officer, preferring foreign seamen to her original suitor, Monsieur Le Blanc, and breaks with conventions of gender and race.

Alongside these puns, Poe represents abortion in terms of artistic self-expression, like the choice of one's perfume or the style of one's handwriting. The cut flower moves from its biological rootedness to the realm of signification, taken up by Marie. If, as Poe's narrator proposes, art is that which modifies nature, then abortion as the modification of an otherwise natural process falls under its purview, remaking one's presence in the world. It can be defined in the same way as Dupin's glasses are, as a corrective to what is God-given about one's physical or natural form. Being alive and named means having been birthed and signed, as much a naturally reproduced creature as an artistic, linguistic entity. Poe reworks the notion of abortion as criminally unnatural for women and experiments with its classification, in his time, as a practice involving "improper arts [or] artificial checks to impregnation."[30] Art and artifice are also creative forces, giving meaning to existence.

The violence perpetuated in the name of life or nature's laws illustrates what Drucilla Cornell calls the "need for re-symbolization of the feminine, [for] a re-imagining." It is not that women require the right to choose, Cornell explains, but that they have the right to abortion itself, to the bodily integrity that an unwanted pregnancy threatens or makes unrecognizable. Defining the self as that which guards against psychic, social, and symbolic division, Cornell stresses its coherence in terms of mirroring and invention. The mind does not oversee the body in a relationship of ownership, Cornell asserts, but experiences it as "a psychic object," both as real and as part of the self's uncanny outlines—as a process of, and with the right to, protection from rupture and dismemberment.[31] As Lorraine Rothman puts it, "Seeing women as creators, not containers, means seeing abortion as refusing to create, not destroying that which we contain."[32] It is possible to interpret Poe's tales as attempts to get to this resymbolization through the depiction of the women as figures who undermine the meaning of the human as it serves Dupin's patriarchal inheritance.

Dupin's decapitation of Madame L'Espanaye and his strangulation of both Camille and Marie come into view as violent proclamations of the

CHAPTER TWO

mind's detachment from and ownership over the body. The proclamation implies a reclamation of the old order, in which the spiritual is distinct from and superior to the material, just as men are to women, citizens to foreigners, enslavers to enslaved. An aristocratic Parisian man, Dupin is assumed to be as intelligent and civilized as his words suggest. He is careful to cast himself as the opposite of the immigrants and laborers in the city. This mode of thinking not only provides his brutality with the cover of whiteness, but it also withdraws the assumption of intelligence from the women, especially when all we are left with is their disfigured bodies. When Dupin speaks hypothetically of the "man long resident in Paris" who is recognized as he walks through town, he begins to set up the rationale for murder. Because when comparing "his notoriety with that of the perfumery-girl," he lets slip the profound insult of this comparison, as a leveling of a hierarchy that puts women and men on the same footing.[33] If he rapes and kills for the sake of civilization as he defines it, then he resembles a crusader reclaiming a holy land and not just a felon who despises women and outsiders.

So much about Dupin's violation of Marie involves his obsessive description of the "volution" of things around her body—the muslin, bandages, garters, hem, a sailor's knot, and the fabric roped around her body for dragging it—as if she were swaddled inside the thicket, awaiting rebirth. Repeatedly referring to the sailor's knot and the hitch, he displaces from the narrative the naval and the umbilical cord that link Estelle Rogêt to her daughter. And this is the point. Described in parentheses that render her incidental, as "(an infirm old lady, seventy years of age)," Madame Rogêt has nothing to say, as far as the investigators believe. "She was heard to express a fear," the narrator adds, "'that she should never see Marie again;' but this observation attracted little attention at the time."[34] This fear is not only prescient but also historical, grounded as it is in Estelle's memory of Marie's first disappearance. She knows something because her fear is realized, and yet it remains unheeded. In the passive grammar of the reports, moreover, no subject hears or observes Estelle; there is only a having heard and a having attracted little attention. Although she escapes Madame L'Espanaye's fate, her parenthetical characterization as a nameless and "infirm old lady" metaphorically cuts her off at the throat. When Dupin takes over to speak, Estelle Rogêt's viewpoint and brief testimony get lost in the volume of sentences he spews.

The more Latin he speaks and the more statistics he spins, the less likely it is for Estelle's role to matter, despite the fact that her words materialize on the page, printed and in quotation marks. As in "The Murders in the Rue Morgue," Dupin aims to put as many details as possible between the sound of the mother's voice and his. For example, where she makes a positive identification of her daughter's clothing, he declares that "our first step should be the determination of the identity of the corpse with the Marie Rogêt who is missing."[35] What Estelle Rogêt actually says is replaced with what Marie Rogêt is imagined to have thought. As she diminishes, he becomes larger than life. The "rigorous masculine expertise of . . . Dupin" becomes, as Elizabeth Miller puts it, the "architecture of narrative estrangement," through which Poe depicts a "culture that makes something out of nothing."[36] This wording perfectly applies to the vilification of abortion in the making of a pro-life culture that simultaneously endorses war and slavery.

Such redirections of significance illuminate the allegory that continues into this tale from the last as the swerving from the maternal figure in the political, legal, philosophical, and medical conversations about "the mystery" and ownership of her own offspring. Poe composes his account out of newspaper and medical reports and Dupin's faux forensics, but he also urges us to back up and reconsider what we read. If we back up far enough, we return to Estelle Rogêt. And if we listen carefully, we can hear the echo between Estelle and Restell, as Poe draws the two figures together and under the purview of those who can get pregnant.

Poe's mode of composition develops the allegory, particularly when he reverses course in extensive paragraphs that end with such assertions as "yet *all* this was satisfactorily disproved" or "this latter point, however, was fully disproved." In other words, certain conceptions develop only so far before he negates them. They are made to look as if they have bearing on the narrative and yet they are included only to be expunged. In addition, the passive grammar by which a story "was composed" or "was disproved" is the grammar that attends descriptions of birth, in which someone is born rather than birthed, and it functions to hide the subject when Marie is "borne across the river, maltreated and murdered."[37] The killer disappears from both the sentence and the scene of the crime.

The passive grammar and the contrived secrets of women function to detract from the secrets of men. Poe sets up the story of Marie's first abortion in the past, describing it as hushed up by her mother, and runs it parallel with the subplot about the men's control over their reputations. Recall that the Prefect meets with Dupin again because his name and honor are at stake and because Dupin's own name is now a "household word," given the allegedly brilliant solution to the murders on the Rue Morgue. The Prefect flatters him by lying about "the simple character of those inductions by which he had disentangled the [Rue Morgue] mystery" because there was nothing simple about it. In this backroom dealing, a vast reward is offered in exchange not for the solution to the crime but for its "development." Thus, where women seek privacy and abortion, so that their very bodies do not split into two persons, influential men seek to protect and establish their names, immortalized separately from their lives, in covert connections with bankers, newspaper men, and government officials.[38]

The unnamed narrator pulls this secrecy around him when he states that he "does not feel at liberty to disclose" what he knows about Marie's death or when his editors "feel it advisable only to state, in brief, that the result desired was brought to pass."[39] His diction enacts the same kind of circumlocution as an abortionist's advertisement, echoing what abortionists called "the desired result" of their remedies and the "prudent considerations" they proposed for their clients.[40] As inexplicit as a terminated pregnancy performed in secret, this editorial statement enacts an excision too, cutting from the body of the text the mystery's conclusion. The editors "take the liberty of here omitting" information as an exercise of freedom and mark their interruption without apology and in square brackets. When it comes to textual reproduction, everything is fair game.

Publishing Marie Rogêt's story as a variation on the historical murder of Mary Rogers (which sold a lot of New York papers in 1841), Poe enters into what Laura Saltz succinctly terms the "circulation of guilt central to the story's economy."[41] Storytelling, publication, and payment interconnect in a transaction that involved laying bare Mary Rogers's corpse once again. I want to stress, however, that Poe's tale moves in a direction opposite of the newspapers' lies and sensationalism. By including the original coroner's report, he secures the fact of murder for both Mary Rogers and Marie Rogêt and uses it to think through the meaning of reproduction. Not only is his tale exceedingly tedious and opaque, and therefore the antithesis of sensational, but it also presents the "beautiful dead woman as so much rotting material and a jumble of dismembered and de-sexed parts," to quote Elizabeth Miller again.[42] This presentation aligns with the decomposition that marks the narrative's composition, through which rotting becomes reproductive in new ways.

Averse from Swerving in "The Mystery of Marie Rogêt"

Fiction and lying may loop together, but they are not exactly the same thing. Poe is careful to maintain that his mystery of Marie Rogêt is not a history of Mary Rogers, even if the one draws on and refers to the other. By incorporating excerpts from the New York papers that reported Mary Rogers's murder as a botched abortion tied to Madame Restell, he folds their lying into his tale and associates them with the murderous Dupin.[43] That is, he pulls the references to abortion from each excerpt, replacing them with asterisks, and moves the insinuations into Dupin's mouth. These cuts arise as decisions about the body of his text and what it will bear and disclose, in a literary experiment animated by abortion's legibility and legitimacy. Recomposing the material surrounding Mary Rogers, Poe modifies its import. Rather than creating a kind of abstract rebirth of her in Marie Rogêt, as if to overtake the material conditions of gestation and delivery, he offers only glimmers of the living woman in the minds and testimony of others, scattering her presence. In addition to the asterisks that switch places with "abortion," other asterisks point to footnotes where the sources for the story reside, expanding the frame of the narrative. Their visible appearance on the page, along with the name Estelle for Marie's mother, gathers into a kind of constellation, one connected with abortion and the night.

Marie comes into the text as the offspring of a star, in a mythic retelling that takes its place alongside Orion's story, with his cruelty and his sailor's cudgel. At the same time, the multiple allusions to the naval officer conjure up the presence of a navel on a body, itself resembling an asterisk, marking the origin of the one body in another's. The names of the two newspapers from which the tale's excerpts are pulled, *Le Soleil* and *L'Etoile*, add to this motif, present as the narrator's source material and as reminders that daylight is distinct from the night's darkness and that the sun is also a star.

By referring to Marie as a "grisette" Poe remakes her again, this time into a mushroom, if we dig past the use of the term that sexualized young working women in the nineteenth century. According to John Loudon's 1822 *Encyclopedia of Gardening*, the grisette is a wholesome mushroom and emits a "graceful, rich scent," distinguishable from the "sickly nauseous smell" of the poisonous kind.[44] The perfumed Marie returns in the fungus that not only flourishes where she dies but also discloses the timeframe and space of her death. In the dark and on the ground, the lowly fungus takes its place, reaching up toward the stars and recording the fact of murder. As a sign of decay's fertility, the mushroom comes into being, rotting into renewal. For

Merlin Sheldrake in *Entangled Life*, "fungi are metabolic wizards" who make and unmake worlds, asking us to "think backward... loosening our grip on our humanness."[45] The mystery of Marie does not necessarily apply to the resolution of who kills her but to the world that might be pulled for reinvention from the hands of the murderous Dupin. "Without Man and Nature, all creatures can come back to life," Anna Tsing says about mushrooms at the end of the world.[46]

When Dupin describes the scene of the crime and ostensibly assumes the voice of the killer, he imagines the "unutterable horror" in this person's mind. But this horror arises not as a consequence of remembering what he does to Marie but upon contemplating the "rudderless boat" into which he drags Marie. A powerful symbol of a godless world, the rudderless boat conveys Dupin's existential panic. It is "cast adrift," Dupin says, again invoking his sense of insignificance in a vast and indifferent universe. A kind of body without a soul, the boat is said to have ribs that press into Marie's back and shoulders, and it replaces her mother to bear her body away from "the land of the living," the world into which Estelle delivered her. "*The rudder is at hand*," Dupin announces before the tale's editors (the "Eds.*... of the Magazine in which the article was originally published"), nameless themselves, cut Dupin's "*following up*" and replace it with their own vague explanation.[47]

All we are we left with is the fact that the rudderless boat is towed by a bargeman "connected with the revenue service" to the barge office, where its rudder might be located. Here, Poe flags the borders of the city, where the barge office processed immigration into New York in the early 1800s.[48] This population growth is the same one captured by the multiple nationalities of the witnesses on the Rue Morgue, perceived from Dupin's pro-life angle as a kind of poisonous mushrooming around solid, genealogical trees.

In a letter about Dupin, Poe gives away certain details about his detective, but in forms of evasion that mirror his fiction. For example, without offering any further information, he asserts at one point that "the 'naval officer' who committed murder (rather, the accidental death arising from an attempt at abortion) *confessed* it; and the whole matter is now well understood" (Poe's italics).[49] Poe scholars tend to read the bracketed point about abortion as an allusion to Dupin's crime-solving prowess and the solution to the mystery. But this does not hold, given the facts of strangulation and rape so clearly maintained by the coroner's account. Rather, the parentheses function in same way as the single quotation marks around "naval officer" do, to flag irony. The sentence emphasizes murder and incorporates a feint that condenses Dupin's invention into a parenthetical remark, at once pregnant with a lie and split open by it.

As Poe's tale progresses through marked-up sentences and paragraphs, it decomposes into its composition. Its extracts, scenes, and memories proliferate like the fungus that springs up where Marie dies, reproductive of the living in different forms: an entirely different kind of resurrection, earth-bound and shadowed from the sun. As in "The Murders in the Rue Morgue," the interplay between reproduction and dissolution is part of the message, gesturing toward the killer's motive and against the intelligence and authority that Dupin performs. In parentheses toward the beginning of the tale, the narrator emphasizes what is true, noting, "(It was at once evident that murder had been committed)." Dupin's parenthetical remarks mirror the narrator's but double into duplicity, striving to shift the real scene of the crime to a sham one: "(if thicket it was)," he says when he recounts the evidence; "(whether from the thicket or elsewhere)"; "(or within other cavities from elsewhere)."[50] We are tasked, as readers, with the necessity of sorting concepts, events, and figures from the subterfuge by which one thing is made to look like another.

"The merely general reader" is contrasted with one who pays "respectful attention," and it becomes a matter of justice, of who speaks for the dead and why. Poe's narrator proposes that we can imagine the living Marie from the fact of her corpse and the impressions she leaves behind, all material evidence of her once having existed. We can also imagine a life for one who was never born along the same lines. But while the space of the mind holds them both and renders them in the same outlines, only one pertains to "the land of the living," a phrase that twice occurs in "The Mystery of Marie Rogêt."[51] And only one suffers in the landscape that Poe creates for her. In addition, a historical Mary Rogers (birthed by her mother) contrasts a fictional Marie Rogêt (conceived of by Poe), and neither one exists (in reality or in fiction) as the version Dupin invents as having died at the hands of an abortionist.

CHAPTER THREE

An Unusual Gaping in the Joints
Delivering the Purloined Letter

> The cushions we probed with the fine long needles you have seen me employ.
> —Edgar Allan Poe, "The Purloined Letter," 1845

> Any smooth instrument of a proper size and length such as the handle of silver spoon or a blade of the forceps will answer the purpose of breaking down and evacuating the contents of the head safely and effectually. But the perforation being completed I have generally introduced the crotchet into the opening in the cranium.
> —Thomas Denman, M. D., *An Introduction to the Practice of Midwifery*, 1832

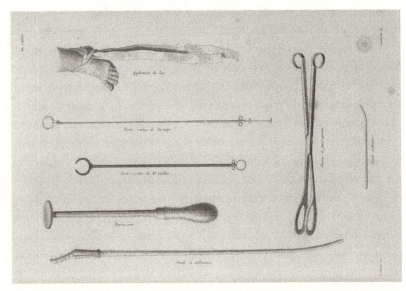

FIGURE 4. Nineteenth-century gynecological instruments. *Obstetrics. Instruments.* Wellcome Collection, University of London. Public Domain Mark 1.0.

In 1846, the sixteenth edition of William A. Alcott's *The Young Man's Guide* hit the streets, maintaining its cautionary message that the world was an awfully smutty place, "abound[ing] in impure publications [and] licentious paintings and engravings, which circulate in various ways." According to Alcott, not only was it crucial for a young man's moral development to avoid such objects, but it was also necessary for him to know their subtle traps: the obscene picture "under cover of a watch case," the seemingly innocuous book steeped in double entendres. To make sure that his readership understood what he meant, Alcott included both a phonetic key to it—"pronounced entaunders"—and a definition: "By this is meant *decent speeches, with double meanings*. I mention these because they prevail, in some parts of the country, to a most alarming degree.... Now no serious observer of human life and conduct can doubt that by every species of impure language, whether in the form of hints, innuendos, double entendres, or plainer speech, impure thoughts are awakened, a licentious imagination inflamed, and licentious purposes formed, which would otherwise never have existed" (Alcott's italics). For Alcott, as for many of his concerned medical and moral contemporaries, the lure of these vices ("not only *social* but also *solitary*") dangerously illuminated the way "to disease and premature death."[1] Such pronouncements formed, of course, an increasingly common refrain of nineteenth-century sexual advice literature directed at both men and women. To take up Michel Foucault's paradigmatic formulation, they were part of the social mechanisms that turned sex into a secret of being and underwrote forms of biopolitical regulation. But what is so interesting about Alcott's account here lies less in its anxieties about human erotic activity than it does in Alcott's sense of having to wage an almost losing battle against a kind of print culture that promoted, in increasingly cunning and indefatigable ways, the very activity he sought to restrict.

If, as historian Ronald Walters shows, we can trace an intensification of concern with the sexual behavior of the white American population to the proliferation of advice literature in the 1830s and 1840s,[2] then we must also see this concern as a motivated response, at least in part, to the creative flair of a certain kind of text passing itself off as something very different from its surface appearance—as something that slips across a guarded threshold, narrowly eluding the vigilant eyes of America's reputable establishment, rather like a purloined letter, the secret contents of which threaten to bring down the entire house. This is how the nineteenth-century market in reproductive control and sexual education operated. Although Alcott does not directly mention it, perhaps for fear of appearing lewd, the publishers of pamphlets, advertisements, and tracts publicly disseminating racy information drew on a vibrant realm of double entendres and euphemisms, particularly in the wake of state laws passed against the sale of contraceptives and the practice of abortion in the two decades before the Civil War. According to Janet Farrell Brodie, nineteenth-century Americans quickly learned that "domestic manuals" and "private medical guides for ladies" carried contraceptive advice and ways of incurring miscarriage and that the necessary products could be purchased discreetly through the mail.[3] Moreover, printed warnings about such insidious materials, by critics such as Alcott for instance, inadvertently effected a broader awareness of the availability of birth control information and erotic materials. By denouncing fornication or abortion, they often disseminated crucial information about it.

In some cases, the denouncement itself was just a cover for an announcement, a kind of deft double entendre governing the appearance of outrage. For example, the July 21, 1839, edition of New York's *Sunday Morning News* carried an article proclaiming that the famous abortionist Madame Restell "persevered in her nefarious traffic" of pills for "married women who had been indiscreet."[4] Following a statement about New York City's "wise statute" against abortion, as well as a warning that Restell euphemistically called herself a "midwife and professor of diseases of women," the author of the article astonishingly reproduces Restell's ad in its entirety: "Mme Restell's Sure Remedies—Price $5 and $10; can only be procured at her office, No 1 East 52nd Street." Within this mixture of admonition and exposition, the extent to which the article actually opposed the distribution of Restell's product is sufficiently obscured.

Such diverse and circuitous routes around genteel morality and state laws did not proceed entirely unnoticed, however, and several states went so far as to draft legislation against the use of any ambiguous language in reports, pamphlets, and advertisements concerning ailments particular to women. Yet, throughout the nineteenth century, the laws against it notwithstanding, ambiguous, euphemistic wording continued to frame the sale of products and procedures. As Helen Lefkowitz Horowitz demonstrates, many purveyors of abortion and contraception also figured out how to blur the "boundary between commerce in contraceptives and works of physiology," adding that "it seemed possible that some authors were using the cover of science to print racy material."[5] In fact, in a fairly early American printing of *Aristotle's Masterpiece* (1817), the publisher seems to have attempted to head off exactly this accusation, avowing in the preface that the book was not intended to "stir up bestial appetites" in its readers but that it was made for women whose modesty precluded them from asking for help "in matters of the womb."[6]

It is from the world of advertisements, books, newspaper articles, and pamphlets on the subject of reproductive control that Poe again takes his lead in "The Purloined Letter," using the same strategies of indirection and innuendo that render abortion inconspicuous but not incomprehensible. That this tale pertains to something physiological, like the two tales before it, becomes apparent when what is crucial is once more passed off as seemingly incidental. Dupin's casual allusion, for instance, to the story of the miser who seeks medical advice by presenting "his case to the physician, as that of an imaginary individual" combines the corporeal with the extortive and elucidates the mode by which Dupin makes his living.[7] Poe thus invites us to listen attentively to what exactly is so pressing about the matter of a letter stolen from a woman's boudoir:

> "Perhaps it is the very simplicity of the thing which puts you at fault," said [Dupin].
>
> "What nonsense you *do* talk!" replied the Prefect, laughing heartily.
>
> "Perhaps the mystery is a little too plain," said Dupin.
>
> "Oh, good heavens! Who ever heard of such an idea?"
>
> "A little *too* self-evident."
>
> "Ha! ha! ha!—ha! ha! ha!—ho! ho! ho!"—roared our visitor, profoundly amused.[8]

If we are the kind of readers who are in the know, then we can begin to hear why Dupin's banter makes the Prefect laugh so heartily—what it is about Dupin's description of the excessively obvious or pregnant nature of the mystery that functions as innuendo for the Prefect's amusement. As Jacques Lacan notes about Poe's tale, the "dialogue may be more fertile than it seems."[9] And yet there is nothing funny about the woman's predicament, given what Poe indicates about Dupin up to this point. Poe circles back to this matter when he has Dupin conclude the story with a description of his penchant for feigned jocularity: how he admits to cloaking his threat of revenge in a "good-humoredly" fashion to disarm his enemy; how he means exactly what he says beneath the lighthearted tone of his words.[10]

Through such maneuvers, the theme of passing also develops, binding the notion of a counterfeit self or appearance to cultural tensions about the sexual freedom of white women. It is this particular anxiety about genealogical reproduction that the tale's most famous critics, Jacques Lacan, Jacques Derrida, and Barbara Johnson, at once detect and overlook in their discussions of its hidden and surface narratives. Each sees the letter in terms of being, but not in relation to birth or gestation. In each of their analyses, the letter's content remains hidden and the tale's significance rooted in absence. Yet they do not account for the fact that Poe's narrator knows exactly what it says. The Prefect reads "aloud a minute account of the internal [and] external appearance of the missing document." It is from the outside in that the narrator communicates the content of the woman's letter, at once protecting himself by omitting what the Prefect details about it and communicating why it is important to "fathom her secret" from this obscured position.[11]

A key hint arises in the tale's attention to the cleverness of the characters who can decode what another character's body tries to disguise or suppress. Thus, although the Minister cannot read an "unexposed" letter, he discerns its significance by tracing its appearance on the table first to the "confusion of the personage," and then to her sudden composure in relation to the "personage who stood at her elbow." Dupin adopts the same strategy, reading the Minister's body language and regarding his "yawning, lounging, and dawdling" as an elaborate performance designed to mask an intensity of energy. Dupin himself engages in similar strategies, such as when he conceals the movement of his own eyes behind dark glasses.[12] If two can play at that game, then so can three. Because the woman in the tale, who also uses the strategy, does not overtly react when the Minister steals her letter, she quickly obscures her despair, splitting her bodily appearance from what she hides beneath its surface or within it. To the man at her elbow, nothing changes. He sees her for what she is: completely visible and above suspicion, like the letter on the table. He does not presume any contradictory meaning to her composure, nor the fact that something on display might also be out of sight.

Poe's narrative connects the physical existence of the woman with the letter, placing their shared and material manifestations into a framework of congruency. In fact, the kinetic shift through which the Minister "perceives the paper" and then "fathoms her secret" effectively merges the woman with the letter, as the one entity encloses the secret of the other. The word "fathom" is telling, too, because its etymological affinity with nautical exploration suggests the sense of literally plumbing something deep and dark. What I want to stress here, or to return to the surface of the tale, is the contextual legibility not only of the letter but also of the woman's body. She may never directly appear to the narrator, may never come forward for a complete description, but she sets all of the events in motion; she contacts the police, devises a reward, and describes the letter to the Prefect, whose own detailed description of it to Dupin and the narrator is not duplicated, only recounted. This sly, secondhand representation on the part of Poe's narrator once again aligns the woman's body with her letter, generating the idea that what she wants back is precisely that alignment, that ability to decide how to represent—and perhaps whether to deliver—something in her keeping. As she works behind the scenes to regain this control, Poe indicates that the potential danger to her body is very real, for his narrator opens "The Purloined Letter" with reference to "the affair of the Rue Morgue and the mystery attending the murder of Marie Rogêt," and therefore casts "The Purloined Letter" as part of a trilogy in which the women compelling the other two investigations are mutilated cadavers.[13] Their wretched fate frames her story, and she seems to know it.

The tale abruptly shifts from the narrator's recollection of the murdered women to the intrusion into his study of the Prefect, an action he casts as a coincidence in light of his present musings. "To any casual observer," he says of himself and Dupin, "we might have seemed intently and exclusively occupied with the curling eddies of smoke that oppressed the atmosphere of the chamber. For myself, however, I was mentally discussing certain topics which had formed the matter of conversation between us at an earlier period of the evening; I mean the affair of the Rue Morgue, and the mystery attending the murder of Marie Rogêt. I looked upon it, therefore, as something of a coincidence, when the door of our apartment was thrown open and admitted our old acquaintance, Monsieur G——, the Prefect of the Parisian police." This is a significant narrative move because it indicates another behind-the-scenes design: a prompting to bear in mind that the narrator is not omniscient but present in the tale, making decisions about what to include and suppress, about what cast as coincidental or interconnected. As a guilty associate of Dupin, who is himself a "partisan of the lady concerned," the narrator finds himself nervously circling around the particulars of the purloined letter.[14] Too much is at stake.

But he is also a storyteller, and his impulse is to urge his reader through artful suggestions and juxtapositions toward the secrets opening up around him. His hinting is rich, and things are laid out with a seeming innocence and frankness. The puns and sexual innuendo cover their own tracks. Thus, if he had to, he could protest that his inclusion of the description of the musket that shoots blanks is just a description of an empty musket and not an allusion to anyone's penis; that the reference to an "unusual gaping in the joints" or to a "secret drawer" simply describes furniture and not a woman's pelvis;[15] that Paris is Paris and America, America. So many echoes and puns obtain from this French setting, permitting an abortifacient to slide into the title of "Rue Morgue" and the purloined letter to transpire as a French letter, the popular term for a condom in the 1840s.[16]

Everything we need to know is indeed on the surface of the narrative. Thus, before proceeding, I want to elaborate on the debate between Jacques Lacan and Jacques Derrida on this point in "The Purloined Letter," along with Barbara Johnson's intervention, in order to accomplish two objectives. First, to address the ontological questions that each of these thinkers brings to bear on and pulls from "The Purloined Letter," and second, to attach these questions to the fact of birth in human existence. In Johnson's words, "The urgency of these undertakings [Derrida's, Lacan's] cannot . . . be overestimated, since the logic of metaphysics, of politics, of belief, and of knowledge itself is based on the imposition of definable objective frontiers and outlines whose possibility and/or justifiability are here [in "The Purloined Letter"] being put into question." Between them, Lacan and Derrida entirely overturn the impression that "much is made of nothing" in Poe's tale, as an early reviewer described it in 1845. And, following them, Johnson elucidates the link Poe forges between language and power, clarifying what it means for subjectivity to be formed within a structure and by a letter.[17]

Because all three analyses take up ontological questions, all three inadvertently point to the same issues and urgency surrounding abortion's criminalization in the 1840s. The lines of inquiry in Lacan's and Derrida's essays through Poe's narrative to questions concerning why "the law holds the woman in position as a signifier," as Lacan puts it, can then be directed to historical concerns that reproductive control liberated women in unpredictable social and symbolic ways.[18] In other words, if Lacan sees at work in "The Purloined Letter" the law of language as it forces the subject into a system of sexual difference, a law he understands as a paternal claim to and redirection of maternal production and identification, then the facts of gestation and birth must be returned to the framework of interpretation. The phallus (understood as patriarchal discourse and injunction) may bring the physiological origin of an embryo in line with the symbolic or spiritual origin of an embryonic subject, but abortion annihilates this narrative of subjectivity. If careful and quiet, only a pregnant person knows if a fetus exists and that its paternal legitimation means nothing if she terminates the pregnancy.

It is precisely in the places where Lacan and Derrida work out such concepts as sign and origin in Poe's tale that the subjects of pregnancy and termination also arise, producing significant crossovers between reproductive decisions and the broader question of framing and truth, contingencies and contracts. The medical archives of early nineteenth-century gynecology permit us to recognize what Poe's innuendo intimates on a literal level. That "a personage of most exalted station" is pregnant by a man other than her husband, "the other exalted personage," and that she possesses the option of abortion, a procedure by which she can erase the only material evidence, apart from the letter, of her affair.[19] Given the presence of arguments in 1840s America that abortion and adultery went hand in hand, it is significant that Lacan calls the woman in Poe's tale the guardian of legitimacy and notes that "we are assured of but one thing: the Queen cannot bring [the letter] to the knowledge of her lord and master." In fact, it is as though Lacan assumes "The Purloined Letter" is about an affair, that it is of course a love letter connected in some way to betrayal and to "the ceremony of returning letters [at] the extinction of the fires of love's feasts" activating the plot. For Lacan, that people in high places commit adultery is a matter not really worth discussing; the exalted rank of the protagonists in "The Purloined Letter" simply saves their escapades "from vaudeville."[20] Yet, the more pressing issue in his analysis involves the way in which the tale functions as an allegory of psychoanalysis and the letter a signifier that possesses its subjects.

As a result, Lacan simultaneously raises and evades the very questions he poses about legitimacy and about the presences of a woman (or "woman") as legitimacy's guardian within a structure of paternal inheritance and naming. What is indicated about this structure if the words of a woman function as the sole confirmation of both the presence of a fetus and the identity of its father? How is inheritance literally possessed as human wealth and directed by legal violence through corporeal lines of sex and race? Lacan traces instead the path by which the letter, associated as it is with absence and femininity, arrives at the place of sexual difference. In a way, my argument follows his route, but toward more tangible sites, back to the reproductive body and its potential for nonreproduction, and back to 1840s America, where the purloined letter also arrives at the place of racial difference. But to be clear, these places or markers of sexual and racial difference are ideological, not stable realities, and their tangibility is grasped through conceptualizations of patriarchy and white supremacy.

According to Lacan, even if Dupin were to rip up the letter, we would still have a kind of metaphysical language, still be subjected to it. Dupin's guarantee of the letter's return to its protector demonstrates the fulfillment of his duty to communicate the sign's conflict with being, Lacan notes. He secures its split nature in relation to, as Derrida puts it, the symbolic absence "between the legs of a woman," "the place of castration." But the woman is more than the letter's guardian or protector. She is also its source, and the condition of its theft points to an identifiable relocation and not necessarily to a timeless law. For Derrida, Lacan's interpretation not only establishes the phallus as a privileged signifier "depend[ing] neither on the signified, nor on the subject," but also erects a kind of "authentic life" for it, one that somehow persists in a realm beyond its material contingencies.[21]

"Materiality," says Derrida, "the sensory and repetitive side of the recording, the paper letter, drawings in ink, can be divided or multiplied, destroyed or set adrift.... If by some misfortune the phallus were divisible or reduced to the status of a part object, the entire edifice would collapse, and this must be [he adds with irony] avoided at all costs." The system of the symbolic, as Lacan thus formulates it, keeps the phallus in its proper place as a "symbol only of an absence" and in the custody of (though not represented by) the woman. Derrida argues that, as a consequence, Lacan invests his interpretation in the "truth" of castration and in the theory of the signifier's "destiny as destination." "What is called man and what is called woman might be subject to [phallogocentrism]," Derrida concedes, but "all of phallogocentrism is articulated on the basis of a determined *situation*.

... An (individual, perceptual, local, cultural, historical, etc.) situation on the basis of which what is called a 'sexual theory' is elaborated." Although he opens up the structure of sexual difference to contingencies of time and place, Derrida's essay stops short of exploring how legitimizing abortion infers obliterating a metaphysics of the sexed and ensouled human.[22]

From Derrida's perspective, the woman in "The Purloined Letter" is a figure who both sustains and threatens the system that contains her. Everything about her leaks its divisions. The power of her letter resides in the writing itself, not in some original essence, for as Poe's tale indicates, the contracts, cast as both fiat and blackmail, bind one figure to another within a structure of fiction and narration. Poe's narrator is deeply invested in writing, Derrida reminds us, and in how it transmits history and inheritance through a network of narrated frames. In this network, and in the absence of any other proof, one could add that a child is the king's if the queen says it is. Derrida's insistence on the importance of the *parergon,* or the narrative frames, in fact creates an analogy with the woman's corporeal existence. Yet, like Lacan, Derrida does not elaborate on the analogy, nor on the pun repeatedly produced through the concept of a woman "delivering" the letter. Like the story's enclosure within other stories, which gets repeatedly overlooked, the woman's body becomes rendered as similarly supplemental, derivative, and ornamental material in relation to the paternal narrative of birthright that is generated through it.

In her essay on Poe, Lacan, and Derrida, Barbara Johnson draws attention to the rivalry between Dupin and the Minister within "The Purloined Letter" and to the rivalry between Derrida and Lacan over it. Pointing where their theories tend to acknowledge and illuminate each other, Johnson notes Derrida's failure to acknowledge his debt to Lacan's *Ecrits* and Lacan's refusal to credit Derrida's grammatology. In her own reading of Poe's tale, she folds their points together in order to address a third rivalry, that of Atreus and Thyestes, the story Dupin refers to in the letter he leaves for the Minister in place of the stolen one. Thus, enclosed within "The Purloined Letter" is an allusion to a tale involving adultery, infanticide, and debts recovered by ruthless violence. In fact, the Atreus-Thyestes reference functions as much more than a literary allusion and becomes a powerful echo, sounding a message down through Poe's tale and into the letters (Dupin's, the woman's) themselves. In Johnson's words, the "story is framed by its own content." Moreover, in the version of the myth to which Dupin refers, it is a purloined letter that informs King Atreus of his wife's betrayal with his brother Thyestes. The queen's own handwriting names Thyestes, not Atreus, as the father of her child. Brilliantly taking all of these debts and rivalries together, Johnson asserts that "the questions [raised by these texts] are legion: What is a man? Who is the child's father? What is the relation between incest, murder, and the death of a child? What is a king? How can we read the letter of our destiny? What is seeing?"[23]

Although Johnson does not track these questions back into "The Purloined Letter," preferring to leave them as latent implications about the contingent nature of power, the tale itself follows them through to prospective answers. It binds the mythological account of adultery to the events at hand and artfully implies that, like Atreus's wife, this "exalted personage" is also pregnant. And although Johnson contends that the "letter's message is never revealed," we are permitted to read all of the other words in "The Purloined Letter" and to consider what we select for detection—to go wide instead of deep. Without disputing the far-reaching, philosophical ideas that Johnson uncovers in or addresses through the tale, I remain unsure about her point that Poe offers "no possibility of a position of analytic mastery."[24] For, as a potential victim of the fierce retribution steadily referenced across both the tale and the Dupin trilogy as a whole, the woman must assume this position and influence the interpretative direction of her letter. It is she who must master the events in an attempt to secure the letter's return to her, and her perspective exists in relation to the narrator's dispersed and repeated references to death and mutilation. She not only faces the prospect of being killed but of also being killed in the kind of frenzy of violence that engulfs the women in the Rue Morgue and Marie Rogêt, as well as the cadavers served up for dinner in the myth of Atreus and Thyestes.

Ostensibly describing a "game of puzzles," Dupin's words here hint at the text's method of disclosing how the woman's hidden letter reflects her "excessively obvious" embodied perspective: "A novice in the game generally seeks to embarrass his opponents by giving them the most minutely lettered names; but the adept selects such words as stretch, in large characters, from one end of the chart to the other. These, like the over-largely lettered signs and placards in the street, escape observation by dint of being excessively obvious; and here the physical oversight is precisely analogous with the moral inapprehension by which the intellect suffers to pass unnoticed those considerations which are too obtrusively and too palpably self-evident."[25]

The letter's content may not be directly presented to us but its message is disseminated throughout (or "stretched" across) the tale and beyond it, in the Atreus-Thyestes myth and in the print culture of Poe's world. These signifiers indicate a signified and even a referent—a fetus, one that the "exalted royal personage" may or may not bring to term.

We are told at the outset, for example, that the woman's urgent concern rests on "the non-appearance of certain results," in such evasive wording that slyly imparts how the suspicion of pregnancy begins with the nonappearance of a certain monthly event. The Prefect later divulges that "the personage robbed is more thoroughly convinced, every day, of the necessity of reclaiming her letter." And again later: "The fact is, it is becoming of more and more importance every day; and the reward has been lately doubled."[26] The passage of time, a pivotal element in the growing size of the reward, gives rise to the implication that, as the days and months pass, the reward is not the only thing growing in size. Mirroring (in terms of urgency and currency) another rapidly multiplying or forming entity, the reward serves both metaphoric and literal purposes in the text. These purposes become especially legible when considered in relation to the words "conceal" and "concealment," which occur no fewer than seven times in the tale and call attention to the legal and public perception of hidden, clandestine pregnancies and suspicious infant deaths.

Poe's nineteenth-century readers would have known that the word "concealment," accompanied by any hint of a missing newborn, denoted a very serious crime. In Dupin's words, "In all cases of concealment, a disposal of the article concealed—a disposal of it in this *recherché* manner—is in the very first instance, presumable and presumed."[27] The two tales preceding "The Purloined Letter" further establish that Dupin stresses the presumable existence of concealment in order to rationalize murder as a form of retributive justice. He extracts money and meaning from the bodies of women, as if he were an obstetrician working with an impacted fetus. Its birth matters more, and its figurative value greater, than the existence and worth of the literal woman who carries the fetus. This is the belief he communicates through the mangled corpses of the L'Espanayes and Marie Rogêt to the woman of "The Purloined Letter." He knows her secret, and she knows his because they are not simply borne by their minds but written out in blood and ink.

"Well, I may venture so far as to say," the Prefect says about the letter, "that the paper gives its holder a certain power in a certain quarter where such power is immensely valuable."[28] The implicit question as to why lineage is traced through paternity thus also moves through the tale, for paternal naming and inheritance involve the sovereignty of the conceptual over the material and a severing of the link to the mother's body. They are also arbitrarily conferred, given that the perpetuation of slavery rested on the denying of the patronymic to enslaved offspring and the tracing of their status through the maternal line. As Barbara Johnson emphatically reminds us, "The Purloined Letter" is after all a "*crime* story."[29] The undoing of the legitimacy of a maternal connection and its subsuming under a paternal claim underscores all of the male rivalries over the letter. The purloining of what belongs to a woman, moreover, takes place in front of her eyes, relayed when the Prefect says, "Its rightful owner saw, but, of course, dared not call attention to the act, in the presence of the third personage who stood at her elbow."[30] That is, she comprehends the system of which she is a part, she perfectly sees how it works, and she maneuvers for latitude within it. It is interesting to note that the Prefect refers to her as the letter's rightful owner, as if it is an incontestable fact despite her position of vulnerability.

Abortion comprises one way of asserting self-ownership at the very least, doubling in the possibility of destroying the letter as this evasive moment of dialogue suggests:

> "[Its] susceptibility of being produced at a moment's notice [is] a point of nearly equal importance with its possession."
> "Its susceptibility of being produced?" said I.
> "That is to say, of being *destroyed*," said Dupin.[31]

As John Muller and William Richardson suggest in their interpretation of Lacan's essay on the tale, "The position of woman as signifier recalls Lévi-Strauss's thesis: that the origin of language and culture involved establishing pacts by means of the exchange of women between groups (for whom the women then symbolized pacts)."[32] Another suggestive pun emerges in the word "letter" if we consider a menstruating body as a blood-letter, circulating within a system of exploitation that determines its value in terms of exchange and patriarchal currency. In addition, the blood-letter is meaningful only if it can be speculated on and multiplied, enveloped in notions of fertility and sealed by white men. And yet the secrets of inheritance, race, and naming remain folded up if a pregnant person refuses to convey them.

In "The Purloined Letter," we are told that the Minister who takes the letter fixes a "large black" seal on it, a seal bearing the D cipher or the Minister's initial. The seal, originally "small and red, with the ducal arms of an S-family," is obscured, and the woman's "diminutive and feminine" handwriting is marked over in a "bold and decided" way. These seals determine the worth and authenticity of the letter and its contents, a letter that, now protruding from a cheap card rack, gives the appearance of "worthlessness." By virtue of the tale's metaphorical dexterity, the image of the letter's placement (the careless thrusting of it, no less) among "five or six visiting cards" insinuates the idea of promiscuity and illuminates the idea that the Minister can take the same entity (the woman, her letter, her fetus) and cast it within an entirely different frame. He possesses the story that can turn something defined as pure into its opposite, something adulterated or prostituted. Suspended in this narrative, the woman risks the loss of her symbolic whiteness; the "soiled and torn condition of the letter" reflects back on her and her offspring. Should the letter's contents be revealed, the possible child would be written off as worthless and illegitimate, a dead end in the line of descent. He or she may look like the real thing but would fall into the same category as a "trumpery filigree card-rack of pasteboard," hanging from an umbilical-like "dirty blue ribbon."[33]

The play of color, of black against blue and red, furthermore, draws definitions of race and blood quantum into the crisis. Given that antebellum white women, especially the "exalted" or blue-blooded ones, were invested with the safekeeping of blood purity against any kind of amalgamation, it is possible that the tale's resolutely unnamed procedure through blackmail generates the homophonic double of "black male" and adds another level of transgression to the secrets of the letter. Although any kind of promiscuity threatened to sidetrack a line of descent from its so-called uncorrupted origin, it was the potential for contamination of white by black that lent the threat such urgency.

As Colin Dayan explains, "Poe moves us back to a time when a myth of blood conferred an unpolluted, legitimate pedigree ("The Fall of the House of Usher" or "William Wilson," both in 1839) and forward to an analytics of blood that ushered in a complex of color: the ineradicable stain, the drop that could not be seen but must be feared ("Ligeia," "The Masque of the Red Death," or *The Narrative of Arthur Gordon Pym* [1838]).... An innate quality (the unseen blood stain) could result in the conversion of a person into property."³⁴ The transformation through blood did not work the other way around, of course. A white man's seal on an enslaved woman's body conferred nothing in antebellum America, as determined by *partus sequitur ventrem.*

Like the tales mentioned by Dayan, "The Purloined Letter" explores the possibility of an imperceptible stain on a family of a "most exalted station."³⁵ It records the fact that adultery, in early nineteenth-century conservative thought, was not just a matter of infidelity but a crime against the blood—an attack on white supremacy and an opening up of bloodlines to uncontrolled circulation. As physician Thomas Burgeland rhetorically asked in his 1837 study *Physiological Observations,* "Would [the abolitionist] feel any objection for his daughter to enter into a matrimonial connexion with one of those beings whose cause he so impetuously advocated?"³⁶ Or as Burgeland's contemporary Hester Pendleton advised, in an oblique reference to Madame Restell, that "infamous lady physician," a woman should not do what she wants and then allow herself to be "probed by a whalebone."³⁷ All of these perils crowd into the purloined letter, a document that is, as we are told, "much soiled and crumpled" as it passes from the woman's boudoir to the Minister's apartment.³⁸

In such a degraded condition, the letter's description yields a subtle pattern of double entendres, especially when it is combined with the space of the Minister's apartment. In the context of nineteenth-century medicine, the letter's position "between the 'legs' of the fireplace," as Derrida notes, introduces a tongue-in-cheek reference to popular theories of a wayward woman's overheated womb—the *furor uterinus* engendered by thwarted and illicit love. Moreover, the sharp instruments used to probe the spaces and furniture should not be tossed aside as irrelevant information, even if they pertain to ineffective police procedure on the tale's literal level of narration. These instruments are stunningly suggestive of surgical abortion procedures, functioning as images of the uterine sound and curette, and the references to cotton wadding and knitting needles intensify what the cushions and drawers signify, as they are probed and opened.

As James Ricci explains in *One Hundred Years of Gynaecology, 1800–1900,* the beginning of the nineteenth century saw the rise of gynecological medicine as "The female genital organs were subjected to minute analysis and [different] areas were described in detail." Hundreds of different kinds of specula were patented and, along with the sound and the curette, were used to "explore the cavity of the uterus."[39] The expansion in numbers of gynecologists and abortionists in the 1830s and 1840s must be understood in light of women's demand for procedures. When herbal abortifacients failed to work, they sought out mechanical abortions, trained to read how abortionists advertised their services in terms of alleviating blocked menstrual cycles and removing uterine obstructions.

Making something illegal or illicit does not repress it, as Foucault reminds us, but rather multiplies the ways of saying and not saying it:

> "Suppose you detail," said [the narrator of "The Purloined Letter"], "the particulars of your search."
>
> "Why the fact is," [replied the Prefect] . . . "we searched *everywhere*. . . . We opened every possible drawer; and I presume you know that, to a properly trained police agent, such a thing as a *secret* drawer is impossible. Any man is a dolt who permits a 'secret' drawer to escape him in a search of this kind. The thing is *so* plain. There is a certain amount of bulk—of space—to be accounted for in every cabinet . . . After the cabinets we took the chairs. The cushions we probed with the fine long needles you have seen me employ. From the tables we removed the tops."
>
> "Why so?" [asked the narrator] "Couldn't the cavity be detected by sounding?" . . .
>
> "By no means, if, when the article is deposited, a sufficient wadding of cotton be placed around it."
>
> . . .
>
> "But you could not have removed—you could not have taken to pieces *all* the articles of furniture in which it would have been possible to make a deposit in the manner you mention. A letter may be compressed into a thin spiral roll, not differing much in shape or bulk from a large knitting-needle, and in this form it might be inserted into the rung of a chair, for example . . . I presume . . . you probed the beds and bed-clothes."
>
> "Certainly: we opened every package and parcel. We also measured the thickness of every book-*cover,* with the most accurate admeasurement, and applied to each the most jealous scrutiny of the microscope. Had any of the bindings been recently meddled with it would have been utterly impossible that the fact should have

escaped observation. Some five or six volumes, just from the hands of the binder, we carefully probed, longitudinally, with the needles."

"You looked into the cellars?"

"We did."[40]

Through droll metaphors for the interiority of the female anatomy (cabinets, cavities, cellars), along with the needles that probe them, this dialogue represents the secret of abortion contained within the purloined letter. "What is all this boring, and probing, and sounding, and scrutinizing with the microscope?" asks Dupin in both a condensed recapitulation of the telling verbs and an almost verbatim duplication of the language of surgical gynecology.[41] Like everything else in the tale, that which is private, secret, and unspoken is at the same time public, clear, and apparent, at least when approached through a particular frame of reference.

As a result, gestures and words meant to disguise information may in fact divulge it. This is Dupin's advantage. Behind his dark glasses and ironic statements, he reads both linguistic and corporeal signs, such as the Minister's fake laziness or the Prefect's vocal hesitations. The question of the body's production of signs also occurs in the tale's attention to handwriting as something unique, inherently recognizable, something that ties, like an umbilical cord, the production of the words to the producer of them. It is because the letter is in the woman's distinctive handwriting that she is in such trouble. Furthermore, Dupin remarks that the Minister will know who fooled him with a new letter because Dupin's own handwriting will be familiar to him. We also observe the Prefect write and sign the reward check for Dupin. In each case the handwriting at once materializes a source and a destination.

But, twice the word "fac-simile" occurs in the tale, thus collapsing any guarantee or endorsement of authenticity.[42] "The Purloined Letter" here opens onto the issue of passing that follows from its explorations of adultery and abortion. In other words, if bodies give something away or express something authentic, it is because a conceptual framework of surface and depth, of the feigned and the bona fide, is already in place. What is counterfeit in one context is sterling in another. Though corporeal material may be sources of signifying innovations, there is nothing inherent in the blood, nothing that yields a timeless secret or racialized value. Even a maternal body, with its pronounced dilation, can be concealed or circumvented, and the question of paternity can certainly be covered up.

Remarking on the success of his detection, Dupin weaves together statements about legitimacy and morality and asserts, "Mathematical reasoning is merely logic applied to observation upon form and quantity. The great error lies in supposing that even the truths of what is called *pure* algebra, are abstract or general truths.... What is true of relation—of form and quantity—is often grossly false in regard to morals, for example.... There are numerous other mathematical truths which are only truths within the limits of *relation*.... Occasions may occur where $x2 + px$ is not altogether equal to q."[43] None of this really makes sense, except that it establishes the same veneer of expertise that Dupin asserts in the previous two tales.

His introduction of a mathematical formula, however, echoes the racial pseudoscience of Poe's time, and the "pure algebra" channels Thomas Jefferson's 1815 theorem for blood quantum in delineations of race into the text. To quote Jefferson,

> The algebraic notation is the most convenient and intelligible. Let us express the pure blood of the white in the capital letters of the printed alphabet, the pure blood of the negro in the small letters of the printed alphabet, and any given mixture of either, by way of abridgment in MS. letters.
>
> Let the first crossing be of *a*, a pure negro, with A, pure white.... Call it, for abbreviation *b* (half-blood).
>
> Let the second crossing be that of *b* and B, the blood of the issue will be +, or substituting its equivalent, it will be +, call it *q* (quarteroon) being ¼ negro blood.[44]

Jefferson then continues through several more mathematical formulas, concluding with "*e*": "But if *e* be emancipated, he becomes a free white man, and a citizen of the United States to all intents and purposes." He also qualifies his position, when it comes to the offspring of enslaved women, stating that his algebra in no way overturns that "which depends on the condition of the mother, the principle of the civil law, *partus sequitur ventrem*."[45] I quote Jefferson at length here because Dupin's calculations and cruelty take their lead from the nation-state and function in conjunction with the rape and extortion legalized by it.

To conclude by returning to the beginning. The initial dialogue between Dupin and the Prefect, in which Dupin's banter about a "mystery [that] is

CHAPTER THREE

a little too plain" strikes the Prefect as hilarious, occurs *before* the Prefect introduces the specifics of the missing letter. By looking backward from the ending, we can see that the crux of the letter and its concealment creep into Dupin's diction, kindling his wordplay and placing him in the center of the crime. Dupin already knows what comprises this "mystery," as the narrator realizes in retrospect and from the sidelines of the dialogue. Thus, the story's epigraph from Seneca (*Nil sapientiae odiosius acumine nimio,* or "nothing is more odious to wisdom than a sharp wit") establishes a hint about Dupin from outside of the story's frame, in one of the narrator's characteristic double moves. This is not a wise man, Poe reminds us through this narrator, but rather someone who satirizes wisdom and amuses himself in the process.

With this conclusion of the trilogy, the narrator brings us closer to the world of influence and money with which Dupin is intimately familiar. He carefully presents Dupin as a facsimile of the Minister D—— and raises the possibility that they are brothers. If they hide this connection it is because it serves them well, sharing what they know without revealing the power that doubles between them. "There are two brothers, I know," the narrator says toward the end of the tale, implying to Dupin that he knows more than Dupin thinks he does and indicating that perhaps Dupin's name is an assumed one, hiding him from view. The narrator's remark about the brothers occurs in response to Dupin's expounding on the "principles of concealment" and relays the message that he gets underway in "The Mystery of Marie," that the dangerous secrets of men hide behind the salacious focus on the secrets of women.[46]

When Dupin retrieves the letter from the locked drawer of his desk, we realize that he has had it all along. This letter's information is corroborated by its own double in the letter stolen from the safe on the Rue Morgue, in a literal and metaphoric line of correspondence between the "exalted" woman (Dupin's sister or sister-in-law) and the abortionist, Madame L'Espanaye. The yarn about the Minister D—— accidentally spotting a letter and seizing the moment is likewise doubled and reversed by the stronger likelihood that this theft was carefully planned and in collusion with Dupin. Once again, motive and cooperation take cover under fabrications involving coincidence and rivalry. The Minister D—— is Dupin's sworn enemy in the same way as an herbivorous ape murdered two women and a botched abortion left Marie Rogêt with a piece of cloth wound around her neck, deeply buried in her once-living flesh. Poe's narrator hides his confession in the contradictions, afraid to come entirely clean, carefully disburdening nonetheless.

Poe thus opens and closes his trilogy with purloined letters, extending the pun on *l'être* from one tale to the next. As he explores the meaning of abortion in the conceptualization of human existence, he indicates why its questions generate such violent responses and redefinitions. For Poe, attempts to disambiguate something so entwined—where existence and nonexistence fold into one another; where a concealed pregnancy that is never announced opens onto nothingness—turn into severing. He presents in his work a kind of Gordian knot and welcomes its thread's disentangling, but only to the extent that it reveals its bending back into the knot. If sliced at that bending, other forms of violence follow. The impetus to cut into tangled forms of existence and deny where they overlap is the same impetus that drives Dupin, as he tears from ambiguity and concealment patriarchal delineations of birthright and inheritance.

PART II

NATION, PLANTATION, ANNIHILATION
Three by Nathaniel Hawthorne

Preamble—"A" Is for Abortion and Agriculture

Hawthorne's fiction pursues many of the same questions as Poe's, in significant echoes of his tales' lexical and allegorical artistry. A purloined letter turns scarlet in Hester Prynne's hands; a strangled grisette resurfaces as a throttled feminist, both borne from rivers and framed by lies; and old patriarchal houses enclose women who modify them from within and treasure their barrenness. Each of the three Hawthorne novels I discuss here shares with Poe's trilogy almost identical philosophical and medical standpoints on the meaning and matter of human existence, and they draw the practice of abortion into similarly striking modes of narrative experimentation and grammatical convolution.

As I argue in this chapter's section on *The Blithedale Romance,* Hawthorne's murderous Coverdale and his confessional narrative surface from hiding and in light of the forensic science that contradicts his words, mirroring the process by which Dupin materializes as a horrifying villain. Where Dupin manipulates reality to the degree that miraculous thorns present themselves at the scene of Marie Rogêt's death, Coverdale insists that Providence selects the site where Zenobia dies on her knees, stiffened into a submissive posture for all eternity. In both cases, the women's bodies carry the facts of the matter inside the textual reproduction of lies about them. Coverdale chokes the life out of Zenobia and conceals her in intimations of abortion and suicide, just as Dupin insinuates abortion into the story of Marie Rogêt or raises the possibility of suicide in "Rue Morgue."

Through Coverdale, Hawthorne explores the stranglehold of a conservative, nationalistic ideology—how it manifests in violent control of reproductive rights, expansionism, and slavery—and turns white citizens into the agents of its enforcement. This is the same question that he raises in the two novels preceding *The Blithedale Romance,* in which Dimmesdale speaks for Providence and Jaffrey Pyncheon asserts his claims to the ancestral house. If Hawthorne's own conservative tendencies flicker in the pages of his work—his own image transpiring in Dimmesdale and Coverdale as writers, or in the genealogical mirror of the Pyncheons' witch-hunting origins—they also exorcise themselves there. For he resembles Clifford too, gazing as he does in a poisoned well, seeing his face dissipate in its uterine depths. It is "Earthly happiness" that Clifford wants to find, not a heavenly afterlife or evidence of his soul.

Margaret Fuller's statement about nationalism and abortion makes particular sense of Hawthorne's preoccupation with America's founding and its metaphors of birth and virgin territory. In Fuller's words, "All attempts to construct a national literature must end in abortions like the monster of Frankenstein, things with forms, and the instincts of forms, but soulless, and therefore revolting."[1] Exploring the meaning of abortion as something malformed and as pregnancy's termination, Hawthorne establishes a nonreproductive ideology at the heart of his novels, spinning complex representations of soulless entities and molecular reinvention into nationalism's undoing.[2]

According to J. Gerald Kennedy in *Strange Nation: Literary Nationalism in the Age of Poe,* "Nationalist ideology, everywhere and always, works to conceal," as it operates to mask brutality in idealizations of culture and genealogy.[3] It is interesting to consider Kennedy's interpretation of nationalism as a mode of concealment, given the medicolegal definition of concealment in the same decades. In the same way as Poe's fiction multiplies forms of concealment, Hawthorne's does too, so that pregnancy, abortion, nationalism, and resistance alternate in the overdetermined spaces of Hester's interactions, Hepzibah's waiting, and Zenobia's decomposition.

Hawthorne frames immortality and decay, white and black, men and women, in patterns of correspondence for which his most reactionary characters speak. What becomes increasingly clear from one novel to the next is the extent to which whiteness and spirituality interconnect in the patriarchal systems that Hawthorne represents, particularly as they are threatened by women who do not insure their reproduction. White supremacy takes hold in relation not only to the image of the human soul as something pure or luminous (and subject to staining by sin and miscegenation) but also to its procreation, the procedure by which this soul must be protected from annihilation by abortion at any stage of gestation.

This interpretation of Hawthorne's understanding of whiteness is buttressed by Willie James Jennings's powerful explication of race and theology in *The Christian Imagination*. Describing the "complex optical operation" effected by modernity's slave-trading empires, Jennings carefully accounts for the processes by which whiteness came to signify proximity to salvation and creation, and blackness the "negative anchor at the bottom of a racial aesthetic." A color-coded hierarchy congealed as a result of dislocation and invasion, in formations of identity that split people from their lands and marked belonging on their skin. Kidnapping and colonialism drew Black and Indigenous bodies "onto a plane of existence that involved constant spiritual and material comparison with white bodies." This visualization extended even further, into the "reaches of literary legitimation": English became spirituality's voice in America; and authorship in English carried this voice through implicit connections among whiteness, literacy, and intellectual superiority.[4]

Hawthorne's anxieties about authorship as a type of creation that mirrors the Author's, a popular term for god in the nineteenth century, course through his representations of race and nationalism. His allegories take place, moreover, inside the agricultural transformations that, as Jennings underscores, enriched Europe and relied as much on extraction as they did on the typological, capitalist, and racialized narratives that justified them. Jennings does not consider how sexualized hierarchies arrived with the plantations' reconfigurations of space and time, but his research opens up ways of seeing how they unfold in Hawthorne's fiction. Thus, where Jennings demonstrates that Christian theology reframed space and bound whiteness to property and production, I trace this reframing in Hawthorne's fiction as it informs a racialized patriarchy's investment in breeding and maternity, so-called natural increase and harvests of souls.[5] In the shadows of Hawthorne's fictional landscapes lies the space of the plantation, where obsessions with whiteness and fertility play out against and include blackness and abortion. His representation of this space incorporates feminist and materialist philosophies of existence, echoing declarations like this one, by Frances Wright: "We are all on the Earth, and they tell us of Heaven. We are matter and they tell us of spirit."[6]

CHAPTER FOUR

Passwords and Countersigns
The Scarlet Letter

> A sentence broken in the midst, where his thoughts had ceased to gush out upon the page.
> —Nathaniel Hawthorne, *The Scarlet Letter*, 1850

> Everyone who stepped on a slave ship became racialized, white and black.
> —Willie James Jennings, *The Christian Imagination*, 2016

When Hester Prynne dreams of fleeing the punitive consequences of her unplanned pregnancy, she contemplates committing murder-suicide at one point. The novel's narrator withholds judgment, viewing Hester's fantasy of bloodshed in terms of revolutionary beheadings and freedom of thought. Just beneath the surface of Hester's quiet, marble-like exterior, such inklings arise and remain entombed, in the same way as "the wild energy" of her mind runs riot in silence, we are told, in the time "before Pearl's birth."[1] As this chapter on *The Scarlet Letter* will demonstrate, it is by means of such allusions to the temporal realm of Pearl's gestation and Hester's seditious thinking that Hawthorne sets abortion's alternative into motion as a form of liberation, at once undercutting the notion that Hester's pregnancy doomed her to the novel's plotline and smashing the fictions of existence that surround birth. Nowhere is Pearl's birth configured in retrospect as inevitable; never is the possibility of Hester's having had no choice insinuated as part of the novel's backstory. On the contrary, acts of choosing repeatedly carve up the way things are in Puritan America, and fate is a lie of the empire founded there.

Hawthorne frames this early American tale of adultery and empire in the context of antebellum white supremacy, its financial investment in slavery equally ontological, and abortion one of its biggest threats. He describes Hester's story in terms of a ledger's entry, as the "error in the balance of an account or an ink-blot on the fair page of a book of record," in a metaphor of calculation and violence connected to the plantation grids that overtook

CHAPTER FOUR

Indigenous lands.² To quote Caitlin Rosenthal in *Accounting for Slavery,* "Standardized plantation account books became like blueprints for factory production—designs for machines made out of humans," and their inventories rested on clear, racialized delineations.³ Plantation owners recorded births and miscarriages (or what they thought were miscarriages) in ledgers designed for tallying profits from sales. Not only did Hawthorne once note that the wished he could publish *The Scarlet Letter* in red ink, but he also returned to this accounting metaphor with more force in *The House of the Seven Gables* and *The Blithedale Romance,* to further illuminate the practice of abortion as that which divested the slave economy of its earnings and shifted the white birth rate into a downward slope.

With *The Scarlet Letter,* he inaugurates his attack on the foundations of American expansionism by depicting a crisis in white genealogical transmission, setting his protagonist in the fictional foreground of an actual institution's brutal perpetuation. That is, when his narrator describes Hester's mind as wild and her prospect of leaving a given, he implies a freedom that is hers and her child's, on the other side of which exists the condition of slavery—the opposite of wild—and its maternal transmission, coded in law as *partus sequitur ventrem.* Inside the novel's impressionistic mode, he pulls Hester between representation and transposition: her story is also another's, but inverted, just as the surface of the brook reflects Pearl's image back to her as "another and the same."⁴

A parallel instance of this complexity arises when Chillingworth directs Dimmesdale's attention to an unmarked grave and proposes that, though it "bore no tombstone," the flourishing weeds around it "manifest an unspoken crime," intimating that the not-bearing of something does not mean that nothing happened, so to speak in a roundabout way of sex. The conscious-stricken Dimmesdale is, of course, supposed to read between the lines about what he hides in his immediate past and beneath the facade of his Puritan respectability. But Chillingworth's insinuation is also Hawthorne's, whose signposting loops together an allegory of concealed deeds with that of colonial violence. For, at the same time as Dimmesdale's buried sexual history is likened to weeds over a clandestine grave, the metaphor extends past it, into what Uncle Sam ("our common Uncle," in the narrator's words) obscures beneath his orderly, mythic "planting in the wilderness." Not only do the weeds appear when pointed out, but they are also black and intentional—as "taking it upon themselves to keep [the dead] in remembrance"—and therefore part of an ideological landscape not entirely under colonial control, if violently marked in black and white. In the same conversation, Chillingworth flips the long-standing, benevolent connotation of whiteness to implicate it as the color of deception, as the gleam of "new-fallen snow" under which "propagate[s] a hellish breed" of anything but innocence.[5]

Hawthorne plays his hand stealthily, signaling that if a breed from hell exists in the novel, then it is the white Puritan settlers themselves. In the harrowing scene of Pearl's interrogation at the Governor's mansion, for instance, the question put to Pearl ("Who made thee?") masks an entire system of seized, branded, and relocated bodies. In effect, what the Governor and his ministers demand to hear reiterated is that their god authorizes them to dispossess mothers of children, by virtue of their race and imperial status. They superintend those "in the dark as to [their] souls"—those plunged in "blacker depths of sin"—and speak for "the Creator of all flesh."[6] The stress shifts almost imperceptibly from souls to flesh: Pearl's proprietorship is weighed and considered; Hester's terrified shrieking turns the mansion into an auction house.

From *The Scarlet Letter* through *The Blithedale Romance*, Hawthorne explores how the possession of a soul as distinct from the body—the one in the hands of an eternal Father, the other conferred by a mortal mother—makes such acts of dispossession possible or even thinkable, especially given the interconnected lexicon of sanctity, immortality, and whiteness that surrounds spiritual existence. As each of the terms becomes intrinsic to one another, blackness in turn becomes impure, immoral, and subject to decay. It transpires in an iconography that was by Hawthorne's time centuries in the making, interacting with unconscious validations of white supremacy. Virginity is "pure as a lily [and] snowy"; iniquity is "black and filthy, ... speckled and spotted"; temptation "bears black fruit." These similes and metaphors have as much to do with authoritarian characterizations of race and lineage as they do with the theological worldview of the Puritans.[7] The latter, moreover, licenses and obfuscates the former.

Working with this iconography of color and corrosion, Hawthorne's narrator slides into his tale a biography of the "Father of the Custom-House," explaining that this man not only fathered twenty children, but also "carr[ied] off the entire burden" of their lives and deaths without "a sable tinge" of sadness. He stands atop a hierarchy, possessed of his whiteness and offspring. "The chief tragic event of the old man's life," Hawthorne's narrator chortles, "was his mishap with a certain goose, ... so inveterately tough that the carving-knife would make no impression on its carcass." This minibiography then terminates in Hawthorne's ferocious reduction of a highly symbolic founding father to the status of meat, declaring him void of a soul, "*an absolute nonentity,*" incorporating him into the tale solely to effect his obliteration (my emphasis).[8] As a result, he tells a tale about abundant breeding and feeding and then reverses it into an existential emptying, taking the notions of legitimacy, livestock, and white immortality down with it.[9] This is the message about flesh and spirit that runs through "The Custom House" as a preface to *The Scarlet Letter*—that no god secures human life for eternity, neither at conception nor after death—quietly establishing it as the awareness at which Hester later arrives, when she thinks about herself as "newly emancipated" from the fictions her world forces on her.[10]

Toward the conclusion, Hester's attempt to flee by ship takes place along a rather straightforward route on the transatlantic slave trade. The ships that disembark surreptitiously in "The Custom House" reappear in the closing chapters of *The Scarlet Letter,* now open to passengers: "The Old World [offered] a more eligible shelter and concealment than ... all of America.... It just so happened that a ship lay in the harbor; one of those questionable cruisers, frequent at that day, which, without being absolutely outlaws of the deep, yet roamed over its surface with remarkable irresponsibility of character. This vessel had recently arrived from the Spanish Main [and] would sail for Bristol." Identifying Bristol as the point of origin for the ship awaiting the protagonists, Hawthorne names a principal slave port of "the mother country." Everything vague about the description above comes into focus at that naming, at least in part. Who comes ashore, vacating the berths, so that Hester and her party might leave? The answers fall inside the network of "pass-words and countersigns" acquired by his narrator while working in the Custom House.[11]

By way of such intricate and elusive details, Hawthorne tells the story that contemporary abortion-historian Rickie Solinger bluntly puts this way: that the United States came into being as a nation-state through "the reproductive capacity of ... an enslaved labor force." The doors of the Custom House open on the commerce and consolidated control of human beings, those whose "ineligibility for citizenship underwrote the exclusivity and value of white citizenship.... *Which men could or could not have sex and children with which women? Which women were coerced to reproduce? Which persons were killed, in part, so that they could not reproduce?*" (Solinger's italics).[12] If one of the meanings of Hester's "A" is America, as Hawthorne scholars concur, then its red threads and gold embellishment make visual the interrelationship among bloodlines, money, and personhood itself. To quote historian Liam Hogan, "By criminalising interracial marriages British Colonists thus wished to ringfence the 'white' and 'Christian' community as the preeminent colonial identity. As Winthrop Jordan summated, their attacks on miscegenation, which can be traced through their laws and correspondence, drip 'with distaste and indignation.' They particularly focussed on controlling the sexual freedom of the white female population, and their patriarchal justice system treated miscegenation between white men and enslaved black women as a far less important issue."[13] In *The Scarlet Letter,* Pearl's illegitimacy and Hester's silence about her paternity stand on this color line, bleeding out the authority exerted over her role in its reproduction.

Imagining everything from committing infanticide to returning to England, away from John Winthrop's imperative to "choose life, where wee and our Seede may live" in his City upon the Hill,[14] Hester disappears only to come back. Pearl remains elsewhere, however. According to both Surveyor Pue and "one of his recent successors in office," she is married—hovering in reproductions of other men's fantasies that Hawthorne's narrator replicates for us: "And, once, Hester was seen embroidering a baby-garment," he reports of the gossip, "with such a lavish richness of golden fancy as would have raised a public tumult, had any infant, thus appareled, been shown to our somber-hued community." And yet no infant makes an appearance, not between the pages of this book. It is sustained rather in the same pattern of hallucination and substantiation through which Dimmesdale's own scarlet letter arrives: a reality of blood or nothing, no more on his flesh than "on a new-born infant's," an image of a birthmark simultaneously conjured as a nonentity and left as such.[15]

One of the novel's first reviewers, New York's Episcopal bishop A. Cleveland Coxe, famously described *The Scarlet Letter*'s intricate artistry as something flowing with "an under-tide of filth."[16] This insight is fascinating because of Coxe's vocal opposition to abortion and his ties to the American Medical Association—his warnings to "his flock against the blood-guiltiness of ante-natal infanticide."[17] Although his review does not mention abortion, he seems to ascertain it in *The Scarlet Letter,* especially when he pairs its message with that of the "late Convention of females at Boston."[18] Baffled by the incongruity between Hawthorne's choice of setting in "the cradle of our country" and the topic of an illegitimate birth, he asks, "Why has our author selected such a theme?" As he builds his case against the novel—its refusal to honor the Puritan "progenitors" and its potential to lead astray the "daughters of America"—Coxe at once incorporates the genealogical terms of Anglo-American nationalism and reveals how insistently *The Scarlet Letter* shatters them.[19] Without quite being able to put his finger on it, he discerns the novel as a threat to the prevailing idealization of America as something born to and bequeathed by the New England Puritans.

The Scarlet Letter indeed stages the birth of the nation in the "mother forest" on the shores of the Atlantic, imagining the soil itself as new or "natal" and the settlement "so newly constructed," only to undermine that very idea or to name it as such. "It was *as if* a new birth . . . had converted the forest land," Hawthorne's narrator writes of Hester Prynne's world, calling attention to the metaphor as an imposition of meaning and a falsehood (my emphasis). He also opens the novel with reference to a "portion of the virgin soil" where the settlement's prison and its cemetery both stand, in a sly witticism that entwines the womb of the place with its tombs. "The spell survives," he explains in "The Custom House" of Salem's effect on him, "just as powerfully as if the natal spell were an earthly paradise," and yet he contemplates it in very dark ways too, as a "place of birth and burial" where long-interred skeletons retain the stain of blood on their bones. He thus sets into motion the American myth of origins—that projected "Utopia of human virtue and happiness"[20]—only to cut it off. The rich, long-standing literary association between textual and sexual reproduction allows him to imagine the terms of a national epic, to reproduce the lexicon of its idealism, and then terminate that conception's progression within his pages. With *The Scarlet Letter,* Hawthorne hints at the possibility that Anglo-America's birthright will find legitimacy under his authorship, but he engages instead in a form of abortion where no such patriotism takes hold.

His narrator moves the representation of a nation as born to or among a people into his tale about Pearl's birth, exploring what it means to see America in terms of biological gestation, as if gestation too is a form of destiny. He then runs this representation against his preference for scrapped sequences and broken chains, "unpremeditated" moments and "latitude of speculation."[21] The novel's main plotline itself, while luring readers into anticipating or expecting the final reunion of Hester and Dimmesdale, is also severed. And it is Pearl who is asked to bear the news:

> "Thy mother is yonder woman with the scarlet letter," said the seaman. "Wilt thou carry her a message from me?"
> "If the message pleases me, I will," answered Pearl.
> "Then tell her," rejoined he, "that I spake again with the black-a-visaged, hump-shouldered old doctor, and he engages to bring his friend, the gentleman she wots of, aboard with him. So let thy mother take no thought, save for herself and thee. Wilt thou tell her this, thou witch baby?"[22]

Pearl "purs[ues] a zigzag course . . . to her mother" with the message, reflecting Hawthorne's insistence throughout the novel that Pearl herself consists of "elements . . . all in disorder, or with an order peculiar to themselves," as well as his insinuations that her birth be likewise detached from the notion of a straight line from conception to delivery. For while his narrator might imagine Pearl in utero, wondering what gets "transmitted to the unborn infant" from Hester, he can only do so retrospectively, interpreting backward from her existence, the discovery of which is accidental.[23] This framework of accident and happenstance (among the forgotten in the archives of the Custom House) then pulls the tale in a different direction, into the chance that neither Pearl nor the book itself might have seen the light of day. Hawthorne's narrator envisions Pearl as "unborn" in order to envelop this scarlet letter in the darkness of its source, its composition, as separate from its destination.

Formed out of "those unquiet elements that had distracted Hester Prynne before Pearl's birth," Pearl also arrives in spite of them, the allusion to unnamed distractions pairing the history of her gestation with vague threats to it. The vagueness here commands our attention. Does "distraction" mean "diversion" (by an external enticement) or "perturbation" (by fears internal to her thinking)? Undermining the representation of Hester's pregnancy as a foregone conclusion, this distraction indicates that she struggles before Pearl's birth in a way that mirrors Dimmesdale's struggle following it. His decision to conceal himself in the shadows reflects on her emergence into visibility. Where he declines visibility, she declines concealment. "What does the scarlet letter mean? . . . Tell me! Tell me!" Pearl's insistent inquiry sustains the link between her and the letter, but Hester refuses to answer her directly. The meaning of the "A" remains unfixed, subject to unraveling, just as the object itself suggests dinner to a "sacrilegious moth" (but a tale to the narrator), and it is from here that most Hawthorne scholarship proceeds.[24]

As Arthur Riss puts it so well, "It is a truth now universally known that the scarlet letter upon Hester Prynne's chest designates much more than adultery."[25] For Laura Doyle, "Hester's 'A' is a layered code," one that gestures toward the concealed violence of American imperialism.[26] And, in Franny Nudelman's words, "Whether considered from a formal or a cultural vantage point, the letter's power lies in its referential latitude, which allows it to accumulate and sustain a variety of readings under the rubric of its own simplicity. Its indeterminacy is indistinguishable from its inclusiveness, and both determine its critical stature."[27] Building on such formulations of the letter's indeterminacy and layers of meaning, I propose another designation for the letter "A," one that reflects or contains the following index from an 1846 issue of *The National Police Gazette:*

>   Abortion, prevention of
>   Abortion, seduction, and murder
>   Abortion, a felony
>   Abortionist, Restell the
>   Abortionist, convicted
>   Abortionists, detection of
>   Abortionists, horrible deeds of
>   Abortionists, more work of the
>   Abortionists, of New York
>   Abortionists, still at work[28]

While I cannot prove that Hawthorne happened on precisely this page, I wish to highlight it as an encapsulation of a cultural phenomenon of which he must been aware and to propose that the A's inclusive indeterminacy aligns the revelation of Hester's adultery with its potential cover up.[29] The letter folds the secret of a declined alternative within it, complicating the view that sex, pregnancy, and childbirth follow one from the other in an escapable train of consequences for Hawthorne's protagonist.

According to Robert Martin, Hester's letter is "not merely of female manufacture but indeed part of a private, mysterious female realm to which one can only have access through the mysterious knowledge of certain 'ladies'"; its "original description as a 'rag of scarlet cloth,'" he further notes, carries the "associations of menstruation and defloration."[30] What if the rag's appearance in the Custom House also carries other, concomitant associations? Advancing along this line of interpretation, the bloodstains following childbirth, a miscarriage, or a terminated pregnancy also crowd into the secrets of the red rag. While its "deep meaning" evades "the analysis of [the narrator's] mind," it communicates something formidable only when he attempts to wear or bear its weight himself: "While thus perplexed,—and cogitating, among other hypotheses, whether the letter might not have been one of those decorations which the white men used to contrive, in order to take the eyes of Indians,—I happened to place it on my breast. It seemed to me,—the reader may smile, but must not doubt my word,—it seemed to me, then, that I experienced a sensation not altogether physical, yet almost so, as of burning heat; and as if the letter were not of red cloth, but red-hot iron. I shuddered, and involuntarily let it fall upon the floor."[31] If we take into consideration the wide-ranging discussions surrounding women's reproductive functions and rights in the 1830s and 1840s, then the female realm of knowledge that perplexes him—very different from that of the "white men" mentioned above—becomes more historically specific, even as it remains guarded and enigmatic. It also coincides with the novel's own status as a kind of stain on America's account of purity of origin and design.

The practice of abortion and its facilitation of nonreproductive sex in New England cities propelled medical and legal debates regarding pregnancy and its regulation in Hawthorne's time, all of which played out in the press, in advertisements for abortifacients, in medical journals, and in the publicized trials of famed abortionist Madame Restell, the figure above named by the *National Police Gazette*. It is this figure in particular who, as I argue, makes sense of Hester Prynne's characterization in "The Custom House," for Hester appears there as a fulcrum for a kind of female underground eager to exchange information about women's experiences. Returning to Boston and donning her "A," she effectively advertises herself as someone who knows what a "surer ground of mutual happiness" between men and women might look like. This is the Hester whom the "Custom House" narrator imagines as an "intruder and a nuisance," an impression that arises from the "record of her other doings" and which, as he says, is *"for the most part"* documented in *The Scarlet Letter* (my emphasis).[32]

CHAPTER FOUR

By the time of the novel's publication, the practice of abortion had expanded into a thriving business, generated by advertising and transforming into a lucrative area of medical specialization. As Janet Farrell Brodie explains in her preface to *Contraception and Abortion in 19th-Century America,* "What began in the 1830s as the focus of a small group of social and health reformers—Robert Dale Owen and Charles Knowlton especially—by the 1860s was the province of a diverse assortment of entrepreneurs and business people."[33] And, reflecting on the drop in the white birth rate of the time, Brodie demonstrates that the demand for abortion and contraception produced the supply, which in turn produced more demand. By virtue of this back-and-forth process, white marital fertility declined in the antebellum period and continued through the century. According to James Mohr in *Abortion in America,* "One indication that abortion rates probably jumped in the United States during the 1840s . . . was the increased visibility of the practice. It is not unreasonable to assume that abortion was more visible at least in part because it was become more frequent. And as it became more visible, more and more women would be reminded that it existed as a possible course of action to be considered." For Mohr, a "dramatic surge of abortion" took place after the 1830s, attributable to its commercialization and to the desire of women (primarily white, married Protestant women) to delay or prevent childbearing.[34] In light of this context, the story of Pearl's birth is interlineated not only with illegitimacy but also with contingency.

As the *National Police Gazette* indicates, attempts to put the practice of abortion outside of women's reach repeatedly failed, and its pervasive footing in the city simply became elusive. With the abortionists "still at work" despite the law, their influence and services proliferated as the kind of open secret to which Hawthorne was drawn. Women knew how to procure what they needed and how to read the abortionists' advertisements, even as those advertisements became increasingly oblique. Indistinct references to menstrual-cycle obstructions, for example, brilliantly evaded censure while delivering the necessary information for obtaining cures. Janet Farrell Brodie meticulously tracks, for instance, the extent to which an "obscure and transitory argot" carried the meanings of what was for sale, with words that played on the promise of "relief for women."[35] At the same time, those who opposed the practice introduced more strident terms, shifting any ambiguity surrounding pregnancy and abortion into definitional clarity. In 1844, the *Boston Medical and Surgical Journal* carried this announcement about abortionists: "The law has not reached them.... Their trade in infanticide is unquestionably considered, by these thrifty dealers in blood, a profitable undertaking."[36] Equating abortion and infanticide, the journal's editorialist here followed the lead of Theodric Beck, whose multiply reprinted *Elements of Medical Jurisprudence* placed abortion as a subsection of his chapter on infanticide and outlined the methods by which both crimes could be detected.

As conservative medical men thus moved birth into their purview and systems of classification, they worked to illuminate the world of women's primary methods of reproductive control, first-trimester abortifacients or surgical terminations, and to redefine the meaning pregnancy itself. That is, they worked to cast the early, ambiguous months of a pregnancy (in which a woman may or may not have been experiencing an obstructed menstrual period) in terms of the last months (in which a fetus clearly presented itself) and to define the entire sequence of gestation as life unfolding. Moving life's origins to conception meant closing what had earlier remained open to interpretation, namely the possibility that nothing as much as everything was happening deep within a woman's uterus. "Society first demanded the crime," Madame Restell announced in 1847. "And by what right does it interfere with the concerns of one who was never born, and therefore never was, and possibly, might never have been, a member of society?" From her point of view, she argued, preventing the suicide of an abandoned or disgraced woman put her on the side of life, of the living.[37]

According to Helen Lefkowitz Horowitz in *Rereading Sex,* practices associated with reproductive control were traditionally communicated through the "secret knowledge of women's vernacular culture," which included the "various means of preventing and terminating pregnancy." With early nineteenth-century migrations of large numbers of women away from traditional communities to urban centers such as New York and Boston, the transmission of this community knowledge was interrupted, creating "the grounds for the dissemination of printed information on abortion and the rise of female abortionists" who freely advertised their services in a public arena.[38] Whereas vernacular birth control practices—passed on like the dark tales to which Pearl refers when she overhears "the old dame in the chimney-corner"[39]—had been disapproved of in a religious context but tolerated under common law, the legibility of this knowledge in the print culture of mid-nineteenth century America provoked a reaction that would lead abortion to be declared, by the 1860s, "the great crime of the nineteenth century," as Edwin M. Hale dubbed it in the title of his third book on the subject.

What I want to establish is the fact that like Poe, Hawthorne was writing at a time when something fairly obscure was coming into light in new ways, accompanied moreover by the consolidation of male medical authority and jurisprudence. Physicians promoted themselves as trained observers who, as James Mohr demonstrates, shifted the status of the early-stage fetus from "potential for life" to life itself.[40] In early nineteenth-century America, abortion was neither rare nor considered morally or legally wrong, as long as the drugs and procedures were administered prior to the quickening, the sensation of fetal movement around the end of the fourth month of pregnancy. However, once these same remedies became more publicly legible in the booming print culture of the 1840s, an intensified discussion surrounding the meaning of fetal life quickly followed. For Mohr, the medical and legal surveillance of women's pregnancy went hand in hand with the professionalization of medicine over the same period, propelled by both existential and financial exigencies. Regular physicians, those with university training, did not want to compete with the "irregulars" dispensing vernacular remedies in the lucrative market surrounding women's reproductive health. The regulars promoted themselves as the protectors of women against quacks peddling poisonous compounds. They also allied themselves with legislators, legitimizing their work as a form of national advancement and calling attention to the declining white birth rate.[41]

In addition to the regulars, the most established phrenologists of the antebellum era, Lorenzo and Orson Fowler, positioned themselves in favor of strict antiabortion legislation. In their best-selling, multiply printed books on marriage, parenting, and human health, they promoted a theory of social reform derived at once from phrenological principles and patriarchal authority. Taking a strong stand against abortion, they published the works of likeminded writers, such as Hester Pendelton, whose book on parenting argued that abortion licensed adultery because it provided women with the means of erasing the evidence of their misbehavior. Addressing the subject in his popular 1846 polemic, *Maternity; or, the Bearing and Nursing of Children*, Orson Fowler communicated the extent to which he believed abortion prevailed in New England, and not just among poor, desperate women: "Many ... women, who stand in high public estimation, have perpetuated this heinous crime, in order to hide their shame. The practice of procuring abortion, or, to use a less offensive expression, inducing a miscarriage, has of late become so common that it requires to be placed before the public in all its naked atrocity. From the increasing number of unprincipled persons who publicly advertise this destructive practice, it is evident that it is extending to a fearful degree in this country."[42] Before 1821, no state in the country had a statutory law against abortion. By 1850, when such arguments had become common currency, seventeen states had criminalized abortion. In 1844, Massachusetts also clarified its position on concealed pregnancies, its legislative report containing the following directive: "Whatever woman conceals the death of any issue of her body, which, if born alive, would have been a bastard, so that it may not be known, whether such issue was born alive or not, or whether it was not murdered, shall be punished."[43] The laws and the medical or pseudomedical declarations shared the same ambition of producing clarity over concealment or uncertainty. They aimed not only to separate legal from illegal, alive from dead, true from false, but also to define borderline areas of activity and secrecy as threatening on a wide social scale.

Such definitional heavy-handedness is altogether thrown out by *The Scarlet Letter,* and the novel retains what David Greven calls a literary "empathy with women's experiences."[44] It does so by skirting the kind of nailed-down definitions demanded by law and medicine, extending ambiguity as concomitant with the creative freedom to choose: how something is read, what shadows to hide in, what ways forward and backward one might take. Hawthorne can then redefine Hester's adulterous sex with the Minister as having "a consecration of its own," shifting the experience into her frame of reference and away from the one that torments Dimmesdale to death. He similarly refutes life's ostensibly inherent value when he has Hester decide that it is "not worth accepting," not for women in the world as she sees it, nor "even to the happiest among them." This decree ushers in her conclusion that "society is to be torn down," as well as her conclusion that not being born at all is, in some cases, preferable to being born.[45]

Indeed, this subject of birth is the "dark question" she raises, first in relation to Pearl's birth, and then to her own. "As concerned her own individual existence," the narrator notes in an almost off-handed way, "she had long ago decided in the negative, and dismissed the point as settled." But the offhandedness carries the insinuation that existence per se is not necessarily sacrosanct, nor fundamentally preferable to nonexistence. "Better he died

CHAPTER FOUR

at once!" Hester exclaims when Chillingworth boasts that he has kept the tormented Minister alive with his herbs and potions.[46] Life, the living, to be truly alive and to experience a "real life"—each of these concepts arises in *The Scarlet Letter,* tapping into the existential questions generated by the abortion debates of Hawthorne's time.

In the early 1800s the theological position that life originated with conception resurfaced in popular medical tracts opposing abortion. Soul, life, and embryo entwined in discussions of human origins and human physiological development. Theodric Beck, for instance, asserted that "to extinguish the first spark of life" was a crime "both against our Maker and society, ... these regular and successive stages of existence being the ordinances of God."[47] In physician Thomas Radford's words, "The value to society of the embryo is as great as the foetus *in utero,* in every way, except as to degree of development."[48] On the other side of the debate, materialist explanations illuminated fetal development and human life apart from abstract values and theological concepts; they conceptualized living entities as material entities, composed of particles like the rest of the known universe, both animate and inanimate. While the pro-life side, to import a useful anachronism here, argued that abortion denied a child "the right of birth" (as the 1844 edition of the *Boston Medical and Surgical Journal* noted), the pro-choice side asked after more precise meanings of the word itself.[49]

For instance, the renowned reproductive rights proponent Charles Knowlton went right to the heart of the issue in his 1825 book on the material organization of the universe, stating, "I shall say that the word life, like the word soul, is a name without a thing."[50] In his *Fruits of Philosophy, or the Private Companion of Young Married People,* published in 1832, Knowlton maintained that the fetus possessed "no more rights than any one of [a woman's] extremities," and that pregnant women required society's sympathy and concern.[51] Holding apart the idea of a fetus from what he considered its actuality (a vegetable state transforming into a "low degree of animal life"), he insisted that "what it *is* while it is a fetus" must not be associated "with an idea of what it will be" (Knowlton's emphasis). Partway through his study, moreover, Knowlton visualized this scenario: "I leave the reader to imagine the misery of the unfortunate female, as alone she weeps, who knows that few months must develop that which will degrade her in the eyes of her community; I say nothing of her paramour, who may be a generous but warm-hearted young man."⁵² For Knowlton, pregnancy was a private matter. Terminating it did not "strike at the peace, the security, and existence of society," as Massachusetts attorney general James Austin claimed it did in 1838.⁵³

Perhaps Hawthorne formed Hester and Dimmesdale out of Knowlton's sketch above; their portrayals are rendered through equally compassionate outlines, and their tale of shame moved along the same path. The alternative route out of such a plotline is one Knowlton also describes: an easily attained abortion. Yet, even if Hawthorne never read Knowlton—though *Fruits* was a bestseller in its time—tracing *The Scarlet Letter* to the fervent antebellum conversation about pregnancy widens its sources, and places its feminist politics in a new light. Consider the following excerpt from A. M. Mauriceau's 1847 *Married Woman's Private Medical Companion:* "What epithet then belongs to him who makes it a trade to win a woman's gentle affections, [and] then abandons her? . . . Why is it that the man goes free and enters society again . . . while the woman is a mark for the finger of reproach, and a butt for the tongue of scandal? Because she bears about her the mark of what is called her disgrace. She becomes a mother; and society has something tangible against which to direct its anathemas."⁵⁴ These questions and statements (regarding abandonment, the "mark" that a woman bears, and the man who disappears back into society) follow one from the other into the tenable backstory of Hawthorne's novel, the private place to which Hawthorne relegates Hester's growing visibility before the novel opens in medias res and Hester steps out of prison and into the shame Mauriceau advises women to avoid.⁵⁵

Yet, we also know that Hester converts this shame when she returns to New England and by "her own free will . . . resumes the symbol." The symbol makes her visible to the Boston women who arrive at her doorstep to ask why "they were so wretched, and what the remedy?"⁵⁶ If we consider that abortionists covertly advertised their products as "remedies" that guaranteed "relief to all female complaints," in the words of one "Madame Grindle, Female Physician," then Hawthorne's oblique wording here may signal something concrete about the women's "continually recurring" troubles.⁵⁷ The stockpiled, alliterative adjectives (describing the women as everything from "wounded" to "wretched") carry suggestions of sexual experiences, of fallenness. Positioned at the edge of Boston, on "soil too sterile for cultivation" and a site concealed from view—or rather "denot[ing] that here was some object which would fain have been, or at least ought to be, concealed"—Hester gives counsel to women.[58] At least this is what Hawthorne's narrator, writing in 1850, lets slip about her return to Boston.

This is not to say that Hester is performing abortions in *The Scarlet Letter*. Rather, her representation stands in relation to that possibility and that threat, without the narrator having to entirely come out of the shadows. He lets his open-ended language run parallel with the medical advice and products that abounded in New England, the kind "designed for females only" or created for the "amelioration of female suffering."[59] In the temporal setting contemporary to him in "The Custom House," the stigmatization of abortionists and abortion resurfaces as a variation on the "persecuting spirit" of the progenitors whom he sees enveloping Hester's story. It does not go away; "the martyrdom of the witches" simply takes on a new form, attaching itself to the sexual independence of antebellum women.[60]

Following Gillian Brown's assertion that Hester introduces a radical break from ownership by men,[61] the mystery of her return to Boston with her scarlet letter may be read as a way of thwarting that authority from within. It is promising to see her not only in the same light as the returning soldier Hawthorne envisions in "The Custom House" (as one "who might be supposed to prize only the bloody laurel on his brow") or the ship captain with a sword cut ("which, by the arrangement of his hair, seemed anxious rather to display than hide") but also in relation to Madame Restell, the scapegoated abortionist of Hawthorn's time.[62] Hawthorne never spells out the word "adultery," compressing it instead into the letter A, nor does he specify what Hester counsels as a "voluntary nurse ... giv[ing] advice in all matters."[63] Instead, he describes her as advertising her hard-won and bloody knowledge to the women who can read her scarlet letter as such, as a code meant only for an initiated reader.

The scarlet letter's intended effect backfires in such a way that it not only reflects what abortionist Madame Restell meant to women but also what she said following her arrest in 1847—that the publicity surrounding her indictment saved her thousands of dollars in advertising. For the women who sought out her abortifacients and procedures, she was their deliverer, and she characterized herself as such: a woman's advocate who provided them with a crucial service that relieved them of the financial and physical burdens of unwanted pregnancies. In an editorial in the *Herald*, possibly written by her husband, the writer pointed out that many of the women who "applied to her for aid" could be directly connected to "men who pretend to be leaders in churches, leaders of fashion, and leaders of finance in Wall Street."[64] In fact, in an anonymously published biography of her in 1847, the otherwise unsympathetic writer conceded that "Restell is to be looked upon as an effect, rather than a cause" of the criminality in their society. This anonymous "Physician of New York" reminded his readers not to commit adultery and reported that Madame Restell recounted "the fears she had allayed, the agonies she had removed, and the sorrows and misfortunes concealed," adding that her house was warm and charming—nothing like "the den of horrors" he had expected it to be.[65]

Six years earlier, the editor of the *Polyanthos* proclaimed that "Madame Restell shows your spouse how she may commit as many adulteries as there are hours, without the possibility of detection" and thus drew on and entwined abortion and adultery in his readers' minds.[66] Between 1839 and 1845, she was indicted six times, and the publication of the detailed record of her 1845 arrest indicates the extent of the public interest in her story. Restell answered her critics through her biographer by ironically inquiring as to why men presumed that their wives and daughters, "once absolved from fear, [would] all become prostitutes." Demanding that the men involved in the pregnancies she terminated be brought forward, she added, "Let there be even-handed justice. There is none at all in making me the scapegoat for others' sins."[67] She never once consented to calling abortion a crime, arguing that she rescued women from the "immense and crushing engine of power" run by men.[68] But as a scapegoat, she became abortion's "representative anecdote" to such a degree that the word "restellism" was coined and circulated by national and international newspapers.[69]

With *The Scarlet Letter,* Hawthorne introduces us to a criminal who is not necessarily a criminal, a scapegoat or "representative anecdote" for the kind of action that, as Hawthorne implies, is not necessarily immoral. Hester's visibility, her scarlet letter, not only initiates her into an otherwise secret world but also one for which she comes to stand, in the name of its suppression. It draws her into mystic sisterhood," in which the "unsunned snow" of one woman seems to have a lot in common with Hester's "burning shame." Retaining the illusion of virginity by avoiding or terminating a pregnancy, someone can hide in plain sight. This is a possibility imagined for Hester when she is described contemplating Pearl's birth—"Had little Pearl never come to her from the spirit world, it might have been far otherwise"[70]—because in this subjunctive, alternate reality, it is not the Minister she imagines as having never come to her.

And it is this subjunctive space that serves to suspend Pearl within the otherworldly realm of her portrayal, as a figure who "hovers in the air and might vanish" and whose first "embryo smile" directs itself at the scarlet letter. She arrives as if filtered through, or in tandem with, the alternative plotline that an abortion might have yielded. Perhaps this is why Dimmesdale observes her playing in an "adjacent burial ground, . . . skipping irreverently from one grave to another." Adjacent, in proximity with tombs, Pearl's placement is powerfully symbolic as a glimpse or instance of Dimmesdale's wish fulfillment.[71] What Lauren Berlant calls *The Scarlet Letter*'s "counter-national symbolic . . . , its hermeneutic of negativity and defamiliarization" applies most powerfully to the characterization of Pearl.[72] For, through Pearl, Hawthorne aligns the strange unreality of America with the composition of the novel itself, binding the existence of all three A's to the existential questions raised by the reproductive rights debates of the early nineteenth century.

Each is detached from an unalterable fate; each retains the ghostly possibility of never having happened at all. "A better book than I shall ever write was there," his narrator remarks about his project. "Leaf after leaf presenting itself to me, just as it was written out by the reality of the flitting hour, and vanishing as fast as written." In this otherworldly process of materialization and erasure, where he writes "from beyond the grave [as a] decapitated surveyor," he locates the birth of the nation and the bearing of this abstraction by its living citizens. Berlant's argument in *The Anatomy of National Fantasy*—that Hawthorne represents his female characters as particularly uncanny in relation to the national narratives of destiny and birthright—makes particular sense in relation to Pearl's detachment from the institutions around her. It is a detachment so profound that she calls being human itself into question. "O Father in Heaven—if Thou are still my Father—what is this being which I have brought into the world," asks Hester, snatching Pearl "to her bosom . . . to assure herself that Pearl was flesh and blood and not utterly delusive."[73] Pearl's uncanniness strikes at the foundations of the patriarchy, with its stake in human definitions and in destiny. If she represents an "accident of birth" (Berlant's term for what national identity obscures),[74] she also gestures toward an alternative accident: birth's occlusion.

If Hawthorne's words about Pearl's history—that "it might have been far otherwise"—run a subjunctive thread through his novel, it is one cleverly initiated by the image of the infanticidal federal eagle in "The Custom House":

> With the customary infirmity of temper that characterizes this unhappy fowl, she appears by the fierceness of her beak and eye, and the general truculency of her attitude, to threaten mischief to the inoffensive community.... Nevertheless, vixenly as she looks, many people [presume] that her bosom has all the softness and snugness of an eiderdown pillow. But she has no great tenderness even in her best of moods, and, sooner or later—oftener soon than late—is apt to fling off her nestlings with a scratch of her claw, a dab of her beak, or a rankling wound from her barbed arrows.[75]

Recasting the federal eagle as an "unhappy fowl ... apt to fling off her nestlings," Hawthorne's narrator pushes us to see "mother" as a similarly overwritten term, as an embodiment forced into being by custom. He drives this idea further when, toward the end of "The Custom House," he formulates a distinction between a "real human being" and the "figurative self [in] public prints." This distinction resurfaces in the tale proper when Hester is first framed on the scaffold as an icon of "Divine Motherhood" and is then witnessed as simply a "fellow creature," emptied out of all human, maternal, and divine markers. She stands on the scaffold, defying the heads of state with the "rankling wound" of her silence and adultery. Her refusal to name Pearl's father—at the same time as she names the child Pearl—also effectively relegates fatherhood to a vast sandbank of potential meaninglessness: just the one grit that got inside, by chance, causing a formation of being. "I am mother's child, ... and my name is Pearl," this child impassively declares to the Governor on meeting him, exhibiting no deference toward patriarchal lineages or authority.[76]

The powerful inferences attendant on Pearl's naming open onto the long-standing existential argument about the nature of the embryo, in which centuries of scientists and philosophers battled over its origin in matter or spirit.[77] The right to terminate an embryo's development, to see the pearl as solely the oyster's artifact, implies in turn that no divine principle sets embryonic development into motion. No soul arrives with the paternal semen and no God secures the very foundations of human existence. Pearl's repeated declarations about her origins—that she is "mother's child" and has no "Heavenly Father"—articulate the threat that her name thus implies. They interconnect with the image of the broken chain links, the "fragments" of which represent Hester's rejection, atheistic in its overtones, of her world's hierarchical ordering: "She cast away the fragments of a broken chain.... She assumed a freedom of speculation, . . . which our forefathers, had they known of it, would have held to be a deadlier crime than that stigmatized by the scarlet letter." Emptied of a soul and severed from a chain that binds human to God, human existence falls into line with the rest of the world's creatures. As a result, the narrator's joke in "The Custom House" about the bipeds with whom he works (and the advantages they have over their "four-footed brethren"[78]) takes on new shades of meaning in a return from *The Scarlet Letter*'s focus on Pearl's origins; it is a seemingly throwaway remark that sends shock waves through the novel because it goes to the heart of the ontological theory carried by Pearl's seditious naming.

Obliquely, methodically, Hawthorne's narrator unfastens human life from a divine, paternal origin and future to consider what it means to look at somebody "merely as an animal" and "ultimately food for worms." It is a proposition that altogether departs from Dimmesdale's fear for his soul and the substance of his sermon "on the relationship between the Deity and the communities of mankind, with a special reference to New England." The impetus to thus "spiritualize" (a process Hawthorne's narrator references at least twice in the novel) permits abstractions such as "America" and "the fetus" to circulate with such vigor; imagined as expected realities or realizations of something intangible in the present, they are borne on and within bodies as idealizations, as arriving in the name of a future one cannot see. In *The Scarlet Letter,* Hawthorne entwines these abstractions, delving into the ways in which they exert such pressure on the "materiality of this daily life," which in itself looks different, depending on the light.[79]

Hawthorne's suspicion of those who demand absolute legibility regarding this material existence arises in his narrator's depiction of Chillingworth's rather gynecological scrutiny of Dimmesdale's interior: "So Roger Chillingworth— the man of skill, the kind and friendly physician—strove to go deep into his patient's bosom, delving among his principles, prying into his recollections, and probing every thing with a cautious touch, like a treasure-seeker in a dark cavern. Few secrets can escape an investigator, who has opportunity and license to undertake such a quest, and skill to follow it up. A man burdened with a secret should especially avoid the intimacy of his physician." Beyond its unrelenting focus on probing and penetrating, this passage intensifies in its disquiet if we take Dimmesdale's feminization here farther, into a wider representational gesture. Namely, if we see this passage as cautionary not only to "a man burdened with a secret" but also to a woman, typically the sex "burdened" with deep, corporeal secrets, then the secret's concealment takes shape as a possible abortion, not to be revealed to the prying "man of skill." Hawthorne flips the sexes in order to confide and to hide the secret of his outlook. A little later on, he switches the "dark cavern" metaphor for a grave, rewording his disgust for Chillingworth's violent persistence and skillfully alluding to Pearl in the reference to a jewel. He notes that Chillingworth works "like a miner searching for gold; or rather like a sexton delving into a grave, possibly in quest of a jewel that had been buried on the dead man's bosom."[80] Here, Pearl is dead (or nowhere) within Dimmesdale, even if alive with Hester. Dimmesdale's unacknowledged, unwanted paternity carries within it, subtly but forcefully, the representation of an unacknowledged, undone maternity.

Dimmesdale's experience of the guilt, moreover, occurs in relation to his thorough investment in "the New England which they were planting in the wilderness" and thus under the pressure of the "A" for America. Caught up in the narrative of Providence, Dimmesdale cannot imagine breaking out of it. To pick up and leave, as Hester urges him in their second forest encounter, is to uproot the metaphoric seed that exists within the framework of this planting. For Dimmesdale, it entails a kind of tearing-out of something before it takes root, and he cannot see that possibility through, especially given his role in the settlement's founding. "I am irrevocably doomed," he thinks, just before Hester announces, "Thou wilt go!" and throws off her scarlet letter. He delays their boarding until after the Election Sermon out of a fear for his reputation, wishing to leave behind an image of himself before "terminating his professional career."[81] *Terminating:* an interesting word choice for Dimmesdale's fretful sense of self-replication in name.

Through Hester, Hawthorne renders the opposite of Dimmesdale's experience, for her sexual secrets are put on display, forced by the scarlet letter into the "broad daylight, and in the presence of . . . a multitude." The reader first sees her clasping Pearl to her breast "not so much by an impulse of motherly affection, as that she might thereby conceal a certain token, which was wrought or fastened into her dress." Her smile indeed acknowledging the irony of the action, she shifts the baby to her arm when she realizes that Pearl is her uncovering. Yet, despite her impulse to conceal the scarlet letter, her smile is "haughty" and her badge "so artistically done," each perhaps signifying the exquisite irony of being condemned for a bastard birth that she knows might have never been—the greater crime of concealment: "She hath good skill at her needle, that's certain," remarked one of the female spectators; "but did ever a woman, before this brazen hussy, contrive such a way of showing it! Why, gossips, what is it but to laugh in the faces of our godly magistrates, and make a pride out of what they, worthy gentlemen, meant for a punishment?" Carefully shaped—each stitch "felt in her heart"—the scarlet letter doubles Pearl's birth as a form of artistry rather than inevitability. Its intricate and "fertile" ornamentation emphasizes display over and above the lure of concealment.[82] Indeed, taking his time and building his descriptions of the letter from different angles in "The Custom House," the narrator raises the possibility that Hester brandishes her choice with it, not just her punishment.

The narrator's primary impression that he might understand the letter's composition only by "the process of picking out the threads" further serves to underscore the ways in which its undoing makes sense of its intricate existence. Which is to say, that what is done, might be undone, might be understood back through its threading to its nothingness and potential to not-be too. "See!" Hester announces to Dimmesdale as she plans their departure from Boston, unfastens the letter's clasp, and tosses the "A" aside. "With this symbol, I undo it all, and make it as it had never been!"[83] Through this lens, Pearl's refusal to cross the creek back to Hester (until she refastens the scarlet letter) moves past the realism of Pearl's childlike fear or recalcitrance and into the otherworldly setting of Pearl's nonexistence; she remains on the other side of the symbolic division, potentially forever, until Hester bears the letter again. This scene additionally replicates the first and unwritten forest scene, the site of Pearl's conceiving, or rather layers on top of it, bringing the words "I . . . make it as it had never been" along with it, as a phrase Hester is capable of uttering.

This is a novel that binds birthing and artistry together with the choice of bearing something (a punishment, an undertaking, an obligation, a child) or not. This latter theme is so subtly drawn as to be barely visible, but it functions incrementally to undermine the doom that appears to preside over the novel's events. Nothing that happens in the novel is fated, even if Hawthorne's narrator is often attracted to the concept of Providence, "betokening" as it does "a celestial guardianship of peculiar intimacy and strictness." Repeatedly, the narrator imagines "the hand of Providence" at work in his characters' affairs, only to retract the notion as an illusion, shaped by an "after-thought." These contrary impulses compete with one another to serve as the frame through which the birth of the nation comes undone too, "from its settlement down to Revolutionary times." Likewise, the narrator presents Hester's story in terms of the seemingly inescapable unfolding of a pregnancy that exposes her to condemnation in "the too vivid light of day." But Hester has a choice in assuming the badge of public shame: revealing the father's name can be exchanged for the scarlet letter. "Speak out the name!" the Governor implores. "That, and thy repentance, may avail to take the scarlet letter off thy breast." Her decision to withhold Dimmesdale's name ("Never!") at once sets the plot into motion and demands an act of will from her partner in crime. And, though the narrator marvels at the "inward and inevitable necessity" compelling Dimmesdale to join Hester on the scaffold, Dimmesdale resists its pull, choosing against necessity to likewise remain silent.[84]

These initial scenes of choice are retrospectively highlighted when Hester later reflects on her agreement to hide Chillingworth's identity: "She had made her choice, and had chosen, as it now appeared, the more wretched alternative." Here, the vocabulary of decision (choice, chosen, alternative) accumulates in a way that not only reframes her confrontation with Chillingworth but also throws light on a wide range of seemingly foreclosed options in the novel. Each event imagined for *The Scarlet Letter* transpires in relation to a declined alternative, one that consistently remains in play as a kind of spirit double of the actual plot: Hester could sign Mistress Hibbins's black book; Dimmesdale could acknowledge Pearl as his daughter; Chillingworth "could reveal a goodly secret" and end his vengeance; and Dimmesdale could escape across the sea, "if thou so choose," as Hester urges in their forest encounter.[85] "The possibility of radical new beginnings is a preoccupation of *The Scarlet Letter*," Brook Thomas affirms,[86] and the paths reserved for its characters tend to split before them into crossroads. Their choices increasingly become substantial elements of the novel's direction, and Providence becomes an excuse for "egotism, [extended] over the whole expanse of nature."[87] So, although Chillingworth may assert his position that "it has all been a dark necessity" and "let the black flower blossom as it may!"—and Dimmesdale may hold fast to "his mission to foretell a high and glorious destiny" for New England—their beliefs simply obfuscate the fact that they choose to follow one course of action over another.[88]

"The novel opens twice," Berlant reminds us, as Hawthorne disrupts the sense of his work's unfolding.[89] One could say that this process also pushes us to observe a boundary line, where the discovery of the "rag of scarlet cloth" in "The Custom House" remains separate from the measured composition of *The Scarlet Letter;* the conceiving (of the tale) is held apart from its material configuration and delivery (as the novel).[90] And, just as Hawthorne's narrator aligns his production with Hester's own—the two scarlet letters thus "endowed with life"—he also backs off, claiming not to author the tale but to edit it. His labor is a carving into with a "steel pen," not a bodying forth, and with no way of knowing what pregnancy is like, he cuts to Pearl, already born.[91]

It seems imperative to see the politics of motherhood in *The Scarlet Letter* in relation to the formation of the American Medical Association, which took place three years before the novel's publication and which pursued, as I note above, strict licensing rules for regular practitioners, especially those associated with midwifery. Seven years later, the association felt compelled to publish this statement in their 1859 *Transactions:* "We are the physical guardians of women. We alone [. . .] of their offspring *in utero,*" revealing the extent of the opposition to this assertion in the very need to issue it so dramatically.[92] As the science of midwifery continued to develop through the study and documentation of dangerous pregnancies and difficult births, it circulated in countless medical publications the very material conditions and contingencies of fetal life. This phenomenon, on the one hand, contributed to the medical control of pregnancy and its classification as a potential pathology; on the other hand, it sustained focus on the dangers experienced by pregnant women alone—"the adult women, whom a thousand social ties engage us to save," as the authors of the 1845 *Elementary Treatise on Midwifery* insist.[93] The midwifery books of Hawthorne's time are filled with case studies of miscarriages and what was called preternatural labor: dystocia caused by partial cervical dilation; heads locked within the birth canal; cephalotomies or fetal decapitations resorted to for saving dying mothers; cesareans described as far too dangerous.

In *The Scarlet Letter,* this history of birth does not come into view through Pearl, but it does through Roger Chillingworth, for his deformed shoulder is described as "misshapen from my birth hour." It is the mark of a harrowing birth, a record of what may be interpreted as shoulder dystocia, and it becomes another of the novel's scarlet letters. Namely, it encodes the possibility of nonexistence, of dying before being born, right onto his body. We might see his misshapen shoulder in terms of a corporeal history—a clavicle shattered for passage through the vagina—then therefor in line with the representation of life's contingency in the novel. Neither the characters nor the "infant commonwealth" is under a "celestial guardianship."[94] It is all just movement, sometimes violent, sometimes illegitimate, across borders and into states of being.

A threateningly nonreproductive ideology enters the text through the abortion debates and the medicalization of pregnancy that took place during Hawthorne's own time. For Arthur Riss, the antebellum slavery controversy about Black humanity informs Hawthorne's exploration of what constitutes a person with rights, adding that "the current arguments over abortion" make sense of that nineteenth-century struggle over personhood as something historically defined.[95] But, if we consider the fact that arguments about fetal personhood circulated in Hawthorne's time too, contributing to legal exchanges as powerful then as they are now, then Hawthorne's complex representation of human contingency takes it force from both the abortion and the slavery debates. It animates Hawthorne's portrait of Pearl as an American accident, her gestation and existence being entwined with her mother's impulsive artistry. Together, the two (nation and child) come into being as strange compositions, entwined with the haunting possibility of never having happened at all but disentangled from either a biological or a heavenly father's control. Whatever forces produce a claim to the land, or a settler's birthright within it, no ultimate meaning accompanies them, beyond the "conception of an oyster-like tenacity [that] clings to the spot where his successive generations have been imbedded."[96] Through his protagonist, Hawthorne explores the reproductive politics surrounding and moving through these generations, including what implicit violence might accompany particular gestational and national theories of embedding in the land. He also gives Hester a name that is one syllable away from oyster.

As Gillian Brown puts it, Hawthorne develops "an account of American nationalism in which national identification continually operates in tandem with resistances to it."[97] He configures Pearl's scandalous beginnings alongside America's, in order to intimate that both are cloaked in illegitimacy and concealed deeds, that both materialize not in relation to a destined plot but rather to labor and within relentless colonial imperatives: the "Indian ... driven with stripes into the shadow of the forest" to make room for "wives and maidens of Old English birth and breeding"; the ships that arrive from "Africa or South America" with unnamed "merchandise, ... readily turned into gold" that berth, surreptitiously, near the Custom House at the entryway to *The Scarlet Letter*.[98] The types that come into focus, of the Indian, the Anglo-American, and the African, underscore the splitting of the "citizen as abstraction" from the "citizen as embodied," to again borrow Laurent Berlant's terminology, a division that Hawthorne repeatedly pulls into view throughout *The Scarlet Letter*.[99] He does so most powerfully by creating a perfect specimen of white womanhood—fertile, beautiful—whose crime of adultery specifically threatens such categorical boundaries with wayward lines of descent.

Hester may bring forth a flawless pearl, "worthy to be ... the plaything of the angels," but she can never guarantee its whiteness against the concealment of the father's name.[100] Like the contraband cargo that slips "directly beneath [the custom officers'] unsuspicious noses" in the docking ships described by "The Custom House," Pearl enters "our beloved country," at once sustaining the implicit pun on "berth" and "birth," and calling attention to the production of meaning at transgressed borders, both corporeal and national.[101] As Laura Doyle argues, the drama surrounding Pearl is a "drama of settlement," understood as the "violence of colonization" originating at the Atlantic ports and continuing westward throughout the 1840s. In a provocative analysis of the novel's representation of colonization, especially as it transpires in its characters' fraught and sexually charged interactions, Doyle further contends, *"The Scarlet Letter* may after all be most fundamentally concerned with the crisis that colonization provokes in Anglo-Atlantic heterosexuality."[102] The insinuation that the ships in "The Custom House" are illegally involved in the transatlantic slave trade bears out or foreshadows this possibility. As Hawthorne's narrator recounts, "Whenever such a mischance occurred, nothing could exceed the vigilance and alacrity with which they proceeded to lock, and double-lock, and secure with tape and sealing-wax, all the avenues of the delinquent vessel."[103] With characteristic innuendo, he thus provides a powerful glimpse of Hester's story, as the sealed-up "delinquent vessel" prefigures what her public branding means to the safeguarding of white America's genealogical passageways and its pretenses to lawfulness.

In 1844, Massachusetts clarified its position on concealed pregnancies, six years before the publication of *The Scarlet Letter,* by this statement in its legislative report: "Whatever woman conceals the death of any issue of her body, which, if born alive, would have been a bastard, so that it may not be known, whether such issue was born alive or not, or whether it was not murdered, shall be punished."[104] In 1845, the Massachusetts Registrar of Births instructed that a "record of stillborn" be kept, as well as a record of "'colored,' if not white."[105] The possibility of concealing a pregnancy, especially as it allowed for its privately administered termination or undocumented stillbirths, enhanced the perceived and combined threats of infidelity and abortion. Even progressive physician Wooster Beach, in his 1848 midwifery guide, argued that "the married, as well as the single, may be the authors of this crime [of abortion], to conceal their guilt or infidelity from an absent husband."[106] While Hawthorne's tale about exactly this kind of infidelity takes its protagonist in the opposite direction, into Pearl's birth, it nonetheless places her in relation to the secrets of women, consistently alluding to Hester's concealed thoughts about the paths before and behind her. The colonial setting, moreover, allows Hawthorne to at once introduce the terms of the nineteenth-century abortion debate and cover his tracks.

Hawthorne closes *The Scarlet Letter* with his narrator standing in a graveyard, gazing on the slate tombstone shared by Dimmesdale and Hester, and musing that its inscription "might serve for a motto and brief description of our now concluded legend; so somber it is, and relieved only by one ever-glowing point of light gloomier than the shadow:—'*On a field, sable, the letter A, gules*'" (Hawthorne's italics).[107] The connotations carried by the substitution of a black slate for a white pearl, combined with the assembly of the words "shadow," "field," "sable," and "letter," supply the outlines for something familiar, another kind of birth. A figure begins to take shape, in a semiogenesis that hovers between the reader's mind and the grave's words, fleshed out by way of the second definition of "gules"—as the throat (gullet) of a roaring, heraldic lion—and recognizable in "sable" as the term characterizing an entire race.[108] Given that "sable letter" is another way of saying "black character," then what we ponder shifts to whom, the general to the specific, and a woman rises from Hester's tombstone. Her red throat opened into a screaming stilled into silence by the nature of inscription, she stands in a field, bleeding perhaps. Her story is Hester's and yet excised from it, recapitulating the novel's disquiet about the accidental nature of existence (on what side of the Custom House's sanction) and the unmarked graves overlaid by the name America.[109]

CHAPTER FIVE

Alleged Necromancies within a System
The House of the Seven Gables

> Be careful not to drink at Maule's Well!... Because, like an old lady's cup of tea, it is water bewitched!
> —Nathaniel Hawthorne, *The House of the Seven Gables*, 1851

> The deficiency of breeding women was very striking, and the perpetuation of abortion common.
> —*The Anti-Slavery Reporter*, 1833

With *The House of the Seven Gables,* Hawthorne exhumes another variation on Hester Prynne, this time as Hepzibah Pyncheon, deliberately childless, and contemporary with his narrator, whose disgust for American nationalism ascends more forcefully to the surface of his tale than it does in *The Scarlet Letter*. Between the strangely disembodied voice of his new narrator and the demonstrably embodied Hepzibah (brilliantly decaying, barren and defiant), Hawthorne also sets up the figure of Uncle Sam, the personification of white national belonging. ("I am at home here, Phoebe," says Jaffrey Pyncheon, one of Uncle Sam's avatars, "and you are the stranger. I will just step in.") Splintering and refracting this personification into the story's different uncles, Hawthorne explores its power, avuncular benignity masking its aggressive reach. He places Hepzibah in relation to it, not only as a descendant of Anglo-American imperialism, itself personified as the first Pyncheon, but also as a configuration of its obstruction. "She made a repelling gesture with her hand, and stood, a perfect picture of Prohibition, at full length, in the dark frame of the doorway": there she resides, inside the definition of "to prohibit," as a barring of something from happening, forbidding its presence or progression.[1] She spends the novel thwarting Jaffrey's attempts to move her out of his way.

In *The Scarlet Letter* we are told that Hawthorne's narrator works in "Uncle Sam's brick edifice . . . as chief executive officer of the Custom

House," as if its shady commerce is just a day's work in the family business, at Uncle Sam's.[2] In *The House of the Seven Gables,* Hawthorne takes up the device more purposefully, converting America into Uncle Sam, Uncle Sam into Uncle Jaffrey, and Uncle Jaffrey into a carcass, the rotting scent of which attracts a housefly across the borders of the house meant to immortalize his name.[3] The process is one of a contraction inward, from patriotic idealism to embodied license, and from the violent, carnivorous expansionism glorified as Manifest Destiny to its personification in rigor mortis and decomposition.

Conceived in 1845 by John O'Sullivan (known by both Poe and Hawthorne), the phrase "Manifest Destiny" shifted into the rhetorical place of Providence as the cover under which Anglo-American colonial violence passed. It also involved a reproductive imperative—to "overspread the continent [with] our yearly multiplying millions"—the white fertility, which, as Hawthorne's novel shows, always comprises the other side of white supremacy's coin.[4] Without ever penning the phrase itself, Hawthorne establishes Manifest Destiny at the center of the romance in *The House of the Seven Gables.* It comprises the "castles in the air" available for his readers' daydreams if we do not wish to confront the plantations extending across the earth.[5] Narrating through a figure detached from what the Pyncheons represent, he portrays Manifest Destiny as the making-fanciful of one's submission to a predatory Uncle who stakes his political life on slavery's expansion into seized territories and by means of enslaved women.[6]

This figure, the above-mentioned Jaffrey, hobnobs with "Insurance Office [and] Bank Directors" (Hawthorne's capitalizations) and eats well. The world is his oyster, there for the shucking and backed by the banks. But what truly drives him is his son, the investment in his perpetuity. For the very conception of the nation requires its immortalization, in a linear temporality that outlasts its citizens' present lives, retaining its ostensible origins in service of its replication. We are introduced to Jaffrey through Phoebe in order for him to be established as an Uncle and as the force of Uncle Sam's pedigree: "The fantasy would not quit her, that the original Puritan, of whom she had heard so many somber traditions—the progenitor of the whole race of New England Pyncheons, the founder of the House of the Seven Gables, and who had died so strangely in it—had now stepped into the shop."[7] The "progenitor of the whole race" works through Jaffrey Pyncheon as ideology, pushing him against Hepzibah and Phoebe, the symbolic obstacles to or conduits of its continuation. The allegorical battle between them involves Uncle Sam's immortality, on the one side, and its contravention on the other.

Because she stands apart as nonreproductive and clear-sighted in her otherwise failing vision, Hepzibah can see the force of the story for what it is: how its promises amass individuals and turn them into objects of its volition and components of its whiteness; how it crashes onward, like an avalanche, indifferent to the lives of those in its path. She tells Jaffrey, "You are but doing over again, in another shape, what your ancestor before you did, and sending down to your posterity the curse inherited from him!" Allied with Hepzibah, and in the briefest of asides, Hawthorne kills off this son, showing his father's objectives and devastations to have been all along a waste of time, pulling others under the weight of his inheritance. In other words, Jaffrey's plotline involves a son on the brink of arriving to assume his birthright, and Hawthorne cuts him from it, as if with a scalpel. "How comes his shadow hither?" the narrator asks of the son's ghost toward the end of the novel. "If dead, what a misfortune! The old Pyncheon property, together with the great estate, acquired by this young man's father, would devolve onto whom?" The tone is fabulously sarcastic, the misfortune already established in the preface as the inheritance itself, in the maiming power of "an avalanche of ill-gotten gold" brought down on the "heads of an unfortunate posterity."[8] The metaphoric and freshly fallen snow blanketing America with the whiteness of a power structure has amassed by the time of *The House of the Seven Gables*.

From the start, Hawthorne's narrator takes ironic shots at the glorious and "populous fertility" of the founding father's plans and rapidly uncovers what the metaphors of whiteness and descent hide, at least in part or without directly using the words "rape" and "breeding": "conjugal relations" that send wives to their graves, one after another; women "worn to death ... by at least nine children"; wives "worn out ... by the remorseless weight and hardness" of the Pyncheon "character". For the youthful Holgrave, everything about the story carries an "indefinite sense of some catastrophe, or consummation," as if the two terms were interchangeable. Each instance functions to indicate the realities that take place behind the scenes, in childbirths that yearly multiply into abstractions of racial pedigree and bank deposits. When Hepzibah exclaims to Jaffrey, "You have forgotten that a woman was your mother!," she illuminates what gets swept into and then buried in the national accounting and patriotism.[9] She also outlives Jaffrey to witness his death in her house, the space originally cleared for Pyncheon posterity, wombs becoming tombs again.

In *The Queen of America Goes to Washington City*, Lauren Berlant revisits the American political myth, explaining this time that "the nation's value is figured not on behalf of an actually existing and laboring adult, but of a future American, both incipient and pre-historical: especially invested with this hope are the American fetus and the American child." (These are Hawthorne's points making their way, I think, from the unconscious of Berlant's earlier work on his fiction and into this book.) "The abstract principles of democratic nationality," Berlant asserts, "have always been hypocritical. From the beginning, entire populations of persons were excluded from the national promise which, because it was a promise, was held out paradoxically: falsely, as a democratic reality, and legitimately, as a promise."[10] This paradoxical configuration is at work in Hawthorne's representation of Hepzibah, whose nonprocreative characterization is uncharacteristically unambiguous and whose confinement in the house runs parallel with her brother's in prison, in an obstetrical argot. She has nothing to do with promises, apart from setting right the wrong done to Clifford.

Standing by her store's rusty scales, she resembles Justice, crumbling but present. Hawthorne's narrator is quick to point out that the "love of children had never been quickened in her heart." "What had she to do with ancestry?," he asks: "Nothing;—no more than with posterity!"[11] From this position, a different story plays out, not the same one over again. Abortion, to clarify, structures the narrative through which Hawthorne conceives Hepzibah. He invokes the possibility of reading her as a barren spinster, but he flips the script. He asks us to pay closer attention to the characterization of this "Woman!" (as Jaffrey calls her when she infuriates him) and rewrites the meaning of barrenness into inventiveness. Hepzibah's story is not one of rejection by men but of choosing to follow a heart disinterested in quickening and empty of conventional attachments, where "Nothing" exists to distract her.

Hepzibah opens a store only to keep starvation at bay. Repeatedly giving away its goods, she is not necessarily moved into capitalism's place, even if implicated in the appetites it circulates. This is a complex issue, involving the possibility that there is no unadulterated outside to the inside in which Hepzibah resides, but what I want to focus on is her role in the novel's thematic investment in divestment, a commercial and legal term to which Hawthorne's narrator twice directly refers: first, in the preface's assertion "that the wrong-doing of one generation lives into successive ones, and, divesting itself of every temporary advantage, becomes a pure and uncontrollable mischief," and second, in relation to his protagonist's actively nonregenerative way of being in the world. "She had spent her life in divesting herself of friends; she had wilfully cast off the support which God has ordained his creatures," he explains of her solitude. The phrase he adds after the semicolon to emphasize Hepzibah's purposeful existence skilfully pairs divesting with the contravening of a divine ordinance. It follows, then, that her refusal to accumulate and her refusal to reproduce come together to underscore her failed attempts to attend church. Before he even names Hepzibah, he establishes her as one of the "dying out" and emphasizes her existence as a conscious decision: "understood to be wretchedly poor, [she] seemed to make it her choice to remain so." It is her way of stopping that "avalanche of ill-gotten gold, or real estate."[12]

Or real estate: in the seeming afterthought of a conjunction, Hawthorne loads the statement, this time signposting the Black lives that constitute the whiteness and wealth conferred by the avalanche, because it was as both real estate and chattel that enslaved Africans were named in the founding documents of the country, the deeds on which the allegorical house rests and then conceals within its structure. For example, Virginia's 1705 charter reads, "That from and after the passing of this act, all negro, mulatto, and Indian slaves, in all courts of judicature, and other places, within this dominion, shall be held, taken, and adjudged, to be real estate (and not chattels;) and shall descend unto the heirs and widows of persons departing this life, according to the manner and custom of land of inheritance, held in fee simple."[13] In this novel about an allegorical house's violent origins and its decay—ostensibly with no bearing on the narrator's contemporary reality—its outbuildings carry the import of its real estate: as enclosures connected with its endowment, as the places where enslaved people lived and died. Here, behind the house and behind the scenes, the transformation of the living into the estate likewise takes place, in the same way as "pencil sketches [pass] behind the original's back." The architectural details of the House of the Seven Gables (the peculiar gables, for instance, or its glittering stones) appear as such in a magician's trick designed to make only one kind of real estate visible to our minds.[14]

Alleged Necromancies within a System

When the smoke clears, the extensive plot of the house ("fringed [by] other enclosures") comes into view as a former plantation. Just as its posts are hammered into the ground to circumscribe it in the opening scenes of the novel, so too are the particularities of its financial and legal expansion, each of which arise in puns involving penetration: the cellar dug, the deep foundations laid, the political connections "consummated." The narrator is sure to point out that Pyncheon ensures the legality of his seizing and penetrating. And though he may vaguely note that this legality fixes "his race and future generations [on] a stable basis," in a statement hazy about the financial details, the words "future" and "stable" fall into place to infer an expected or predictable reproducibility—a banking on a point of origin and its extension in time.[15] The law makes it so, translating the offspring of both freeborn and enslaved women into slavery's future, who are racially conceived in advance of any other category of naming.

Such forms of imprecision are necessary for the sake of brevity, or so we are told. Significant portions of the house's two hundred years of "mortal life" require cutting, otherwise "it would fill a bigger folio volume, or a longer series of duodecimos, than could prudently be appropriate to the annals of all New England." As a result, something unspeakable surrounds the whole story, imprudent, and causing its teller to remain reticent. He never tells us what makes the first Pyncheons so rich, never specifies what their financial security involves. Their founding concerns a "golden fertility of human culture," and we are tasked with questioning what it denotes and why New England's history requires extensive editing.[16] To quote Saidiya Hartman,

> Gestational language has been key to describing the world-making and world-breaking capacities of racial slavery. What it created and what it destroyed has been explicated by way of gendered figures of conception, birth, parturition, and severed or negated maternity. To be a slave is to be "excluded from the prerogatives of birth." The mother's only claim—to transfer her dispossession to the child. The material relations of sexuality and reproduction defined black women's historical experiences as laborers and shaped the character of their refusal of and resistance to slavery. The theft, regulation and destruction of black women's sexual and reproductive capacities would also define the afterlife of slavery.[17]

CHAPTER FIVE

The fiscal stability associated with Hawthorne's Pyncheons thus appears to involve another invocation of *partus sequitur ventrem* and the "golden fertility" it secured. It is crucial to see Hawthorne's childless, female protagonist configured on the outside of this system, keenly aware that some women are "kept white and delicate"—or look that way—because others are kept Black and enslaved.[18] The "No, in thunder" that Melville hears booming across *The House of the Seven Gables* surfaces from within all the divestments associated with Hepzibah, particularly in the refusal to be oriented toward procreation.[19]

In *Birthing a Slave,* Marie Jenkins Schwartz demonstrates that "breeding women," a familiar term in antebellum commercial activity, were sold for as much as fifteen hundred dollars because their future children meant that the enslavers' own children would be financially secure. When the international slave trade ended in 1808, the "'problem' of slavery's perpetuation" resolved itself in violent acts of procreation, shrouded in the phraseology of natural increase.[20] Discussing the rape at the foundations of American wealth and banking, North and South, Ned and Constance Sublette include an excerpt from William Wells Brown's 1847 address to the Female Anti-Slavery Society of Salem: "*Were I about to tell you the evils of Slavery . . . I should wish to take you, one at a time, and whisper it to you. Slavery has never been represented. Slavery can never be represented*" (their italics).[21] The hushed tone seems to make a scandalmonger out of the speaker, but the issue of representation strikes a powerful note. How does one depict the countless acts of sexual violation survived by individual women and girls as they disappear into the archives of banking, property, interest, and credit?[22] At the same time, it is also "unsurprising," to quote the Sublettes, "that a planter who denied the humanity of the people he held captive would have thought of his laborers as breeding stock. . . . Slaves, whose legal status was comparable to that of livestock, were expected to provide a farm owner with marketable children." Sexual violence underwrote slavery; it belonged to the "portfolio of privileges" of those running the system.[23]

As Hawthorne's narrator weaves his words from the official documents to which he has access, he makes room for what is whispered or said "under [one's] breath" about Jaffrey Pyncheon, who is primed for government and yet nothing if not a rapist. "Brutish . . . ruffianly in his propensities," he is predatory and insatiable. In the allegorical struggle between him and Hepzibah, his role is to get past her to the hole in her house, where "the secret of incalculable wealth" hides on a legal deed. The threshold, it seems, must be penetrated before the secret is revealed, which lies beyond a simple claim to riches to imply something more: a kind of nascent power, awaiting animation. To be more precise, the hidden parchment does not function as a receipt, dispatching a cache of wealth; it carries the potential for wealth's limitlessness, incalculable as such. Its secret is procreative, not finite. It secures enslavement along the mother's line as a rape- and race-based system. Clifford Pyncheon's proposition that a "crimson curtain, broad enough to hang in folds," be placed over the portrait in front of the hole brings all of the anatomical inferences into focus.[24]

The parchment's nomenclature as a "concealed deed" establishes it as an object and an action, something tangible in the present and something shameful about the past. At the same time, given the legal denotation of "concealment" as a covered-up abortion or pregnancy, the parchment also conveys a history of noncompliance and rebellion along with that of rape and forced reproduction. Like the water of Maule's Well, which is "productive of intestinal mischief," according to the "old women of the neighborhood," the concealed deed bends the Pyncheon history into its own undoing.[25] Even if it comes down the centuries with the house and in relation to what its "father had wrested from the wild of hand of Nature," it also retreats from patriarchal reach and into concealment. A bloody curse surrounding it, the parchment molders before it delivers on its promises, resembling the brackish well water that comes with a warning as do certain cups of tea. Abortive, it resides inside a space associated with penetration to symbolize a secret from another angle, subtractive of wealth, productive of decay and mischief. Folded and vellum, the parchment doubles into itself as skin and words incapable of animation.

It seems that Hawthorne knew what most plantation owners suspected by the mid-nineteenth century about the practices of enslaved women. For, not only did they have access to the details of "highly esteemed pharmacopoeia" for reproductive control, garnered from both African and Native American traditions, but Black women also obtained the prepared pills, teas, and powders that were marketed across the United States to white women.[26] Liese Perrin argues that the practice of birth control among enslaved people took place as "both a form of resistance [and] as a form of strike." It closed down a lucrative facet of the labor expected of them and in solidarity with one another. That the strike involved the very crop for which their lives

CHAPTER FIVE

were extorted to cultivate is particularly inspired: "Their understanding of the properties of cotton root was especially useful. In parts of Africa, wild cotton plants did grow, but the main source of cotton was from cotton trees, which were much bigger than the cotton plants in America. Despite this slight difference in appearance, when slave women found themselves knee-in the cotton fields of the American South, it was not difficult for them to recognize the plant and continue using cotton roots as a natural form of birth-control." They also ingeniously made abortifacients out of indigo, the material of ink and therefore of writing itself. Oral testimonies gathered from once-enslaved Africans and their descendants confirm the practice of abortion throughout the nineteenth century; written calculations in slave ledgers of births, nursing periods, and the times between births corroborate the evidence of it. Again in Lisa Perrin's words, "The WPA [Works Progress Administration] narratives contain several interviews which give details of various substances which were used as contraceptives and abortifacients. Lu Lee, an ex-slave and midwife, from Texas, described how pregnant women 'unfixed' themselves by taking calomel and turpentine, and explained that, when the turpentine manufacturers became aware of this practice, they changed the recipe, thus rendering turpentine useless as an abortifacient. Lu Lee revealed that indigo, another plant which was frequently grown on plantations, was also used to cause miscarriages."[27] According to Angela Davis, this history was never really a secret. "Black women have been aborting themselves since the days of slavery," Davis maintains in "Race, Birth Control, and Reproductive Rights," and the high numbers of miscarriages tell a story about oppression. Self-determination is part of the picture. The other part involves desperation.[28]

By midcentury, physicians had enough data on both free and enslaved women's menstrual cycles and pregnancies that they could trace trends in infertility and intervene in them. Plantation physicians worked hard to interpose themselves between midwives and the women who trusted them, setting up small hospitals or practices, for example, and requiring women give birth there. The rise of American gynecology and obstetrics as powerful fields of medical specialization took place as an early nineteenth-century phenomenon. It correlated with new perceptions of population statistics and national advancement. And while this is not to say that direct correspondences among slavery, abortion, and clinical medicine accounts for all of the facets of this development, it is to contend that a lucrative and extensive market in forced reproduction fills out the biopolitical picture of American medical specialization. For example, both South Carolina and Virginia produced legislation in the early 1850s requiring physicians and midwives to record the birth rates among enslaved women, at a time when the criminalization of abortion was well underway across the United States, and aimed to curtail the practice among free women too.

In *The Development of Gynaecological Surgery and Instruments*, one of the first overviews of the field's clinical history, James Ricci exclaims that nothing in "the entire realm of medicine was more dramatic than the sudden change in gynaceological therapy" of the nineteenth century, and yet he cannot account for exactly why this dramatic shift took place.[29] He candidly admits his inability to make sense of this transformation in the field. Filling in a missing piece of the puzzle, Marie Jenkins Schwartz explains it this way: "Priding themselves on their modern attitudes and scientific approach to plantation management, owners sought physician assistance in increasing fertility among slaves. Doctors responded, putting themselves forward as scientific caregivers who were uniquely to be trusted with African American women's ailments."[30] The study of "woman" in general at the US medical schools extended into the practice of plantation medicine, Schwartz notes, and she pinpoints the 1840s as a time when declared specialists in gynecology increased in number and found themselves drawn into the world of slavery's perpetuation. Their work on the nature of fertility and what impaired it reinforced interest in gynecology's scientific claims, publications, and developments.[31]

In "The Comparative Fecundity of the Caucasian and African Races," an essay frequently excerpted and reprinted in medical journals following its publication in 1851, Southern physician E. M. Pendleton observed, "Every practitioner of medicine in the South is aware that an opinion generally prevails among the planters, that the blacks have a secret unknown to the whites, by which they either produce an incapacity to bear children, or destroy the foetus in embryo. . . . It cannot be denied that about towns and cities there are a great many unfruitful colored females; so much so, that it has become almost proverbial." Despite the numbers he gathered and his facility with statistics, he did not believe that the "puzzling barrenness among our slaves" could be traced to "nostrum taking and vending."[32] ("Savin, rue, and tea beware/ Wives who'd have a mother's care," warned *The Medical Times* in 1845.[33]) And although concerned about the nature and conditions of slave labor, as hard on their bodies, Pendleton viewed enslaved men and women through livestock metaphors (in relation to "gregarious quadrupeds") and failed to see them as intentionally terminating their pregnancies, despite prevailing suspicions. He advised that a "more rapid increase" could be achieved by informing enslaved women that they carried "immortal beings" whose destinies were "in some way, committed to their trust" and by encouraging paternal authority in enslaved men.[34]

As Barbara Bush-Slimani puts it in her study of childbirth and abortion on Caribbean plantations, "Where sexuality and reproduction were concerned, slave women were doubly oppressed by black and white patriarchy, gender and racial oppression. In refusing to 'breed' as well as perform hard labour on the plantation, slave women were both subconsciously and consciously protesting their slave status, harsh conditions in their productive labour and the erosion of their African cultural heritage." As early as the mid-1700s, overseers in Jamaica had started documenting infertility among their enslaved labor force, noting their suspicions about the use of abortifacients on plantations. As physicians explored the problem and published advice (about, for instance, keeping good notes on fertility cycles and discrediting African midwives), news traveled to the United States, and Jamaican data became a point of reference for their plantation statistics. Despite the suspicions of the Jamaican planters, however, physicians in both Jamaica and the United States still found it difficult to comprehend that Black women actively controlled their reproduction. All the evidence pointed to knowledge of abortifacients, use of instruments, and the option of infanticide—and yet "the enigma of low fertility" circulated through the medical papers.[35] Given the framework of livestock within which the term "slave breeding" existed, they failed to see the facts of human defiance in front of them.

Drawing on a world that banked on fertility and aware of what livestock denoted, Hawthorne establishes his allegorical house as an obligatory reproductive space from the start, his narrator defining it as the site "where children of the Pyncheon blood were to be born."[36] The grammar brilliantly performs concealment and evasion. Nobody actively gives birth here, and the subject of the sentence seems to be "children," in an ergative that reads like an imperative for them to get themselves born. It resembles the statistical framework of obstetrical charts, birth crunched into an anticipated rate of increase. Not exactly subtle in his representation of the Pyncheon patriarch's "stern rigidity of purpose," Hawthorne's narrator describes the house's origin as the ground's splitting open into "shavings, chips, shingles, and broken halves of bricks, [and] virgin leaves," a scattering into images of labor and afterbirth, turbulent and explosive.[37] The Pyncheons come down the line, and the house's grounds expand and contract.

When the narrator cuts to the present time of 1851, the House of the Seven Gables still stands, functioning as the place of Hepzibah's confinement. The lexicon is obstetric as Hepzibah waits for Clifford in a "strange mingling of the mother and sister," her life a kind of pregnant pause. And yet if Clifford returns "a child again," he is also a "necromantic miracle, . . . abortive." His role is to join Hepzibah at the end of the Pyncheon line, their reproductive years long behind them and the house fertile only with decomposition. Hawthorne extends this paradoxical formulation into the representation of the space as pregnant with the ghost of Alice Pyncheon, in the same way as his novel bears a story within a story about her undoing through the secret of the concealed deed. As his narrator momentarily gives way to Holgrave, who recounts tale of the virginal daughter on whose inviolable pedigree the structure of white humanity rests, the focus remains on obstructed reproduction. Turned into the medium of the dead Pyncheon's legacy, Alice confronts the curse: "Finally, when [the ghost] showed a purpose of shouting forth the secret, loudly enough to be heard from his own sphere into that of mortals, his companions struggled with him, and pressed their hands over his mouth; and forthwith—whether that he were choked by it, or that the secret itself was of a crimson hue—there was a fresh flow of blood upon his band." The impasse transpires as an erupting of blood combined with Alice's inability to deliver what her father wants from her. Abortion, miscarriage, stillbirth, and violent parturition shade together, preventing the ghost from "disburthening himself of the trust."[38]

Holgrave's story also functions to illuminate the omissions in the wider narrative of the founding or land grab and the curse, given that it recapitulates and compresses the sequence of these events but adds in missing details. Thus, at about the midpoint of *The House of the Seven Gables*, the wider story stands still, opening onto a retelling, in which a "shining, sable face of a slave" appears at a window in the house. This word "slave" is new, and it signifies another terminated biography in the architecture of its telling: just a glimpse is afforded us before Alice herself comes briefly into view. This enslaved person's existence, to put it another way, surfaces as part of the Pyncheon history but is never borne out. Appearing solely to disappear, she or he underscores the holes in the official account and extends the trope of abortion into what is cut from the story. Holgrave says that he follows the "chimney-corner legend," but adds in parentheses "(without copying all its extravagances)," as he shifts into his narration about Alice.[39] If "(extravagances)" refers to an enslaved person's rendition of domestic secrets (as embellishments left out of transcriptions), then what is cut is not synonymous with nothingness. Holgrave's decision to pare down the tale points to something unmentionable, its profligacy contained in parentheses.

It is also clever of Hawthorne to write about Holgrave reading his article aloud, to turn the story he prints back into an oral story, emphasizing a catching at the throat or a holding back. In a kind of whirlwind of sexual and textual reversals, indecent puns spin around the convergence of ingurgitation and blood, wickedly eddying into so many of the other moments in which oral and sexual appetites take each other's place. Choking and swallowing repeatedly occur in the novel, implicit in allusions to such as activities as the "quaffing [of] passionate love," blowing bubble pipes, going "down on [one's] knees," and "gushing up to find words." Even the chimney's "sooty throat" experiences the wind's "intimacy" and takes it in.[40] The innuendos build, signaling the demise of the Pyncheons in what the medical world term termed "contrary sexual instincts," also known in Hawthorne's time as welcome "checks to the population": the kind of queer activities that did not involve procreation or which intentionally bypassed it, departing from the belief that "the great object of the sexual function [was] the reproduction of the species" (to quote William Alcott).[41] Each of the novel's main characters is childless, including Uncle Venner if we do not count his pig as kin. Ways around procreating also inform the narrator's choice to describe different processes, four times, as abortive.

Hawthorne's narrator says in the preface that he will not force a moral on his readers, requesting rather that we "may perhaps choose to assign an actual locality to the imaginary events of the narrative." This explication is not so much a coy allusion to its political allegory as it is a form of differentiation from the ways in which noses, minds, and bodies are repeatedly assaulted and penetrated by the production of propaganda internal to the Pyncheons' self-mythology. There is a moral to Hawthorne's story; he just does not want to impale it, he says, as if "sticking a pin through a butterfly."[42] Rather, he works to remove ideas that bore into minds, pulling up nailed-down illusions and classifications of being. He raises the prospect that the frightening experience of hunger (represented by Hepzibah's near starvation and Uncle Venner's itinerant scrap collecting) might be part of the actual and philosophical divestments he proposes. To put this differently, he proposes that one must be willing to go hungry, if that is what it takes to change everything. The assurances obtained by plantation agriculture for those not enslaved by it, along with the ideological sustenance that white supremacy provides, must be reckoned with and emptied out.

Thus, backward from the story of Alice's death to the description of the house's "ceremony of consecration" as a "belching forth that impregnate[s] the whole air," the curse of blood pertains to America's excessive appetite for breeding and feeding. Hawthorne's narrator describes the inaugural feast by means of ergatives that once again erase the laboring subjects of the sentences: "An ox roasted whole, or, at least, by the weight and substance of an ox, in more manageable joints and sirloins. The carcass of a deer, shot within twenty miles, had supplied material for the vast circumference of a pasty. A cod-fish of sixty pounds, caught in the bay, had been dissolved into the rich liquid of a chowder."[43] The significance of this menu also extends beyond its ergatives and excess, to include the transformation of animals into parts and words. Whole bodies become rendered as palatable dishes and euphemisms.[44] Their dissolution into "manageable joints" and chowders points to the distortion of enslaved humans into "merchantable goods" and livestock themselves.[45]

The feast signifies the crime at the founding of the house as the establishment of a plantation. Its violent roots go deeper, into the separation of animal bodies from human souls, out of which the hierarchies of flesh ascend into national allegories.[46] That the air becomes "pregnant" with the scent of immolation is consistent with the representation of the soul's incarnation at conception. Immolation and incarnation, to clarify, are sophisticated turns on cooking and copulating, just as empire is a sophisticated way of saying land-grab.

This representation of meat follows from *The Scarlet Letter*'s as Hawthorne casts the invasion of Maule's territory by "civilized man" as the "work of blood."[47] The phrase is as indeterminate as the scarlet emblem itself, multiplying into possibilities about bleeding as exploiting and draining, or preserving and marking. If we take it to entail something like ideology, "the work of blood" denotes the kind of labor and thinking that draws the human species apart from other animals and then carves humans into the racialized categories of white, Black, and Indigenous blood. These categories are not real in spite of their violent effects, Hawthorne implies. They comprise the work of blood by which Black men and women are named in livestock ledgers and Indigenous worlds are presumed extinct. In the end, the ceremony of consecration at the novel's beginning pairs fire and blood in the production of "woman," "slave," and "livestock" as cauldrons into which beings dissolve, consumable and regurgitated according to the Pyncheon predilections.

To echo Derrida's formulation, the sovereign requires the beast, standing as he does on the side of the fault line across from which everything nonhuman resides. The race-based slavery instituted by the Anglo-American founders is informed by this line. It is a history marked by debates as to whether people of African descent had souls and if Indigenous territories were mapped by Satan himself.[48] In *The House of the Seven Gables*, when Hawthorne's narrator refers to the "absurd delusion of family importance" inherited by the generations of Pyncheons after the founding, he means their sense of birthright, for which they do not have to toil.[49] Being born white and therefore unquestionably possessed of a soul, they profit from delusion, the work of blood having established an abstract and immortal superiority for them.

Clifford Pyncheon's fear that a "dark face" stares back at him from Maule's Well literally reflects the delusion of whiteness that he inherits. He is made doubly conscious of it when he gazes upon the immigrant and his monkey just outside his window. What Hawthorne stresses through Clifford's terror is the experience of being mirrored by other races and animals as the confrontation of white humanity with loss on a "spiritual as well as physical level."[50] When the monkey stretches forth its hand, it replaces god's. While this awareness might be considered terrifying, it is also liberating. Everything about this novel celebrates the passing into nothingness of the "epoch of Adam's grandchildren," this lineage generated, ostensibly, without Eve's participation in it and distinct in creation.[51] Only after an atheistic gutting can kinship and life be reorganized into the revolutionary notion of one "fellow-being, moulded of the same elements," facing another.[52] This statement is characteristically beautiful, and the pun on "mould" produces a kind of doctrine of decaying together. Molding purports both composition and decomposition, in a simultaneity that configures conceiving as concurrent with rotting. Once released from the stranglehold of "life at conception," death becomes life's essence, not its digression or evacuation, and there is nothing to fear.

Early in the novel, Hawthorne brings these positions into conversation with his narrator's moments of reflection on the process of writing. He says, "It would be an omission, trifling, indeed, but unpardonable, were we to forget the green moss that had long since gathered over the projections of the windows, and on the slopes of the roof [and to] the flower-shrubs growing aloft.... The decay of the roof gradually formed a kind of soil for them, out of which they grew." How can an omission take place as both trifling and unpardonable? When the narrator backs up to address the omission, he takes us into the representation of a fertile decay as it is enacted by his paradoxical sentences. Weird formulations are required for radical thinking and none seems more strange than this convoluted, description of Holgrave's thoughts: "He had that sense, or inward prophecy,—which a young man had better die at once than not to have, and a mature man had better never have been born than utterly to relinquish,—that we are not doomed to creep on forever in the old, bad way, but that, this very now, there are the harbingers abroad of a golden era, to be accomplished in his own lifetime." Double negatives and reversals through assertions of possession and relinquishment characterize the phrase isolated between the double dashes. They try to convey human existence as meaningful only as a form of disentanglement from the "bad way" into which it is drawn. Otherwise never coming into existence is preferable.[53]

Perhaps it goes without saying that Hawthorne follows Poe's lead in "The Fall of the House of Usher" to narrate rot and negation into the architecture of life and whiteness. Where "minute fungi" rise from the tarn in an alliance with the miscarrying Madeline to bring down the house, toadstools infiltrate the Pyncheon grounds, joining Hepzibah (that "mildewed piece of aristocracy") in a vibrant pact with the forces of disintegration.[54] Inside the "desolate, decaying, gusty, rusty, old house of the Pyncheon family" Hepzibah resides, "impregnated with the dry-rot of [the house's] timbers," heir to a meaningful barrenness. In the same way as Poe's House of Usher births Madeline from within its own tremoring over the dark tarn, the dormant deed inside the house's hole configures this architectural space as violated and female, reversing the equation through which human lives become property and enslaved as such. This renewal therefore turns on a termination, of all that is classified in the service of white supremacy, breaking from a sense of history as "little else but a series of calamity, reproducing itself in successive generations," as Hawthorne's narrator describes it in *The House of the Seven Gables*.[55] The fissure that marks the spectacular collapse of the Usher house resides in the Pyncheon house as a secret hole, similarly overdetermined as an anatomical space through which death passes into birth, vibrant and soulless.

Like Poe, Hawthorne takes such fissures and holes into his sentences, incorporating barrenness, emptiness, and nothingness into their syntactical presentation. Throughout *The House of the Seven Gables*, bracketed phrases or qualifications cut into sentences and force their meanings to double back and come apart. "Nothing flourished in the ... pitiless atmosphere" of the house, the narrator tells us, "*except* the moss ... and the great bunch of weeds" (my emphasis). Not nothing, then, flourishes. Along these lines, Phoebe's chamber is described as empty of life, before a qualification cuts into and redirects the statement's import. Her room is "untenanted for so long—*except* by spiders, and mice, and rats, and ghosts—all overgrown with desolation. And Hepzibah's kitchen appears utterly vacant, until the narrator revises the scene. He says, "It was touching, and positively worthy of tears (if Phoebe, the only spectator, except the rats and ghosts aforesaid, had not been better employed than in shedding them), to see her rake out a bed of fresh and glowing coals, and proceed to broil the mackerel." The parentheses introduce the description's undoing, revising the emptiness as a space actually occupied by rats and ghosts.[56] It is important to stress that these ghosts are not to be read as spectral entities or disembodied spirits but as the material traces of once-living entities. They linger in the mold generated by the humidity of their breath in the past and as the fungus that lives in the soil's decay.

Hawthorne scholar Samuel Kimball describes Hawthorne's prose as "contraceptive." Focusing on *The Scarlet Letter,* Kimball says that Hawthorne's "radically self-subverting speech-acts" replace metaphors of conception with contrary conceptions, functioning therefore as contraceptive. He takes as a key instance in *The Scarlet Letter* Hawthorne's placement of the imperative "Be true!" inside levels of fiction, as a self-conscious moment that establishes truth's fictionality. Such contradictions send tremors into the "linguistic and ethical, not to mention sexual and reproductive," codes of patriarchal authority and refuse to clear space for any "transcendental guarantor" of meaning.[57] Playing on the words "generative," "conceiving," and "contravening," Kimball argues that Hawthorne illuminates patriarchal power in terms of lexical structures founded on the generation of truth, reproduced as metaphysical and named as such by men.

Kimball clarifies this point via Louis Althusser's description of ideology as that which forms being in advance of birth: "Everyone knows how much and in what way an unborn child is expected.... It is certain in advance that it will bear its Father's Name, and will therefore have an identity and be irreplaceable. Before its birth, the child is therefore always already a subject, appointed as a subject in and by the specific familial ideological configuration in which it is expected once it has been conceived."[58] For Kimball, Hawthorne's contraceptive thinking in *The Scarlet Letter* pushes against the force of this interpellation, a point I not only agree with but also see at work in *The House of the Seven Gables,* especially when the Pyncheon name is described as immortality intermittently embodied.

Holgrave's famous rant against "Dead Men" and the "Rotten Past," through which his fury becomes directed at "great-grandchildren," combines the reproduction of stale ideas with that of children. "We shall live to see the day, I trust ... when no man shall build his house for posterity," he states. And when he feels himself drawn into what seems to be a marriage plot, Holgrave cannot decide whether he is heading toward a "catastrophe, or consummation," as if the terms are interchangeable: "A feeling which I cannot describe—an indefinite sense of some catastrophe, or consummation—impelled me to make my way to this part of the house."[59] Just as the phrase is suspended inside the sentence and firmly held there between double dashes, so too is Holgrave's proposal to Phoebe suspended inside the narrative, their wedding left unwritten. What I mean to emphasize here is that the possibility of their marriage does not overturn Holgrave's earlier scoffing at the whole idea. It remains part of the sequence of ideas. In the same way, when Holgrave asks Phoebe about assuming his name, she does not answer him, veering off instead to address Uncle Venner. What is set into motion is not brought into being.

As the narrator notes in his preface, "The final development of a work of fiction, may add an artistic glory, but is never truer, and seldom more evident, at the last page than the first."[60] He calls this development a "crowning"—an obstetrical term for fetal presentation at birth—in order to assert that plots and ideas may break off without delivering what their sequence seems to initiate. Instead, they fall at odd angles to the plot, halted in time and with little "use of immortality," like the mechanical pantomime he intricately describes.[61]

"Unrelentingly political," as Robert Levine puts it, Hawthorne's novel "poses considerable challenges to the orthodoxies of his day," specifically resisting the "the blood-based Anglo-Saxonist nationalism and expansionism of the O'Sullivan Young-American Crowd."[62] Throughout the novel, paradoxical formulas and reduplications twist the foundations of entire scenes and go undercover to attack the sacrosanct underpinnings of white birthright. They push us to see that for a "fair Alice" to secure America's coveted center, a "Black Scipio" is violently held apart from her, and an Indigenous Maule removed from the path. Levine asserts that Hawthorne proposes human entanglement over lineage, brilliantly ascertaining weaving as another of the novel's powerful tropes. This entanglement includes the nonhuman entities who slide into Hawthorne's sentences and quietly reside with Hepzibah. She shares with them a "mechanism of animal life," each alive only as different configurations of elements. All around her, spiders spin webs; objects rust and transform; mushrooms grow where oaks fall; dust moves in. As her teeth chatter and fall out of her head, Hepzibah's decay seems tragic only from within an old anthropocentric story, with its delineation between life and death. The most beautiful phrase in the novel, regarding existence as a "substantial emptiness, a material ghost," captures the philosophy that begins with the "original atoms" in the preface and moves through Hepzibah's detachment from god.[63] For William Scheick, the novel's ultimate secret is that death resides at the center of existence and confirms a "dreadful message" about nothingness, terrifying to contemplate.[64]

But perhaps the terror might be taken as a redirection. As Holgrave asks Phoebe after the storm, "Phoebe, is it all terror?—nothing but terror? Are you conscious of no joy?"[65] The "eye of Heaven" or "the eye of the Father," to which Hawthorne's narrator refers throughout the novel, remains vacant or "withdrawn," conferring a godless universe on its human inhabitants. And yet this paternal abandonment initiates a starting point from which everything might be justly rearranged.[66] Hepzibah's paradoxical reformulation of Providence's nonexistence (such that "its vastness made it nothing") takes place as a breath of fresh air. An "invigorating breath," it draws animation from air's ostensible emptiness.[67]

"The gloom has not entered from without," Hawthorne's narrator announces. "It has brooded here all day, and now, taking its own inevitable time, will possess itself of everything."[68] The tone of such a pronouncement is at once eerie and conspiratorial, drawing us toward nightfall's symbolic presence as a "double-handful of darkness" that turns white and gray into "sable."[69] By means of the furtiveness of this description, through which blackness goes under cover of the setting sun in a room, the narrator signals the end of the world as the white patriarchy knows it. "Tomorrow! Tomorrow! Tomorrow!" he calls out, ironically imploring for the future from his entrapment in the darkening world.[70] Against this entrapment, Hawthorne covertly deals his blows, crafting his gothic tropes into white supremacy's worst nightmare. Once human life is divested of its spiritual singularity, all manner of other conceptual props go down with it: Race, Truth, and the American fetus itself.

"The black mould always clings to my spade, as if I were a sexton," Holgrave exclaims, longing for "the greatest of renovators and reformers" to help him turn over the soil and let it breathe. In a skillful allusion to the Free Soil Party, Holgrave's outburst aligns his digging with abolitionism, the "rank weeds" of injustice inside the rich soil. (When Jaffrey dies, we learn exactly what side he served because his "warm and merry guests . . . conclude that the Free Soilers have him.") The blackness and mold that maintain the prospect of new growth are complex images, functioning in the same way as the dark night does, as literal phenomena and as metaphors for the Black human beings from whom meaning is extorted to make the white family tree look immortal. Working on the ground instead of praying heavenward, the latter being repeatedly described as useless, Holgrave aligns reform and abolition with his labor. "I dig, and hoe, and weed, in this black old earth," he explains, conveying the sense of an overwhelming task: the extirpation of a deeply rooted system.[71]

Holgrave's digging with his spade replicates Hawthorne's nudging with his pen, both aimed specifically at the plot bequeathed by the founders around 1750 and "unctuous with nearly two hundred years of vegetable decay." The decay is not the problem here; it is the unctuousness attached to it, the stranglehold of empire and agriculture on the earth, in service of Uncle Sam. It is no accident that when Clifford and Hepzibah flee the house for a day, leaving it empty but for Jaffrey's corpse, they encounter a ruined church and an abandoned farm: "The world had fled away from these two wonderers. They gazed drearily about them. At a little distance stood a wooden church, black with age, and in a dismal state of ruin and decay, with broken windows, a great rift through the main-body of the

CHAPTER FIVE

edifice, and a rafter dangling from the top of the square tower. Farther off was a farm-house in the old style, as venerably black as the church, with a roof sloping downward from the three-story peak to within a man's height of the ground. It seemed uninhabited." Church and Agriculture, two frameworks of Black enslavement, are emptied of human inhabitants and falling apart. The imagery is altogether postapocalyptic, the "great rift" reminiscent of Usher's house. When Hepzibah kneels down at the end of the chapter, she asks, "God—our Father are we are not thy children?," but nothing follows, just the blank page. Hepzibah's prayer—described as at once "abortive" and "too heavy" to send up to heaven—participates in an existential terror that is also a way out of a cosmos of worshipped fathers and favored children.[72]

The route to follow is the one struck by the "eccentric old bachelor" in the Pyncheon past who once attempted a restitution of the great crime of his house. He is a different kind of uncle, not "unctuously benevolent" like Uncle Jaffrey and, like the other protagonists, detached from breeding. While the narrator explains that his one paragraph about this particular man is really just a digression, requiring just "a few words," it is the space where an entirely different story arises as a ghostly alternative to the one that entrenches itself. Here, along this eccentric route, we learn that the old bachelor imagines returning what his family stole and making amends, if not reparations. By "rummag[ing] old records," the man looks backward, contemplating how to substitute "right for wrong" instead of looking toward increase.[73] Queer, childless, and oriented toward divestment, his characterization transpires in relation to the novel's abortive threads.

By the time of the old bachelor's generation, his family's crimes include both the conquest of Maule's land and the slavery perpetuated on it. The latter crime emerges as he observes the "black stain of blood, [now] patrimonial property" in his history and desires to change his will, the documentation by which manumission was often conferred. The narrator remarks that the old man veers into relinquishment of his property only to retain it "in the line marked by custom," but this is not correct.[74] Rummaging back through this digression, we recall that the old bachelor does not preserve his last will and testament before he dies. He is murdered before he can change it. By the time Hawthorne's narrator arrives at the conclusion of his paragraph, he seems to have forgotten the murder that opens it. Or he ironically forgets, resuming with the plotline, the straightness of which Hawthorne repeatedly exposes as the kind of forward-facing that turns falsifications of history into something like Manifest Destiny.[75]

The novel's attention to eccentricity combines with its ironic force too, throwing off the seemingly intended meaning of scenes and ideas. The opening paragraphs that describe the golden age of the seventeenth-century Puritans, for instance, seem as if they are recounted through clenched teeth. As the "queerest of rhetorical devices," in Lee Edelman's famous formulation, irony involves the nonreproduction of sense by sound, doubling into an uncanny echo.[76] It is a mode of concealment, therefore, making available a different meaning from within the "alleged necromancies within a system."[77] Alert to it, we can see how that meaning operates as an undermining, as rust on iron. It follows, then, that the fixed and "iron will" of the Pyncheons becomes subject to the irony permeating their tale. All of the swords, nails, hinges, and stakes are overtaken by rust that operates like an abortifacient disintegrating every phallic thing. Again, closely reading the intricacy of this novel yields the possibilities on the other side of the dominant ideology of life. We can comprehend the corrosion and irony as we do the mold and the fungus that proliferate throughout the house, from within the necromancy that attends Maule's Well and inhabits the house's decomposition.

Indeed, an instance of high irony occurs when Clifford proposes that electricity might offer a revolutionary model for understanding materiality and then takes as his example a telegraph message carrying a birth announcement: a new technology speeding up an old patriarchal paradigm. The telegraph's message is transmitted to an "absent husband," informing him that "an immortal being, of whom you are the father, has this moment come from God."[78] Every word of this message is out of step with the novel's endeavor. Even if electricity gives evidence of a kind of vital materialism, to borrow Jane Bennett's term,[79] Clifford gets it backward. A residual conservatism marks the telegraph, ironically compressing into conciseness the god-father-birth paradigm that the novel takes pages to pull apart, including the fact that the telegraph bears no signature, reiterating maternity's irrelevance in its delivery.

And yet, as a queer bachelor himself, Clifford reaches for comprehension of the materialism that surrounds him and attempts to understand time as a spiral that curves backward, into a prepatriarchal, nomadic antiquity that curves forward into the present too. He desires an "earthly future," he says. If everything comes to be recognized as self-organizing matter, ironically vital and inanimate, decaying into other dynamic formations, then an earthly

CHAPTER FIVE

future shifts into place for him, leaving no room for the lure or the lie of an eternal future. It is telling, for instance, that when Hawthorne's narrator expresses pity toward Clifford he says, "There seemed no necessity for his having drawn breath, at all;—the world never wanted him," replacing birth with a having-drawn of breath. In other words, following such patterns of materialist philosophy, Hawthorne views living on earth as a matter of breathing, as a kind of oxygenation threatened by choking, and not as life, unfolding from conception. Clifford's earthly future arrives with his breath, which is like the wind that blows through the house and animates its voice: "The old house creaks again, and makes a vociferous, but somewhat unintelligible bellowing in its sooty throat—(the big flue, we mean, of its wide chimney)—partly in complain at the rude wind, but rather, as befits their century-and-a-half of hostile intimacy, in rough defiance."[80] The brackets, dashes, and punctuated clarification, for example, "—(the big flue, we mean, of its wide chimney)—," calls attention to the metaphor that confers animation on things and reconfigures them in relation to others. The implication is that every entity in and around the house exists in the interactions between air and atoms, as variations on the elements and not according to a chain of command that begins and ends with god and in utero.

"It was the belief of the Stoics," Wooster Beach explains in his *Improved System of Midwifery*, "that the soul was not combined to the body until the act of respiration, and that the fetus was inanimate during its residence *in utero*." Perhaps Hawthorne took his ideas from here, at least in part. Like Beach, most midcentury obstetrical handbooks included explorations of physiological origins and, in Beach's words, the "similarity or analogy between the reproduction of vegetable, animal, and human life."[81] Intricate color plates of chickens and eggs accompany Beach's arguments, at once delineating a sequence from embryo to hatchling and illustrating the dead creature in relation to the eggs symbolizing her species' life.

In *The House of the Seven Gables*, a family of backyard chickens makes its way into the narrative, serving both literal and metaphoric purposes, as we are repeatedly reminded. The Pyncheon chickens replicate the notion of "progenitors, derived through an unbroken succession of eggs" and remain "mixed up with [the family's] destiny."[82] On the one hand, they are straightforwardly chickens, charming birds who share the same space as the human residents. On the other, they stand in for the enslaved humans otherwise written out of the novel. For although the scholarly impulse is to read them as feathered and comical versions of the declining Pyncheons themselves, they may not at all brandish white plumage and neither do they reside on the inside of the house. Confined to its grounds and "mixed up with" the Pyncheons, their story as livestock runs alongside that of the white inhabitants. Repeated hints about agricultural trends and the exotic nature of the chickens, moreover, make it possible to read the birds as black and therefore part of the allegory that obscures slavery from the house's founding.

This is to say that the representation of the hens' infertility combines with their slaking their thirst at Maule's Well to underscore its metaphoric role in the novel and the undoing it represents. When Hepzibah feeds Clifford a hen's carefully guarded egg, as if out of indifference to her own reproduction, the bereaved hen's point of view also comes into focus. The egg is hers, Hawthorne's narrator insists, and "not to be estimated either in gold or precious stones."[83] While the wording here may seem hyperbolic and the chickens' fury comically rendered, the allegorical level carries another meaning entirely. Hepzibah's casual pilfering of another's offspring sheds light on the history into which she is born. It is also not a positive development when the chickens become more fecund toward the end of the tale, especially given that this fecundity coincides with the windfall of an inheritance earlier represented as crushing in nature and criminal in origin. The story of the chickens remains structured by the novel's irony and smokescreens, and the future of their eggs remains suspended and unwritten, in the same way as Phoebe's reproductive future is.

CHAPTER SIX

The Blithedale Romance and Abortion's Conditional Perfect

> And having nobody but myself to care for.
> —Miles Coverdale, *The Blithedale Romance*, 1852

> The fetus is incompetent to think about power as contingent. It speaks only of God's creation.
> —Lauren Berlant, *The Queen of American Goes to Washington City*, 1997

The Blithedale Romance follows fast on the heels of *The Scarlet Letter* and *The House of the Seven Gables* as another meditation on the scene of the crime denoted by the name America, Hawthorne again facing the complexities of inheriting something so heavy. Picking up where he leaves off in the two previous novels, in *Blithedale* he drives home his dejected estimation of the country as little more than a white man's revenue system generated by enslaved labor on stolen land. It is a site crowded with metaphors, carved as such from a "mother forest" into a letter A, and then again into a great house. Here, it becomes "this experiment," the Blithedale farm: all permutations on American exceptionalism, all rife with unquiet graves. To begin once again with Lauren Berlant. "Characters in his *Blithedale*," she says, "are the site of history's burial: the 'unwedded bride' is the analogy for that which we do not know, and—given Coverdale's particular feelings about Zenobia—that which we, as readers and citizens, do not want to know.... To write the complete American history on its utopian trajectory would be to write the history of scandal (mass killing) and to read a series of failures, ... a record of the obsessions of a failed storyteller."[1] The "hitherto unwedded bride" to which Berlant refers is Hawthorne's tongue-in-cheek rendition of the cliché of virgin land, placed in the mouth of a narrator who clings to the concept while trying to obscure it.

According to Berlant, such clichés and their attendant elusiveness communicate the ways in which utopian rhetoric drives "Native Americans [toward] ... the farthest margins of representation."[2] This metaphor for virgin land also reintroduces from *The House of the Seven Gables* the reproductive imperative underscoring that rhetoric. The were-to-be-born children on the inside of the Pyncheons' architecture become here the progeny of a "hitherto unwedded bride," both phrases functioning as interpellations as much as descriptions. For by defining a woman in retrospect as already married before the fact, the paradoxical expression "unwedded bride" stakes a claim from the future, in the same way as the conceptualization of the "unborn" does.

This is the grammar of "incipient citizenship," to borrow Berlant's phrase, in which the bodies of white Americans are configured as gestating both their own orientation toward heterosexuality and the nation's procreative, utopian future. In a manipulation of scale, the magnification of fetal significance layers over America's fracturing political spaces and, as Berlant shows, sutures them into its ideal of a foreordained national becoming. As a result, women's desire "for other kinds of creative agency ... becom[es] an obstacle to national reproduction"; their bodies must buttress a "nation-making function," always potentially maternal.[3] With *The Blithedale Romance,* Hawthorne lays this thesis out in narrative terms, situating Zenobia's lush, fertile corporeality at the center of Coverdale's story, but also nonmaternal and dead, entombed within the space of his textual reproduction of her.[4] In the final, physical contestation between her body (its deliberate deviation from gestating incipience) and his (the muscular, self-defined conservative), she loses.

As I note in the preface, the word "unborn" was already in print well before Hawthorne's time, and by the 1840s it had acquired phantasmagorical overtones. For example, in his fascinating polemic *Man-Midwifery Exposed, Or the Danger and Immorality of Employing Men in Midwifery Proved* (first published in 1849), physician John Stevens refers to the unborn as he condemns the rise of men in obstetrics and their excessive utilization of instruments and forceps. He makes several references to an eighteenth-century pamphlet titled "Petition of the Unborn Babes to the Censors of the Royal College of Physicians of London,"[5] in which the petitioners describe their casualties before birth and demand consequences for those who seize them: "If we cannot leave our Dwellings, and make our Appearance," they write from beyond the grave, "so soon, as is expected ... we are forthwith drag'd out of our Habitations by Hooks, Pincers, and other bloody Instruments."[6]

CHAPTER SIX

Stevens then includes an updated petition, in which the unborn ask that men be barred from obstetrics in the new year, and he adds his own flourish following their last paragraph: "[Here followed several thousands of small signatures which proved even above the power of clairvoyance to recollect]."[7] These excerpts illuminate *The Blithedale Romance* from interesting angles, especially the scenes involving Priscilla's otherworldly attachment to the nonmaternal Zenobia and Zenobia's own violent delivery from the river.

Throughout *Man-Midwifery Exposed,* Stevens repeatedly quotes American medical journals and underscores the similarities between British and American practitioners, demonstrating the extent to which medical concepts and developments traveled in print across national borders. It is important to note too that the "Petition from the Unborn Babes" was written out of a sense of urgency regarding fatalities associated with the excessive use of forceps. By giving voice to these apparitions, they did not intend to supply antiabortion positions with particularly powerful scenarios of souls awaiting entry into the world, appealing for a safe passageway. But they did insist on notions of fetal innocence, demanding in the voice of the so-called unborn that they be visualized as faultless, even when their uterine position meant death for the person in labor.

As I argue in this chapter, Coverdale clings to similar scenarios and envisions Blithedale as the place in which new souls will take form. His thinking is represented along the same lines as Colonel Pyncheon's before him, in which the actualities of pregnancy and birth are incidental to the paternal design. When Coverdale's vision is overwritten by Hollingsworth's, he kills Zenobia in order to cast him as a murderer, terminating Hollingsworth's particular conception of the future by stifling him with guilt. Zenobia's murder is the substance of the confession toward which the novel moves, the "one secret—I have concealed it all along," as Coverdale says, and that which is "essential to the full understanding of my story."[8] His pages carry this secret like a concealed pregnancy, enclosing the image of Zenobia's kneeling corpse, bent in such a way that reads nothing like a drowning. Coverdale reproduces this image wrapped in convolutions of abortion, pregnancy, stillbirth, and murder.

Threatening to come apart at the seams, the novel carries both Coverdale's romance of the nation and Hawthorne's simultaneous undoing of that attempt. What looks like utopianism from one angle, Hawthorne insists, is a murderer's confession from the other. The American epic that Coverdale sets out to write ("we must all figure heroically in an Epic Poem") thus materializes as its opposite, this novel, a not-epic—part monstrous birth, part abortion.[9] On the one hand, Coverdale's victory over Zenobia makes for a darkly pessimistic vision, as Tony Tanner maintains.[10] Every hopeful reform fails on a land stained by genocidal conflict and entrenched in slavery. On the other hand, Coverdale's victory is only partial, and its lies fall into decipherable patterns on the surface of a narrative that Hawthorne also pens. Zenobia's feminism does not fail, and its template can be recomposed, in the same way as Poe holds Marie Rogêt's body and story apart from the patriarchal fictions that close in on them.

Like the complex point of view developed in *The House of the Seven Gables,* this one splinters too, with Coverdale functioning both as a patriotic subject and as the object of Hawthorne's cutting irony. Introducing a figure who speaks with nostalgia about the America of New England Pilgrims, Hawthorne works against the grain of its seemingly harmless longing, showing it up for what it is: another variation on the white supremacy tackled in the previous two novels. As Coverdale's idealism buckles under Hawthorne's materialism, the novel illuminates creative transformations from within its unclassifiable form. "It needs a wild steersman when we voyage through Chaos!" Zenobia declares. "The anchor is up! Farewell!"[11]

A central feature of *The Blithedale Romance* occurs as Coverdale's struggle against chaos. Speaking for Providence (by now a cliché for Hawthorne and yet another capitalized noun for Coverdale), he tries to make death fit a pattern and explain away violent imperialism as "the advancement of our race" from both the future and the past, and as "human progress." Declaring Native Americans vanished, as if by a stage trick, Coverdale defines them as lost to history and parenthetical. "It was still as wild a tract of woodland," he proposes about the land, "as the great-great-great-great grandson of one Eliot's Indians (had any posterity been in existence) could have desired."[12] In Tony Tanner's words, Native Americans are "literally . . . bracketed out of American history" by Coverdale's syntax and thinking.[13] They are also bracketed in, but distorted through yet another cliché, the convenient colonial trope of the disappearing Indian. Hawthorne works this trope into Coverdale's insinuation that those who are brutally dispossessed in fact simply take themselves out of the picture. "It is for this reason," he remarks with confidence, "that the stricken deer goes apart, and the sick lion grimly withdraws himself into his den," in a metaphor that serves his story rather

CHAPTER SIX

nicely. For it allows him to underscore the connection he forges between the genocide of the Native Americans as a form of race suicide, and the murder of Zenobia as a suicide for love. Both lies, they obscure the military enforcement of the Indian Removal Act and the violent energy produced by appeals to utopian patriotism.[14]

When Coverdale raises the subject of Zenobia's death in the final chapter, titled "Miles Coverdale's Confession," he quickly sweeps it aside and emphasizes that the true loss entails "the experiment [and] its own higher spirit"—his "infant community," as if Blithedale were a real child. "More and more," he says, "I feel that we had struck upon what ought to be a truth. Posterity may dig it up, and profit by it."[15] Evoking an abstract, future Posterity, Coverdale offers this book as the medium by which one might disinter the spirit of Blithedale and give it birth. He does so while standing on the soil near Zenobia's grave, the site from which he narrates the whole tale. Drawing on the interplay of "womb" and "tomb" once again, Hawthorne keeps it readily at hand, not because it is an easy trick or worn-out pun but because the act of abortion literalizes the metaphor in the conservative worldview he confronts. A womb can turn into a tomb and then back again, Coverdale implies.

The future for which he speaks originates in a very particular lineage and must be fortified against those whom Coverdale observes with particular disgust: the "big, red, Irish matrons [and their] innumerable progeny," for example. This evocation and exaggeration of immigrant fecundity forms the basis of his reactionary politics, in which Coverdale fears the contamination of his inviolable America. "There are some spheres," he notes, "the contact with which inevitably degrades the high, debases the pure, deforms the beautiful." This coy white supremacy occurs as another reverberation of Puritan election from the past into the present, unavailable to the ears of immigrants, materialists, or the kind of women "with bold intellectual development." The America of the original New England colonies—providential, a "beacon-fire ... kindled for humanity"—thus occurs as an ontological inward turning, putting the lie to the openness that the beacon signals. It involves a closing of ranks around a white inheritance, glowing against the shadows projected along its outward edges.[16]

And it is for this reason that key scenes take place at Eliot's pulpit, the "omphalos of his experience," in Berlant's words, and the ground on which Coverdale believes American exceptionalism stands. For Berlant, the novel's "crisis of national-utopian politics" centers here because Coverdale's glorification of Eliot neither addresses Eliot's missionary failures nor the violence of King Philip's War associated with them.[17] Indeed, the history that Coverdale understands allows him likewise to compress centuries of African slavery in America into one line about destiny and artistry. Forcing disconcerting details through an aesthetic sieve, he says, "Human destinies look ominous, without some perceptible intermixture of the sable or the gray."[18] A nod to the mixing that the slave trade made unavoidable too, Coverdale covers all bases in his version of events, excusing any "intermixture" as attenuating the superior glare of whiteness.

Accomplishing a feat of symbolism, moreover, he kills Zenobia at Eliot's pulpit. The remarkably phallic stone that rises "some twenty or thirty feet" from the ground at this site is in fact "a shattered granite boulder, or heap of boulders, with an irregular outline and many fissures." Zenobia's murder occurs here precisely because her feminism represents a fissure in the symbolic integrity Coverdale feels duty bound to protect. The feminist dies at a birthplace of the American experiment, killed in the name of its future. In the contradictory logic of the pro-life ideology under Hawthorne's concomitant scrutiny all along, the elimination of the one makes way for the life of the other. Zenobia's strangulation is the fact of the tale's very conceiving, the confession about which Coverdale's last line aborts just as he is about to deliver it. The stuttering, punctuated statement ("I—I myself—was in love—with—Priscilla") cuts apart what "rises in my throat" for disclosure.[19] This surprising revelation, unforeseen because untrue, takes place as a choking at his throat.

Page after page, Hawthorne carefully crafts his narrator's investment in the posterity of the nation-state, establishing it as the romance of that state's violent incursions into Indigenous territories: white borders multiplying outward from a mythical point of origin in the pilgrims and the founding fathers. Theirs is the "high enterprise [we] were carrying" in anticipation of the next generation, the prototype of which is established by Priscilla's blossoming at Blithedale.[20] For Lee Edelman, this is precisely the form of conscription that makes abortion, prostitution, and homosexuality all comprehensible in light of each other, as practices that do not embrace the promises symbolized by the unborn child. With his now-famous capitalization of Child, he explains:

> The Child, that is, marks the fetishistic fixation of heteronormativity: an erotically charged investment in the rigid sameness of identity that is central to the compulsory narrative reproductive futurism. And so, as the radical right maintains, the battle against queers is a life-and-death struggle for the future of a Child whose ruin is pursued by feminists, queers, and those who support the legal availability of abortion. Indeed, as the Army of God made clear in the bombing guide it produced for the assistance of its militantly "pro-life" members, its purpose was wholly congruent with the logic of reproductive futurism: to "disrupt and ultimately destroy Satan's power to kill our children, God's children."[21]

Coverdale's tale is that of a capitulation to the politics of reproduction. His project has nothing to do with actual social reform, harboring as he does a hatred for reformers "for all futurity." His allegiance to Blithedale is his way of securing himself in place in an American superwomb that permits him a kind of rebirth, this time as whole, not "crooked." Its very possibility is his love object, always just out of reach—the pure idea, awaiting its materialization or incarnation, in the same way that "Nature shap[es] out a woman before our very eyes."[22]

The Blithedale Romance is haunted by Zenobia's death, as Hawthorne critics concur, but its ghostly nature is also an effect of Coverdale's panegyric to the unborn, where "beings of imagination are compelled to show themselves in the same category as actually living mortals." Coverdale may not write the Epic Poem (capitalized like Nature, outdoing her), but he will clear the path for that "future poet" over whom he "will bend unseen": his literary heir, his form of immortality. "They will have a great public hall, in which your portrait, and mine, and twenty other faces that are living now, shall be hung up.... Though our posterity will really be far stronger than ourselves, after several generations of a simple, natural, and active life.... In the course of ages, we must all figure heroically in an Epic Poem; and we will ourselves—at least, I will—bend unseen over the future poet, and lend him inspiration, while he writes it." Hollingsworth accuses Coverdale of complete nonsense, aligning this moment with the preface's cautionary words against confusing the "creatures of [one's] brain" with "the actual events of real lives." As the author of the preface repeats, Brook Farm is not Blithedale; Hawthorne is not Coverdale; and real bodies in the present and the past do not belong in the same category as the "imaginary progeny" of some fantasized future. The imagined must be held apart as such, from the actually alive and their real claims to legitimate personhood.[23]

The preface recedes and Coverdale's story begins, with Blithedale represented as an embryonic entity. Murdering in the name of its life, Coverdale establishes a variation on Manifest Destiny, even as he acknowledges that nation building exacts a heavy price and betrays no limits. In parentheses, inside the Fauntleroy chapter (the setting of which is "one of the middle states") in a telescoping inwardness, Coverdale writes, "Society (unless it should change its entire constitution for this man's unworthy sake) neither could nor ought to pardon" Fauntleroy's ways.[24] Deep inside the book resides this story-within-a-story, in which a bracketed aside communicates the revolution for which the Blithedale experiment should stand, just as in *The House of the Seven Gables* the parentheses split the body of the sentence to undo its message from within, conveying the same imperative for the society and its constitution. The word "constitution" is of course the brainchild of the founding fathers, misconceived and regenerative of slavery and empire building.

The pro-procreative reach of the American empire extends itself into Coverdale's compulsive representation of ontological hierarchies and patriarchal conceptions. Throughout the novel, he repeatedly represents his ideas as generative sparks that penetrate his mind from the spiritual realm or to which he gives birth. "I had conceived the idea," he says at one point, in a kind of redundant duplication of the same thing. And, at least twice, he quotes Zenobia opening sentences with the words, "I cannot conceive," subtly denigrating her mind's ability and her body's ostensibly maternal purpose.[25] The threads come together when Coverdale sees his colleagues' reform movements as misconceptions forming inside their minds, in contradistinction to his utopianism.

"I began to long for a catastrophe," he admits. "If the noble temper of Hollingsworth's soul were doomed to be utterly corrupted by the too powerful purpose, which had grown out of what was noblest in him; if the rich and generous qualities of Zenobia's womanhood might not save her; if Priscilla must perish by her tenderness and faith, so simple and so devout;—then let it be so! Let it all come!"[26] The central clash between Coverdale and Hollingsworth, I maintain, involves far more than the broken bond of an intense, homoerotic friendship. It is symbolized by Coverdale as Hollingsworth's abortion of Coverdale's nascent and imaginary empire.

When Coverdale learns of Hollingsworth's plan to redirect Zenobia's money through Priscilla to his reform project, he speaks in horror about the "new life" undone and the "mortal existence" threatened by it: "'And have you no regrets,' I inquired, 'in overthrowing this fair system of our new life, which has been planned so deeply, and is now beginning to flourish so hopefully around us? How beautiful it is, and, so far as we can yet see, how practicable! The Ages have waited for us, and here we are—the very first that have essayed to carry on our mortal existence, in love, and mutual help! Hollingsworth, I would be loth to take the ruin of this enterprise upon my conscience!'"[27] Blithedale is a prophesied birth in this outburst, its gestation just underway and anticipated by the Ages, temporally pregnant with and awaiting "us." So idealized, its uprooting (of what is "now beginning to flourish") denies him the metaphoric paternity through which he immortalizes his name.

Coverdale experiences Hollingsworth's words as being "penetrated ... with his own conception" and forced into an inferior position. A "pregnant silence" follows their conversation.[28] The line of associations through an embryo's soul to a white America steadily runs through the novel, connecting patriarchal connotations of the word "conceiving" both to the immaterial nature of thought and to the spiritual role of insemination in reproduction. Of all the possessions mentioned and passed around in the novel—from Zenobia's hair ornament and inheritance to Priscilla and her purses—the most valuable one is the soul, conferred from a male god at conception through men and made evident by men in art. What matters is what originates in, imitates, and returns to an eternal realm of thinking and being. When Coverdale describes Westervelt as being "of time," he means it as a grave insult, consigning Westervelt to the realm of other animals, nature, and decay.[29]

The genealogical chain between humanity and divinity that breaks in both *The Scarlet Letter* and *The House of the Seven Gables* likewise crumbles in *The Blithedale Romance* but only at the edges of the terrified narrator's consciousness. Coverdale's fear of being seen as insignificant intensifies into a fear of being abandoned in a godless universe. "I was beginning to lose the sense of what kind of a world it was," he confesses. "Our great globe floated in the atmosphere of infinite space like an unsubstantial bubble.

No sagacious man will long retain his sagacity, if he live exclusively among reformers and progressive people, without periodically returning into the settled system of things, to correct himself by a new observation from that old stand-point."[30] Coverdale's readjustment to the world requires reasserting his idealism, repudiating materialism, and scoffing feminism.

Coverdale starts with Zenobia's resistance to maternity. He repeatedly brings the archetype of Eve into focus in order to establish Zenobia's worth solely as a reproductive entity. That she resembles Eve, he says, is "born of a thought that passes between men and women." When Coverdale looks at Zenobia, he sees a perfect specimen of the breed who wants no part of its perpetuation. "I wanted a clear path," she says. But the simplicity for Coverdale of "having nobody but myself to care for" is a revolutionary ambition for Zenobia.[31] A clear path means an unobstructed one, with nothing or nobody in the way. Coverdale then envelopes Zenobia in the secrets of women, hinting that her independence has something to do with concealment, a word that runs through the novel, marking almost every chapter in which Zenobia appears. His insinuations of abortion and infanticide have no bearing in reality, except to point to the body buried inside Coverdale's own story as an actual murder.

By introducing the ghostly Priscilla in the way that he does, withholding for pages and pages that she is Zenobia's half sister, Coverdale further implicates Zenobia in secrecy and deception. In the atmosphere of his romance's "phantasmagorical antics," Priscilla's mysterious nature (a "sprite," "another kind of creature," "ghost-child," "a gentle parasite," "a figure in a dream") and unexpected arrival at Blithedale read like the haunting of a mother by an abandoned child or even a fetus. Not only does Priscilla "tak[e] shape" there—her smile "like a baby's first one"—but she exhibits some strange umbilical link to Zenobia. Appearing out of Hollingsworth's coat like a magician's trick, or "fall[ing] from the clouds" like a stork's package, she goes straight to Zenobia, only to be thrown off. "You have been my evil fate," Zenobia tells her.[32] Even if the reality of Priscilla's relationship to Zenobia lies elsewhere, the story that plays out around them involves Zenobia's failed maternal instincts toward Priscilla. Once Moodie discovers this failure from his paternal point of view, he viciously turns on Zenobia, waving his phallic walking stick and rewriting his will. Because Coverdale discloses the nature of Moodie's connection to Zenobia in his own time, he pushes us to read Zenobia's punishment as righteously delivered by every single

CHAPTER SIX

father surrounding her, from the founding fathers of Blithedale (Coverdale and Hollingsworth) and her biological father to God himself.

At the same time as Coverdale admits to spinning most of this romance out of conjecture, he asserts that what he knows or intuits arrives from a spiritual realm outside of his body. This representation of thought becomes increasingly sinister and turns him into an agent of god's wrath. A concept "strangely forces itself upon [him]" and intuitions "impel" him, he says, "often against my own will." They arrive in the same way as offspring are conceived, "from the beneficent hand of God," as he is sure to remind us, but they read like rape. The effect of these descriptions is cumulative, turning Coverdale's mind into a receptacle of an immaterial agent and his body into its physical activation. "Our souls, after all, are not our own," he remarks, the proof of which occurs as "our abortive effort to resume an exclusive sway over ourselves" when god pulls the strings.[33]

Casting himself as the instrument of a higher force, Coverdale returns Zenobia's soul to its original lender. He is just the middleman in an inevitable transaction, he subtly pleads. Backhandedly confessing to Westervelt at Zenobia's graveside, he contends that Providence's "holy hand" makes perfect sense of her death. Coverdale says, "And there was a secret burthen on her, the nature of which is best known to you. Young as she was, she had tried to live fully, had no more to hope, and something, perhaps to fear. Had Providence taken her away in its own holy hand, I should have thought it the kindest dispensation that could be awarded to one so wrecked."[34] He loads his sentences with connotations that Zenobia combined abortion and suicide by drowning with her "secret burthen."

Coverdale also takes the principal image of encasement in preformationist embryology and argues that by killing Zenobia he simply sends Zenobia back through those layers to God. In effect, by choking her, he does her a favor, especially if she dies while kneeling in prayer:

> One hope I shared; and that, too, was mingled half with fear. She knelt, as if in prayer. With the last, choking consciousness, her soul, bubbling out through her lips, it may, had given it up to the Father, reconciled and penitent. But her arms! They were bent before her, as if she struggled against Providence in never-ending hostility. Her hands! They were clenched in immitigable defiance. Away with the hideous thought! The flitting moment, after Zenobia sank into the

dark pool—when her breath was gone, and her soul at her lips—was as long, in its capacity of God's infinite forgiveness, as the lifetime of the world.[35]

Bent forever into the fetal position, Zenobia's final "bubbling" exhalation imitates her first inhalation in the world. Liberating her soul from her body, Coverdale intimates that this is the only form of emancipation worth worrying about for women. Zenobia, her mind once "fitly cased" in her body but "full of weeds," is now divided and redistributed between God and Nature.[36]

According to Barbara Stafford, exploring what she calls the "*imperium* of the soul over the body*,*" preformationism marks the history of philosophy and medicine precisely where conceiving doubles as the act of thinking and procreating. Under the tenets of preformationism, "disembodied embryonic thoughts" precede embodiment in expression, logically mirroring the manifestation of spirit by body at conception. For Stafford, "utopian idealization [follows from] the polemic concerning the nature of reproduction [and] abstract perfection": an idea, like a soul, remains distinct from matter, even as it sets into motion material events. The endeavor of art is to come as close to spiritual perfection as possible. Thus, a "malformed idea" resembles a "premature birth," something gone awry when spirit comes into contact with the inferior realm of matter.[37]

Running contrary to the preformationist schools, epigenetic and other materialist philosophers debated the nature of classification, hybrid species, and corporeal defects, their theories crucial to developments in natural history and comparative embryology. For instance, Karl Ernst von Baer, in his monumental study *On the Development of Animals* (1828), illuminated a common stage of embryonic growth across animal species, famously asserting that entities developed through layers of tissue and self-existent energies and not out of preexisting forms.[38] According to historian Adrian Desmond, conservative scientists responded to such claims as atheistic, working hard throughout the rest of the nineteenth century to cast their rivals' research and findings as developments in extremist evolutionary thought. Desmond explains their vehement reaction as that of an aristocratic class repudiating any reduction of "man to a lowly parentage." High in a hierarchy themselves, they spoke for and traced divine designs in the natural world. Pointing to the ability to imagine archetypes and exempla, they asserted the separation of mind and matter, as well as the superiority of humans over other animals, in an "apotheosis of the animal structure."[39]

This system lies behind Coverdale's depictions of the link between the origin of an idea and the origin of life. From truth and man to woman and animals, each remains in its place on a stable scale, each with its own nature, descending toward a closer proximity to matter. And though the four pigs on the Blithedale farm correspond in number with the four protagonists of his tale, Coverdale balks at the possibility of a kinship with them, for they are "buried alive" in their soulless flesh.[40] Only radical materialists, the likes of whom the self-described conservative despises, attempt to smash the ranks that hold men above women, humans above other animals, sentience above the mud in which other creatures wallow.

When Coverdale finds himself confronted with this point of view in the Boston lecture halls and theaters, he remarks, "It is unutterable, the horror and disgust with which I listened, and saw, that, if these things were to be believed, the individual soul was virtually annihilated, and all that is sweet and pure, in our present life, debased, and that the idea of man's eternal responsibility was made ridiculous, and immortality rendered, at once, impossible, and not worth acceptance. But I would have perished on the spot, sooner than believe it." Among the horrors Coverdale lists within the scope of materialism is the mesmerist's ability to distort what he claims is stable to human nature, such as maternal and heterosexual love in women. It produces the kind of woman, as he says with dismay, who "thrusts away her child," even when lactating, "with her babe's milk in her bosom," or who expresses little grief for a dead husband and moves on to the next man.[41]

Female reformers similarly destabilize all that is natural, their attacks on society revealing "an instinctive sense of where the life lies, and [are] inclined to aim directly at that spot."[42] Another abortion image, the well-aimed knife extinguishes the "religious sentiment" and puts in its place a "nothingness" that Coverdale apprehends with revulsion.[43] In *The Blithedale Romance,* Hawthorne thus reverses the existential wonder that takes hold in *The House of the Seven Gables,* exploring what it might look like for a character to resist modernity with everything he had, clinging to a paternal god, panicking at the prospect of annihilation.

Coverdale's panic also arises in the places where his self-presentation fails to cover what he sees as his own defective or malformed existence. Despite all of the characteristics that secure him at the top of the nation's hierarchical ordering, he harbors an enigma of self that could, if exposed, bring him crashing down. There is a distinction, he says, between "what is offered to the public, and what is kept for the family." Appealing to God and Nature, he tries to come back from the far edges of the human species to which he feels banished. Even the cows whom he has milked and from whom he demands recognition fail to honor him, chewing their cuds as he throws the "rotten fragment of an old stump" at them. It would seem almost pathetic—Coverdale's moments of ontological anxiety—if it were not for the fact that he keeps "a death-grip" on his sense of white, human supremacy.[44]

"The nation rejuvenates itself," Berlant explains, by making civic identity synonymous with "public heterosexuality [and] reproduction."[45] This is the cover that Blithedale provides, the success of which Coverdale ties to a "posterity ... far stronger than ourselves, after several generations," and the toiling to "the advancement of our race." Through the "romantic story" of "Father Hollingsworth and Uncle Coverdale [painted] in my shirt-sleeves," he projects himself beyond the present, reproduced in art and narrative, bypassing sex with a woman.[46]

According to David Greven, Coverdale's compulsive reflections enact a tragically phobic queerness, a horror at the part of himself that he cannot seem to escape, as it flickers in all of the eyes and mirrors into which he looks. Greven writes, "The subversive energy of *The Blithedale Romance* lies in the manner whereby Hawthorne exposes Coverdale's act of seeming masculine dominance—wielding the gaze, voyeuristically devouring what he sees—as indicative of a hopelessly unsuccessful embodiment of male power. The novel can be read as a critique of developing antebellum forms and theories of American masculinity; an evocation of queer threats to it; and a treatment of the issues of effeminacy that personally plagued Hawthorne."[47] Coverdale's attachment to Blithedale becomes a way of straightening out and saving his soul. For if he experiences his queer identity, in the temporal framework of the novel, as coming under new biopolitical redefinitions, then escaping into the narrative of the nation-state permits him both a cover and a purpose.

Inside its borders, he finds an orientation toward the future and the "children to be born among us," without having to marry a woman. A "crooked stick ... not the easiest to bind up into a faggot," as he says of himself, he remains unsure if it is nature or nurture that makes him so.[48] If Coverdale's story is taken as tragic, then his sense of exile from within Blithedale—always

CHAPTER SIX

on the outskirts of conversations and plans—arises as the exclusion of queer lives from the national project and its forces of legitimacy. Its world does not include his kind. Nonreproductive bodies, Coverdale fears, are perhaps "abortive creatures" themselves.

Although the etymology of "faggot" had not yet arrived at its viciously pejorative definition for "homosexual" of the early twentieth-century, its association with femininity was firmly in place by the time of the novel's inception. Its connotations of queer desire, moreover, point to something about Coverdale without giving him entirely away—an open secret, an invitation to read his bachelorhood in a different light. According to Jordan Stein,

> Style, rather than discourse, could provide the basis for a characterization of *Blithedale* as a queer novel before "homosexuality." A passage like the one with which I began, claiming that the characters' remove to Blithedale "seemed to authorize any individual, of either sex, to fall in love with any other, regardless of what would elsewhere be judged suitable and prudent," only appears to be a frank claim of homosexual desire under conditions where it's possible to imagine "homosexual desire" as a legible libidinal position. The point here is not that there was no "homosexual desire" in 1852 (an unverifiable assertion), but only that such things may not have been adequately legible for this statement to feel frank rather than, say, queer.[49]

Even if "homosexual" had not yet come on the medicolegal scene as an established category, Coverdale not only communicates its internalization but also repeatedly presents marriage as a corollary of social order and inclusion.

Who he is and what he thinks he should do split him down the middle. Where Fauntleroy/Moodie slips into the darkness and illegitimacy that the state produces on the other side of its civic intelligibility, Coverdale moves back and forth between the city's enticements and Blithedale's discipline. Indeed, the story within a story about Fauntleroy/Moodie communicates by indirection what Coverdale stands to lose should he be similarly discovered, which is to say everything. He folds this brief biography into his recollections, as a kind of parenthesis about "empty years" and unspeakable shame, "prodigal expenditure" and "unnatural light."[50] The Moodie biography is his queer interior, to echo Castiglia, burying his knowledge that his wealth and inheritance can be stripped from him.

The Blithedale Romance and Abortion's Conditional Perfect

Coverdale follows Zenobia to Blithedale because he wants to know how she pulls it all off, how it is possible that "the great event of a woman's existence had been consummated, [and] the world knew nothing of it."[51] Gazing on her, he searches for the key to sex without consequence and to sexuality outside of marriage, but private and sheltered. Between abortion, contraception, and infanticide, at one end, and same-sex love, luck, and physiological complication, at the other, the notion of consummation without evidence produces multiple lines of conjecture through her body, none of which includes virginity. "Poor child," says Silas Foster on pulling her from the river. She is a dead child here, not a fallen woman nor the "enigma of the eternal world" for Coverdale to solve.[52]

This enigma accompanies Coverdale's multiple allusions to spiritual incarnation, through which he communicates his belief that eternity intersects with time, human souls with animal bodies. Zenobia is "womanliness incarnated"; "wisdom . . . incarnates itself" at Blithedale; the Deity takes a "mortal and masculine shape." Staring at the painting in the "Old Acquaintance" chapter, for instance, Coverdale observes the representation of meat, the animal flesh that experiences no incarnation. It is a moment that recalls his interactions with the animals at the farm. As art, their flesh is ideally reproduced, brought into affinity with the realm of the soul where time is stilled as eternity. The paintings, he says, emit an "indescribable, ideal charm, [taking] away the grossness from what was fleshiest and fattest, and thus helped the life of man," again asserting this form of creation as superior to childbirth, where flesh and fat confer death as well as life.[53]

Coverdale earlier describes his illness in much the same way, as diminishing his flesh and allowing "the soul to get the better of the body." He describes it as an "avenue between two existences," out of which he crawls (like a baby, through a vaginal or "darksome doorway") and into a second life: "In literal and physical truth, I was quite another man. I had a lively sense of the exultation with which the spirit will enter on the next stage of its eternal progress, after leaving the heavy burthen of its mortality in an earthly grave, with as little concern for what may become of it, as now affected for the flesh which I had lost."[54] With each anecdote, he aims to convince his ideal reader (God, most likely, or himself) that eternity is real and that he prepares his soul for it. Although Hawthorne resurrects the figure of the resolute bachelor in Coverdale, this is not an archivist rummaging in ideas and rethinking the patriarch's will, as the old bachelor does in *The House of the Seven Gables.* Instead, he pushes Coverdale along a different path, as someone particularly vulnerable to the appeal of conservative forces, "neurotically processing," to quote Gale Temple, the changes around him.[55]

Discussing Coverdale's shattering sense of identity, Richard Millington flags two of the novel's quotations and places them in juxtaposition: "Nothing else; nothing but self, self, self" and "But what, after all, have I to tell? Nothing, nothing, nothing!" The first phrase is uttered in anger by Zenobia and the second pondered by Coverdale. Seeing in these phrases striking moments of "cultural diagnosis," particularly of the middle class's self-absorbing emptiness, Millington contends that Coverdale's narrative comprises the composition of a self against "the vicissitudes of identity." While he makes a powerful case for Coverdale's evasion of "some unspoken knowledge," Millington also skirts the edges of what that knowledge is and all of the ways in which Coverdale in fact speaks it. He takes Priscilla's purse, for instance, as an "ideal image of the adequately guarded self,"[56] but it is much more problematic than that, or rather it stands in for the vaginal aperture out of which Coverdale believes the self comes—as destined to be that self, and not contingent on the historical forces that form it. Here, at this entryway into the world, the juxtaposition between self and nothingness in the novel gets underway, moving toward Zenobia's death as Coverdale's ultimate assertion against the potential meaningless of birth. Holding fast to "my poor individual life," he cannot conceive of being alive in terms of the "substantial emptiness, a material ghost" for which Hawthorne's protagonists speak in *The House of the Seven Gables.*[57]

Thus, the misogynist rant that Coverdale attributes to Hollingsworth is also his own, a condensed version of a philosophy he extends across the novel:

> Man is a wretch without woman; but woman is a monster—and, thank Heaven, an almost and hitherto imaginary monster—without man, as her acknowledged principle! As true as I had once a mother, whom I loved, were there any possible prospect of woman's taking the social stand which some of them—poor, miserable abortive creatures, who only dream of such things because they have missed woman's peculiar happiness, or because Nature made them really neither man nor woman!—if there were a chance of their attaining the end which these petticoated monstrosities have in view, I would call upon my own sex to use its physical force, that unmistakeable evidence of sovereignty, to scourge them back within their proper bounds.[58]

The words "monstrosity," "abortive," and "hitherto," as well as the colluding and capitalized pair of "Heaven" and "Nature," are hallmarks of Coverdale's diction, making it difficult to know where he ends and another character begins. His world a hall of mirrors, he searches for his soul and comes up with little more than someone looking at someone else, who is himself looking in a mirror, in infinite regress. If this is the case, then "the beneficent hand of God" again withdraws, as it does in Hawthorne's two previous novels, relegating existence to the purview of the maternal bodies otherwise absent when Coverdale desires "children to be born among us." Immortality is nothing more than a patriarchal story, told to "every mother's son of us," but it propels Coverdale's identification with Blithedale in the same way that Priscilla attaches herself to Zenobia, likewise driven to her by a father's tale.[59]

Of course Coverdale requires a giant uterine hermitage into which he can crawl and reorient his thinking: a "hollow chamber, of rare seclusion," encircled by an arterial kind of vine curling in tendrils between the branches of trees; dark, an "aerial sepulcher of its own leaves"; and easily accessed via a passage between branches that not only "yield" but also "close again" behind him as he crawls upward and into it.[60] This "sepulcher," a word that recurs in relation to it, becomes for Coverdale his private property in the otherwise communal setting, and it symbolizes his individuality, as he describes it. He imagines thrusting his head out from deep within it, to the surprised delight of his companions, as Hawthorne makes sure we catch the vaginal insinuations of the earlier details.

Inside of it, he smokes his cigars in its still atmosphere and daydreams about his "spiritual aspirations," as well as honeymooning with Hollingsworth. At the same time as it is hilariously irreverent, this sketch forms an image par excellence of the pro-life position that one's individuality begins in utero—as the unborn state of a destined birth, set into being by the spark (of a cigar lighter in this case) and carried all the way through to the person contemplating those origins. Inside his leafy womb Coverdale also ponders why "Nature thrusts some of us into the world miserably incomplete" in a moment of reflection about what brings women together with men, why that "yoke" exists.[61]

Investing in Blithedale becomes a kind of eternal-life insurance, a way into immortality and out of emptiness. Thus, when Hollingsworth's reform project threatens to overturn Blithedale as Coverdale conceives of it, he mobilizes

CHAPTER SIX

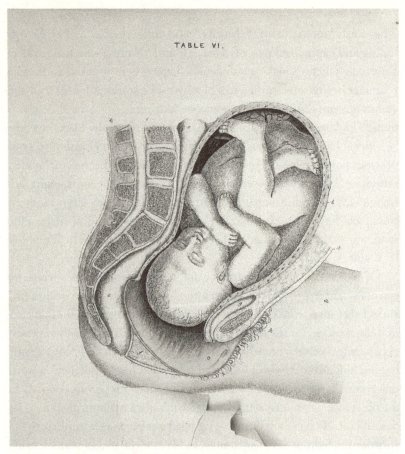

FIGURE 5. George Spratt's *Obstetric Tables, Comprising Graphic Illustrations* (London: Published for the author by John Churchill, 1835). Copyright of the University of Manchester. Used by permission of CC-BY-NC 4.0, https://creativecommons.org/licenses/by-nc/4.0/.

to protect it. The maneuvering is complex, with abortion and birth metaphors underpinning Coverdale's rationale for murdering Zenobia in order to crush Hollingsworth for rendering him purposeless. He also describes Hollingsworth's plan as a choice that cuts into the progression of fate:

> It is enough to say that Hollingsworth once more brought forward his rigid and unconquerable idea; a scheme for the reformation of

the wicked by methods moral, intellectual, and industrial, by the sympathy of pure, humble, and exalted minds, and by opening to his pupils the possibility of a worthier life than that which had become their fate. It appeared, unless he over-estimated his own means, that Hollingsworth held it as his choice (and he did so choose) to obtain possession of the very ground on which we had planted our Community, and which had not yet been made irrevocably ours, by purchase. Our beginnings might readily be adapted to his great end.[62]

By killing Zenobia, Coverdale turns her into an instrument of abortion, controlling the narrative that effects the transformation. He imprints the image of her corpse on Hollingsworth's mind and conscience, not only by showing it to him but also by connecting it to him and his rough usage of her. Coverdale's goal is to get Hollingsworth—whom he casts as the abortionist of Coverdale's Posterity—to perceive himself as a murderer and terminate his own life's work. In a form of quid pro quo, he renders Hollingsworth similarly futureless. And it works. The last scene with Hollingsworth shows him to be propped up by Priscilla, overcome with guilt and impotent.

Coverdale likewise empties out Zenobia's feminism by framing her death as a suicide for a man. When Zenobia earlier accuses Hollingsworth of "flinging her aside ... a broken tool," she employs a metaphor that Coverdale makes literal with her corpse. He shuts down the work of two reformers with one death. Just as Coverdale wraps his words around Zenobia, wringing them of political significance, so he wraps his hands around her neck, forcing her from her literal and metaphoric standing, and into a posture of submission to him. He bends her into an eternally kneeling position, communicating his own reestablished footing in the cosmos: upright, unquestioned, and manly. The feminist who desires an unencumbered, unobstructed existence tilts the world in the direction of the materialists whom Coverdale abhors. Through feminism and materialism, Coverdale shudders, "the individual soul was virtually annihilated."[63]

According to Thomas Strychacz, "Hawthorne strikes a qualitatively different attitude toward allegory in *Blithedale* than in his previous works.... The reader becomes aware that Coverdale [as a first-person narrator] is actively creating fantasies of womanhood derived from his cultural inheritance of art and of patriarchal structures of the home and economy." His brilliant reading of the search for Zenobia's body in the "Midnight" chapter takes him into the "psychopathological aspects" of Coverdale's mind as it projects on and distorts everything he sees, including the otherwise natural imagery of the river. Highlighting Hollingsworth's "hooked pole" and Silas's rake (as "he pok[es] it as far as he could into the water"), Strychacz shows the extent to which Coverdale's rage is at work in the scene, in language that gestures toward a "bizarre and vicious rape." Hawthorne places the river pool, Strychacz points out, next to a "stump," which Strychacz takes to be symbolic of impotency or diseased male potency. It makes sense that what the men pull out of the water or deliver is therefore a corpse, death instead of a living body. "The search for Zenobia," he says, "[occurs] in terms of a perverted form of birth, or abortion."[64]

To add to Strychacz's reading, the words "born" and "bore" also occur throughout the chapter—"the drift of the stream had again borne us"; we "bore her out"; "we bore Zenobia"; "we bore our burthen"; "I have borne it"—and follow from the powerful image of a crouching corpse hooked and pulled from a watery tomb.[65] The phrases come together to portray Coverdale as laboring with the prototype of the drowned Ophelia, which he then wishes to deliver to Hollingsworth. Confronted with a horrifyingly bent body, Coverdale's conceiving fails, however, to materialize in reality. And the awfulness of rigor mortis chronicles a very different account of the corpse's coming into being.

Throughout the novel, Coverdale narrates in nostalgia, hoping to restore a genealogical connection to "the Pilgrims, whose high enterprise ... we had taken up, and were carrying it onward and aloft, to a point which they never dreamed of attaining." Killing in the name of this "high enterprise," so that what the Pilgrims "dreamed of" or conceived in the past is birthed in the future, becomes a gestational imperative for those who see themselves as the Pilgrims' purest descendants in the present. To paraphrase Coverdale, white America originates with the first settlers as an embryonic and divinely sparked nation, the life of which must be protected, "carried onward," and made manifest in the future. "The first-born child is yet to come!" Coverdale announces, in the same speech that anticipates the first death, as a form of martyrdom, sanctifying the ground.[66] Almost every reverie of Coverdale's involves a man, his wife, and his children, repeatedly cast through spectral idealizations, as "yet to come into existence," or long dead but "coming out of their chill graves" in some kind of ghostly rebirth.[67] Heterosexual, implicitly white, and reproductive, it is this family unit that makes America great again and again. Spaces must be cleared for this genealogical line to perpetutate itself, according to conservatives like Coverdale. Because he does not contribute to its sexual reproduction, he offers instead its textual reproduction, spinning white America into an "atmosphere of strange enchantment." The realities of colonialist wars in these spaces, systematically wiping out Indigenous worlds and expanding into slave states, make their way into Coverdale's consciousness, even as he tries to hold them at bay.[68] The idealized "high enterprise" of America involves, in reality, livestock production and plantation agriculture, the problems Coverdale glimpses when he stares at the pigs and cows on the Blithedale land.

According to Gillian Brown, Coverdale takes pleasure in looking in order to occupy at a safe distance from intimate contact with the world. Enacting "a consumerism without buying," he displaces his desires, especially when he feels moved into Hollingsworth's orbit and feminized as a result. "Visual pleasure in certain objects," Brown explains, "defends against a homoerotic attachment. . . . A dead woman's shoe marks the horizon of an individuality vested in femininity as she vitiates the female." Zenobia's shoe, as Brown intricately interprets it, "substitutes for the woman who substitutes for the man." Coverdale holds on to it, "all these years," warding off the castration anxiety that fetish objects also evoke.[69]

The shoe is also a piece of evidence lifted from a crime scene, where four footprints occur at the riverside, not two. As John McELroy and Edward McDonald contend, in the only essay to date that directly names Coverdale a murderer, Coverdale's story distorts justice and displaces desire: "Leaving aside for the moment the fanciful metaphor of Zenobia struggling against Providence, the posture of this rigor mortis is that of a person forced to her knees by an overpowering adversary standing in front of her and applying a choking force, while she, her hands clenched to the assailant's wrists, tried with all her to stop him from choking her. . . . By strangling Zenobia 'Judge Coverdale' meted out 'justice' to a 'fallen woman' who disdained his affection, and he also punished her lover, whose life is destroyed by guilt for her death."[70] This conclusion discomfits them, even as they establish it, mainly because Coverdale's motive is more intricate than they take it to be. At one point, McElroy and McDonald contend that it is possible to see Zenobia's death as a suicide, overturning their argument entirely.

Beverly Hume also contends that the issue "is not whether Coverdale literally murders Zenobia" but that he uses his narrative as a metaphorical

CHAPTER SIX

weapon to both create and cover up his homicidal longings. Hume argues that seeking out a literal level of meaning or a literal murder does a disservice to the great ambiguities of Hawthorne's prose, asserting too that forensic pathology was a "young science in the early-nineteenth century."[71] But everything about Zenobia's corpse points to a murder on the shore, cutting through Coverdale's insistence on suicide by drowning.

Forensic pathology and medical jurisprudence were highly developed fields by the mid-nineteenth century, in almost all areas, from the chemical identification of different poisons in bodily organs to the precise detection of drowning as a cause of death, including how to determine whether or not a person discovered in a river had been murdered on land. In 1810, Benjamin Rush taught the subject at the University of Pennsylvania and published his lectures in 1811. Theodric Beck's *Elements of Medical Jurisprudence* was in its tenth edition in 1850, two years before the publication of *The Blithedale Romance*. That Beck included his brother John's work on abortion as a subsection of his "Infanticide" chapter is significant in the development of antebellum positions on terminated pregnancies.

The excerpt illustrates John Beck's detailed approach to infanticide, including the ways in which "infanticide" shifts as a term into "feticide" and "abortion" across the chapter's categories. Together with chapters 5, 6, and 7, on the subjects of rape, pregnancy, and delivery, the weight of the book lies with the crimes committed against and by women. Along with the other chapters, each centers on the means by which one thing can be passed off as another: a murder for a suicide; a pregnancy faked for money; an abortion passed off as a miscarriage. Medical jurisprudence, as far as the Becks were concerned, was a field committed to shining a hard light on bodies in order to differentiate between unreliable and reliable testimony, fiction and truth, especially with regard to two main issues: justice for the so-called unborn, and protection against fraudulent inheritance claims. Who or what one professes to be (say, a virgin, or a member of a particular family) could be ascertained or verified by the readable corporeal signs meticulously represented in their writing.

Toward the end of the infanticide chapter, Theodric Beck imagines this scenario: "That a young female of character and reputable connexions and possessed of tender sensibility may have been betrayed by the arts of a base seducer, and when reduced to a state of pregnancy, to avoid the disgrace which must otherwise be her lot, may stifle the birth in the womb, or after

CHAPTER VIII.

INFANTICIDE.

BY JOHN B. BECK, M.D., ETC., OF NEW YORK.

PART I.—History of Infanticide, as it has prevailed in various nations, ancient and modern. PART II.—Fœticide, or criminal abortion —The period of gestation when a child ought to be considered as alive.—Signs of fœticide deduced from an examination of the female.—Where the death of the female follows the abortion.—Anatomical examination of the parts after death.—Hydatids and moles considered as occasioning all these signs.—Signs of fœticide deduced from an examination of the substance expelled from the female.—Modes in which fœticide is perpetrated.—Involuntary causes of abortion.—Circumstantial evidence.—Murder of the child after it is born alive.—Of the age of the child.—Of the child born alive without respiring.—Of the child born alive and respiring.—Proofs of the latter.—1. Proofs drawn from the respiratory organs.—Configuration and size of the thorax—situation of the lungs—their volume—their shape—their consistency or density—their absolute weight.—The static test.—Ploucquet's test.—The specific gravity of the lungs.—The hydrostatic test.—Consideration of objections to it.—Rules for applying the hydrostatic test.—2. Proofs drawn from the circulation.—Difference between the blood of the fœtus and of the child after respiration.—Peculiarities in the organs of circulation before and after respiration—the foramen ovale—the ductus arteriosus—the ductus venosus—the umbilical vessels—the cord.—3. Proofs drawn from the abdominal organs—the liver—the intestines—the bladder.—Consideration of the general objection to these proofs, that a child may respire and yet may die before it is fully born.—General inferences in relation to the foregoing proofs.—Modes of perpetrating infanticide.—Accidental modes in which a child's life may be lost.—Congenital malformations.—Congenital diseases.—Circumstantial evidence—Method of conducting examinations in cases of infanticide.—Cases and illustrations. PART III.—Of infanticide in its relations to medical police.—Laws against it in different nations.—Foundling hospitals.—List of American and British cases of infanticide.

FIGURE 6. "Infanticide" chapter from Theodric Romeyn Beck and John Beck's *Elements of Medical Jurisprudence*, 11th ed. (Philadelphia: J. B. Lippincott, 1860).

CHAPTER SIX

it is born, in a state of phrenzy, imbrue her hands in her infant's blood, in the expectation of throwing the mantle of oblivion over her crime."[72] It is possible to compare this portrait with Zenobia's, particularly as Coverdale paints it. He seems to bank on his reader's familiarity with an anecdote such as this one. And if the "mantle of oblivion" may be reworded as a "veil," one of the key images of *The Blithedale Romance,* then Coverdale further implicates Zenobia's secrets in the kinds of crimes that forensics tried to make clear: "So young as I beheld her, and the freshest and rosiest woman of a thousand, there was certainly no need of imputing to her a destiny already accomplished; the probability was far greater that her coming years had all life's richest gifts to bring. If the great event of a woman's existence had been consummated, the world knew nothing of it, although the world seemed to know Zenobia well."[73] Somewhere between the "destiny already accomplished" and the "probability" that it has not, Zenobia hides her past, moving through the world just outside of Coverdale's narrative reach.

Joel Pfister's lucid claim, that throughout Hawthorne's oeuvre, men use women as the raw material of their fantasies,[74] highlights the extent to which the image of the fallen woman serves both Coverdale's confessional narrative (as his crime's rationalization) and his intricately fashioned revenge plot (in a straightforward appeal to Hollingsworth's own misogyny). Purposely visiting Hollingsworth in the penultimate chapter, Coverdale checks to see if his plot succeeds or fails:

> Priscilla threw me an upbraiding glance. But I spoke again, with a bitter and revengeful emotion, as if flinging a poisoned arrow at Hollingsworth's heart.
>
> "Up to this moment," I inquired, "how many criminals have you reformed?"
>
> "Not one!" said Hollingsworth, with his eyes still fixed on the ground. "Ever since we parted, I have been busy with a single murderer!"
>
> Then the tears gushed into my eyes, and I forgave him. For I remembered the wild energy, the passionate shriek, with which Zenobia had spoken those words—"Tell him he had murdered me! Tell him that I'll haunt him!"—and I knew what murderer he meant, and whose vindictive shadow dogged the side where Priscilla was not.[75]

Coverdale's tears do not gush for either Hollingsworth or Zenobia. If they flow out of a sense of forgiveness, it is for Hollingsworth's theft of Coverdale's investment in Blithedale, not for Zenobia's murder. The tears arrive as a kind of substitute consummation, following the thrill of the realization that his death blow hits the mark inside Hollingsworth's conscience.

Coverdale closes the chapter moralizing and crowing that Nature takes Zenobia's body "without a sigh or complaint" or rivalry with God over her soul. And though *The Blithedale Romance* seems to end there, with Coverdale surprisingly announcing that he been has been standing near Zenobia's grave the entire time, it extends into one more chapter. "There is one secret—I have concealed it all along," Coverdale announces, as he invites or entices his reader to back up through the pages in search of the moments when this secret's concealment might show itself.[76] This retrospective movement is significant because it is the same one that Hawthorne subtly directs us to undertake in the previous two novels, such as when the old bachelor in *The House of the Seven Gables* reads his family's history and decides to right its wrongs, or when the narrator of *The Scarlet Letter* reminds us that the country's graves carry the story he fails to tell.[77] In each case, the dead once existed, leaving footprints and graves in the soil. The unborn leave traces only if noted by those who carry them or by those who seek them out, armed with medical technology and legislation.

With *The Blithedale Romance*, Hawthorne reflects on John O'Sullivan's 1839 call in "The Great Nation of Futurity" for a representative writer committed to "propagating and extending [America] through present and future": "Why cannot our literati comprehend the matchless sublimity of our position amongst the nations of the world—our high destiny—and cease bending the knee to foreign idolatry, false tastes, false doctrines, false principles? When will they be inspired by the magnificent scenery of our own world, imbibe the fresh enthusiasm of a new heaven and a new earth, and soar upon the expanded wings of truth and liberty?"[78] With an eye on the past that O'Sullivan fails to mention, Hawthorne offers Coverdale, whose embrace of epic archetypes draws murderous energies from him, and whose existence and wealth are never traced back to any sources in labor or records of inheritance. Veiling his history, Coverdale fits the bill of a spokesman for virgin land and the fertility of white womanhood. Because through this lens, American borders have nothing to do with territory and plantations, and

CHAPTER SIX

whiteness has nothing to do with race. Everything falls away, including the actualities of gestation and childbirth from the meaning of life.

Hawthorne positions a feminist within this wider national story in order to explore the modes by which it buries her philosophy of existence. Inside Coverdale's pages, she is already dead, but the retrospective narrative returns her to the land of the living, not just as a distortion of Coverdale's memory but also as something his guilt demands of him. In other words, it is possible to heed what she says while alive specifically from within the genre of a confession because he tries to come clean through it. Tangled together with his duplicity are glimpses of a reckoning with the materialism and feminism that animated Zenobia before he kills her. They float in his consciousness along with the image of her corpse, as forms of tangibility from which he recoils into idealism.

Contrasting fate with choice in a discussion about maternity, he recalls Zenobia asking, "How can [a woman] be happy, after discovering that fate has assigned her but one single event, which she must contrive to make the substance of her whole life? A man has his choice of innumerable events"—to which Coverdale responds, "A woman, I suppose, by constant repetition of her one event, may compensate for the lack of variety."[79] His retort comes across as comical by virtue of its lewd connotations, but it is treacherous. It sums up the ideology through which destiny takes the form of her dispossession, in a direct reflection of the dispossession that arrives from her past with Moodie, hemming her in between a divine father and an actual father, both prepared to punish her.

Coverdale then shifts the notion of choice from Zenobia's repudiation of maternity into the act of suicide she ostensibly commits, out of her own free will. She "fall[s] on her own sword," he lies, in a telling and imperial metaphor for the penetration to which he finds her body particularly suited. He justifies killing her by turning her body into a fertile medium in the ground. Zenobia "bequeath[s] us no earthly representative," but she yields "a crop of weeds" through Nature's ever-productive womb.[80] If we resist being comforted by Coverdale's stale metaphors, the plantation beneath Nature's skirts materializes along with the horror of American expansionism.

In a compelling turn, however, Hawthorne reimagines Zenobia's story, this time through Westervelt and in the form of the conditional perfect: "What an actress Zenobia might have been! It was one of her least valuable capabilities. How forcibly she might have wrought upon the world, either directly in her own person, or by her influence upon some man or a series of men, of controlling genius! Every prize that could be worth a woman's having—and many prizes which other women are too timid to desire—lay within Zenobia's reach. . . . She would soon have established a control over [her heart] and loved again."[81] With a "might have been" for Zenobia, he frees her momentarily from her enclosure in Coverdale's unbearable version of things and conceives of her as acting in and on the world, not pressed into it. It is not moderation or abstinence that he contemplates for her either, but rather partnerships with a "series of men" and prizes that do not connote offspring. Promiscuity and sex work may be insinuated here, but potential and love make their ways in too, all of which break from the oppression that marriage and pregnancy exemplified for Zenobia. As Poe does with Marie Rogêt, Hawthorne shifts Zenobia into a space over which God and Nature do not preside and where the artistry of her existence expresses itself in delicate outlines, like a signature signed in chalk.

CONCLUSION

> Loth to confess, unable to conceal.
> —Virgil *The Aeneid,* book 6, "The Underworld"

Toward the end of *The House of the Seven Gables,* Hawthorne's narrator reflects on the tree in front of the Pyncheon house and conjures up the golden bough in Virgil's *Aeneid.* Alluding to its function in book 6, in which the Cumaean Sibyl helps Aeneas descend into Hades, he imagines obtaining access to a hidden and dangerous realm of knowledge: "This aged tree appeared to have suffered nothing from the gale. It had kept its boughs unshattered, and its full complement of leaves; and the whole in perfect verdure, except a single branch, that, by the earlier change with which the elm-tree sometimes prophesies the autumn, had been transmuted to bright gold. It was like the golden branch that gained Aeneas and the Sibyl admittance into Hades."[1] The tree signifies the opposite of gold's resistance to decay here, as it points toward the dying at the heart of its living leaves, the surrounding verdure made possible only by seasonal cycles. In *The Aeneid,* Aeneas seizes the golden bough in order to make contact with the dead, urged along by Apollo's voice, for which the Sibyl acts as its medium.

The underground temple through which Aeneas passes existed in reality, having been carved into the base of a mountainside in Naples centuries earlier. Virgil did not see it for himself but he describes it in accurate terms, drawing on the stories of those who did descend into its dark and sacrosanct world. Here it is, in John Dryden's 1697 translation of *The Aeneid,* along with Dryden's penchant for parentheses:

> A spacious cave, within its farmost part,
> Was hew'd and fashion'd by laborious art
> Thro' the hill's hollow sides: before the place,
> A hundred doors a hundred entries grace;
> As many voices issue, and the sound
> Of Sybil's words as many times rebound
> Now to the mouth they come. Aloud she cries:
> "This is the time; enquire your destinies

He comes; behold the god!" Thus while she said,
(And shiv'ring at the sacred entry stay'd).²

In the sixth century, the cave's entrance was destroyed and the temple consigned to oblivion, but it was rediscovered in 1932 and is now open to visitors. Neither Hawthorne nor Poe would have known of its existence in reality, except as it was represented in mythic accounts and associated with propitiations to Laverna.

The cave is as striking as Virgil describes it to be, although he exaggerates the number of doors. A series of trapezoid-shaped archways leads to the Sibyl's room, which is off to the left and at the very end of the temple; the arches resemble keyholes or mouths, and the acoustics are formidable. All manner of calculations of lunar cycles remain inscribed into a rock surface near the well-worn stairway into the temple. They denote attention to menstrual cycles and reproductive rites.

It is telling, in the context of women's secrets, that T. S. Eliot places the Cumaean Sibyl at the opening to *The Waste Land,* not in her splendor but rather outwitted by Apollo and pleading to die from within a tiny bottle. The epigraph that contains her mournful voice is followed by Eliot's antiabortion epic, in which a fortune-teller appears alongside women who discuss abortion and false teeth, all of whom materialize in relation to a barren landscape parched and longing for rain. It rains at the end of *The House of the Seven Gables* too, but from a sky where no heavenly father exists for the novel's protagonists. If the rain that falls in Hawthorne's novel signifies cleansing and renewal, it is emetic, like an abortifacient, not baptismal.

By metaphorically placing the Cumaean Sibyl at the entrance to a house emptied of a paternal god, Hawthorne draws attention to it as a pathway into the past where women's secrets reside. This realm is at once threatening and threatened, subtractive of life and subject to misinterpretation. Like the fortune-tellers' residence on the Rue Morgue in Poe's tale, the seven-gabled house is breached by those who want access to what the women try to keep safe and out of sight. Aeneas's humble request to enter the Sibyl's domain in Virgil's story does not furnish a pattern for Dupin and Jaffrey as they assert their rights to take what they want.

And yet Hawthorne's allusion to Aeneas obtaining entry from the Sibyl carries his irony through to the end. His narrator notes, "This one mystic branch hung down before the main entrance of the Seven Gables, so nigh

CONCLUSION

the ground that any passer-by might have stood on tiptoe and plucked it off. Presented at the door, it would have been a symbol of his right to enter, and be made acquainted with all the secrets of the house."[3] At the same time as "the secrets of the house" open up, they are potentially drawn into the light where propaganda likewise shines. It is not so glorious that Aeneas receives the Sibyl's permission to pass into the Underworld; her mysteries are subsumed by the narrative of the founding of Rome, the empire that emerged out of rape and slavery.

Poe's classical allusions work in similar ways, incorporating glimmers of rituals surrounding women's realms that are also subject to distortion. Dupin sullies Laverna's name by uttering it, but Poe also delivers her to us, renewed or cleansed by her association with the laundress who protects the L'Espanaye women's privacy.[4] Throughout his trilogy, Poe makes references to myths and symbols—the Gordian knot; Theseus's thread—in order to demonstrate how their ancient meanings and ambiguous curvatures are stiffened into patriarchal narratives of conquest and hierarchy. Like Hawthorne's, his fiction provides us with routes back into spaces of knowledge where unyielding hierarchies of life dissolve into older correspondences among the living and in conversation with the dead. We are asked to pay close attention, not only as a form of suspicion by which their unreliable narrators might be detected but also in terms of widening their tales' frames of reference and knowledge.

Reviewing Hawthorne's work in 1847, Poe proposed that he aim to write comprehensible prose once in a while:

> [Hawthorne] has the purest style, the finest taste, the most available scholarship, the most delicate humor, the most touching pathos, the most radiant imagination, the most consummate ingenuity; and with these varied good qualities he has done *well* as a mystic. But is there any one of these qualities which should prevent his doing doubly as well in a career of honest, upright, sensible, prehensible, and comprehensible things? Let him mend his pen, get a bottle of visible ink, come out from the Old Manse, cut Mr. Alcott, hang (if possible) the editor of "The Dial," and throw out of the window to the pigs all his odd numbers of "The North American Review."[5]

CONCLUSION

This reference to writing in invisible ink reflects on a mode of popular entertainment and political intrigue in the eighteenth and nineteenth centuries. A medium of concealment and communication, invisible ink makes for a fascinating correlation with the oblique tactics of abortion's advertising in the 1800s: imperceptible to those unfamiliar with the means by which the messages become clear.

At the same time, the notion of something latent surfacing into visibility—in the way that a parchment held against a flame makes manifest the words penned in invisible ink—also seems to lie behind the powerful image of Manifest Destiny as John O'Sullivan saw it. To quote once more from his 1839 "Nation of Futurity": "The far-reaching, the boundless future will be the era of American greatness. In its magnificent domain of space and time, the nation of many nations is destined to manifest to mankind the excellence of divine principles; to establish on earth the noblest temple ever dedicated to the worship of the Most High."[6] A providential map exists, as he implies here, and it is up to white Americans to make its already-written legend readable on the surface of the continent and its principles reproducible into the future. Poe and Hawthorne, as I argue in this book, turn against this rhetoric in their fiction, by making the slavery and land grabs latent in this map equally available for manifestation and by repeatedly terminating destiny's plotlines.

In *Abortion in America*, James Mohr quotes in full an 1847 Massachusetts law designed to criminalize the very hint of making abortion's availability possible for a pregnant person. It is one sentence in length:

> Whoever knowingly advertises, prints, publishes, distributes or circulates, or knowingly causes to be advertised, printed, published, distributed or circulated, any pamphlet, book, newspaper, notice, advertisement or reference, containing words or language giving or conveying any notice, hint, or reference to any person, or to the name of any person, real or fictious; from whom, or to any place, house, shop or office where any poison, drug, mixture, preparation, medicine or noxious thing, or any instrument or means whatever, or any advice, direction, information, or knowledge, may be obtained for the purpose of causing or procuring the miscarriage of a woman pregnant with child or preventing, or which is represented

CONCLUSION

as intended to prevent pregnancy, shall be punished by imprisonment in the state prison for not more than three years or in jail for not more than two and one half years or by a fine of not more than one thousand dollars.[7]

The breathless intensity of the drive to cover all the bases indicates the lexical dexterity of abortionists and their clients as they claimed control over their reproductive bodies and practices. It reveals the extent to which information about abortion circulated in the 1840s and how attempts to drive it underground only inspired more sophisticated forms of circumlocution and doublespeak. Resisting the call to contribute to a nationalist literature fitting of a new empire, Poe and Hawthorne took a page from the abortionist's handbook and crafted devious narratives in which appeals to god and nation hide the opposite message from one angle of light and disclose it from another.

Notes

Preface

1. See Judith Ranta's *Women and Children of the Mills: An Annotated Guide to Nineteenth-Century American Textile Fiction* (Westport, CT: Greenwood Press, 1999) for an overview of the approximately ten ballads and tales that address or allude to abortion the 1830s, 1840s, and 1850s.
2. This was the phrase used at the trial of Lindsey Ingalls, an abortionist who raped Elvira Mitchell in 1847, and was found guilty. For excerpts of the *Capital Trial of Dr. Lindsey A. Ingalls, of Lowell, Mass., for a Rape*, see Ranta (*Women and Children*, 121–22).
3. Eliza Richards, *Gender and the Poetics of Reception in Poe's Circle* (Cambridge: Cambridge University Press, 2004), 52. I want to note from the start that I replicate the words "men" and "women" in this book, but only for ease of reference, often substituting "pregnant people" for "pregnant women." I do not wish to exclude trans women and men from the terminology or experiences attendant on "men" and "women" or to imply that sexual reproduction is implicit to the reality of these words. Cis-gendered individuals, in addition, are not the only subjects harmed by reproductive ideology and are not the only individuals who resist and/or embrace sexual reproduction.
4. Thomas Low Nichols and Mary Gove Nichols, *Marriage: Its History, Character, and Results* (New York: T. L. Nichols, 1854), 307.
5. Friedrich Engels quoted in Judith Orr, *Abortion Wars: The Fight for Reproductive Rights* (Bristol, UK: Bristol University Press, 2017), 48. On both sides of the Atlantic, medical reports and the penny press seemed endlessly to circulate tales of infanticide, at once scandalizing their readers and conveying the crises attendant on unwanted, forced pregnancies. The subjects of concealed pregnancies, stillbirths, and abortion made for similarly captivating narratives, and they were increasingly classified as variations on infanticide by conservative physicians in the early nineteenth century. And this attention to women's criminality set into motion heated debates about men's roles in sexual misconduct and why fetal life took precedence over living women.
6. Margaret Fuller quoted in Kathryn Harrison, "Vindication," *New York Times*, April 19, 2013.
7. Celia Morris, *Fanny Wright: Rebel in America* (Champagne: University of Illinois Press, 1984), 3, 184. See also the anonymously collected *Twelve Letters to Young Men, on the Sentiments of Miss Frances Wright and Robert Dale Owens* (Philadelphia, PA: Thomas Kite Printer, 1830) for a series of arguments about prohibiting her, as a woman, from public speaking.
8. Jordan Stein, "Rappaccini's Son," *J19: The Journal of Nineteenth-Century Americanists* 9, no. 1 (Spring 2021): 145–54, 146.
9. Kenneth Silverman, *Edgar A. Poe: Mournful and Never-Ending Remembrance* (New York: HarperCollins, 1991), 26.
10. Edgar Allan Poe, "William Wilson," *Poe: Poetry, Tales, and Selected Essays* (New York: Library of America, 1996), 338.
11. Leland Person, "Queer Poe: The Tell-Tale Heart of His Fiction," *Poe Studies* 41, no. 1 (2008): 7–30.

12. Joel Pfister, "Hawthorne as Cultural Theorist," in *The Cambridge Companion to Nathaniel Hawthorne,* ed. Richard H. Millington (Cambridge: Cambridge University Press, 2004), 35–59, 36.
13. Its criminalization in the nineteenth century coincided with new forms of regulating sexuality. As the print culture of Poe and Hawthorne's time popularized ways of categorizing criminality, the abortionist and the sodomite came into view in an increasingly hostile lexicon regarding monsters in human form or unnatural deviations from natural laws. Conservative publications and editorials in the 1840s used this lexicon to push back against the freethinkers, contraceptive-advice lecturers, liberal booksellers, physiological societies, and informed workingwomen. Janet Farrell Brodie explains it this way: "The power to curtail pregnancies and thus to separate sexual intercourse from reproduction threatened to alter the relations between man and woman, to diminish the power of husbands over their wives and of parents over their children, especially over their daughters" See Janet Farrell Brodie, *Contraception and Abortion in 19th-Century America* (Ithaca, NY: Cornell University Press, 1994), 154–55.
14. Eliza Richards also makes the point, with regard to Poe's work, that it is not a "highly crafted" version of women's writing, not "concatenated," as Baudelaire described it (*Poe's Circle,* 57).
15. Meredith McGill, "Poe, Literary Nationalism, and Authorial Identity" in *The American Face of Edgar Allan Poe,* ed. Shawn Rosenheim and Stephen Rachman (Baltimore, MD: Johns Hopkins University Press, 1995), 271–304, 282, 295.
16. Please also see "Charles Dickens and the American Copyright Problem," Creative Law Center, accessed May 12, 2021, https://creativelawcenter.com/dickens-american-copyright/.
17. "Virtual Event: Scott Peeples and Michelle van Parys at Buxton Books: *The Man of the Crowd,*" Princeton University Press, posted October 20, 2020, https://press.princeton.edu/events/virtual-event-scott-peeples-and-michelle-van-parys-at-buxton-books. In the event description, Peeples discusses his argument in *Man of the Crowd: Poe and Edgar Allan Poe in the City* (Princeton NJ: Princeton University Press, 2020.).
18. Shawn Johansen, *Family Men: Middle-Class Fatherhood and Industrializing America* (London: Routledge, 2001), 53.
19. See Marvin Olasky's opening chapter in *The Press and Abortion, 1838–1988* (Hillsdale, NJ: Lawrence Erlbaum, 1988), which includes these quotations from the *National Police Gazette* (April 25, 1846, and February 21, 1846, respectively), 10–11.

Introduction

1. Quoted in Allan Keller, *Scandalous Lady: The Life and Times of Madame Restell, New York's Most Notorious Abortionist* (New York: Atheneum, 1981), 187, 188.
2. "Anthony Comstock—His Work and Ways," *Index: A Weekly Paper Devoted to Free Religion,* vol. 9 (Boston, MA), September 19, 1878.
3. Madame Restell's words, in her advertisement in the *New York Herald,* April 13, 1840.
4. "Madame Restell Dead: Or Was Her Reported Suicide All a Sham and a Pauper's Body Buried for Hers?," *Boston Daily Globe,* April 15, 1878.
5. Madame Restell quoted in A. M. Mauriceau, *The Married Woman's Private Medical Companion* (New York: Liberty Street, 1847), 131.
6. This is according to George Walling, former New York chief of police, in his *Recollections of a New York Chief of Police* (New York: Caxton Book Concern, 1887), 436.

7. Madame Restell quoted in Karen Abbott, "Madame Restell: The Abortionist of Fifth Avenue," November 27, 2012, Smithsonian Magazine, https://www.smithsonianmag.com/history/madame-restell-the-abortionist-of-fifth-avenue-145109198/.
8. See Thomas Crist, "Babies in the Privy: Prostitution, Infanticide, and Abortion in New York City's Five Points District," *Historical Archaeology* 39, no. 1, 2005, 19–46, 24. Janet Farrell Brodie, *Contraception and Abortion in 19th-Century America* (Ithaca, NY: Cornell University Press, 1994).
9. Kate Manning, *My Notorious Life* (New York: Simon & Schuster, 2013), 415.
10. Madame Restell quoted in A. Cheree Carlson, *The Crimes of Womanhood: Defining Femininity in a Court of Law* (Urbana-Champaign: University of Illinois Press, 2009), 111.
11. Madame Restell quoted in James Mohr, *Abortion in America: The Origins and Evolution of National Policy, 1800–1900* (Oxford: Oxford University Press, 1978), 107.
12. Mohr, *Abortion in America*, 199.
13. *Sunday Daily News,* July 21, 1839.
14. Gustav Lening, *The Dark Side of New York Life and Its Criminal Classes from Fifth Avenue down to the Five Points* (New York: Fred'k Gerhard, 1873), 466.
15. Nathaniel Hawthorne, "Rappaccini's Daughter," in *Tales and Sketches,* ed. Roy Harvey Pearce (New York: Library of America, 1982), 975–1005.
16. Nathaniel Hawthorne, "The Birth-Mark," in Pearce, *Tales and Sketches,* 764–80, 777. As popular radical lecturer Henry Clarke Wright notes in his *Unwelcome Child; Or, The Crime of an Undesigned and Undesired Maternity,* a compendium of his research and lectures on the problem of unplanned pregnancies (which go back to the 1830s), an unwanted fetus was a "hated intruder"; (Boston, MA: Bela Marsh, 1860), 58. "'Get rid of it!'—as the phrase is," he explains, referring to women's quest for abortions (Wright, *Unwelcome Child,* 6). Hawthorne scholars Lee Person and Brenda Wineapple also briefly consider "The Birth-Mark" in relation to abortion. See Person's *Cambridge Introduction to Hawthorne* (Cambridge: Cambridge University Press, 2007), 57; and Wineapple's biography *Nathaniel Hawthorne: A Life* (New York: Random House, 2004), 175. Monika Elbert, moreover, brilliantly notes Hawthorne's comprehension of prison or plantation surveillance; she sees "Rappaccini's Daughter" and "Artist" in relation to "The Birth-Mark" as tales that similarly incorporate nineteenth-century vocabularies about women's fertility; Elbert, "The Surveillance" of Woman's Body in Hawthorne's Short Stories," *Women's Studies* 33, no. 1 (2004): 23–46, 29.
17. Nathaniel Hawthorne, "The Artist of the Beautiful," in Pearce, *Tales and Sketches,* 907–31.
18. Rodney Hessinger in *Seduced, Abandoned, and Reborn* discusses the steam-powered press as "exponentially boost[ing]" the production and range of books in New England in the late 1820s; *Seduced, Abandoned, and Reborn: Visions of Youth in Middle-Class America, 1780–1850* (Philadelphia: University of Pennsylvania Press, 2013), 129.
19. Mohr, *Abortion in America,* 48.
20. William Sanger, *The History of Prostitution: Its Extent, Causes, and Effects throughout the World* (New York: Harper & Brothers, 1858), 482.
21. Mohr, *Abortion in America,* 47, 50.
22. Susan Klepp, *Revolutionary Conceptions: Women, Fertility, and Family Limitations in America, 1760–1820* (Chapel Hill: North Carolina University Press, 2017), 269.
23. Brodie, *Contraception and Abortion,* 51–53.

24. Brodie, *Contraception and Abortion*, 166.
25. See, in particular, Klepp (*Revolutionary Conceptions*, 179-214) on the eighteenth-century's pharmaceutical history.
26. Janet Farrell Brodie, "Menstrual Interventions in the Nineteenth-Century United States," in *Regulating Menstruation: Beliefs, Practices, Interpretations*, ed. Etienne Van de Walle and Elisha P. Renne (Chicago, IL: University of Chicago Press, 2001), 39-63, 54.
27. See James Ricci, *One Hundred Years of Gynaecology, 1800-1900* (Philadelphia, PA: Blakiston, 1945), 26. The dangers of perforation do not seem to be the cause of the disputes at the conference, as Ricci briefly notes them.
28. See, for instance, John Halliday Croon, *Manual of the Minor Gynecological Operations and Appliances* (Edinburgh: E. and S. Livingstone, 1883), 137.
29. Mohr, *Abortion in America*, 65.
30. Ricci, *One Hundred Years*, 38.
31. See Joseph Needham, *A History of Embryology* (1939; repr., Cambridge: Cambridge University Press, 2015), 204.
32. Kristin Luker, *Abortion and the Politics of Motherhood* (Berkeley: University of California Press, 1985), 31.
33. Charles Meigs quoted in Ricci, *One Hundred Years*, 29.
34. The fetus was even at times declared a citizen, as this 1846 overview of American criminal law demonstrates: "The civil rights of an infant *in ventre sa mere* are equally respected at every period of gestation"; Francis Wharton, *A Treatise on the Criminal Law of the United States* (Philadelphia, PA: James Kay, Jun. and Brother, 1846), 308.
35. Hugh Hodge, *Foeticide, Or Criminal Abortion: A Lecture Introductory to the Course on Obstetrics and Diseases of Women and Children; University of Pennsylvania, Session 1839-40* (1872; repr., Collingwood, Aus.: Trieste, 2017), 5.
36. Brodie, *Contraception and Abortion*, 267.
37. Horatio Storer, *On Criminal Abortion in America* (Philadelphia, PA: J. B. Lippincott, 1860), 14.
38. Barbara Johnson, "Apostrophe, Animation, and Abortion," *Diacritics* 16, no. 1 (1986): 28-47, 35.
39. According to Luker, physicians' official rhetoric often departed from practice, in which the "embryo's rights remained conditional, set in relation the 'woman's right to life'" (*Abortion*, 35).
40. Luker, *Abortion*, 200.
41. Barbara Duden, *Disembodying Women: Perspectives on Pregnancy and the Unborn*, trans. Lee Hoinacki (Cambridge, MA: Harvard University Press, 1993), 104.
42. Duden, *Disembodying Women*, 70.
43. John Beck, *An Inaugural Dissertation on Infanticide* (New York: J. Seymour, 1817), 28.
44. Duden, *Disembodying Women*, 56.
45. Karen Newman, *Fetal Positions: Individualism, Science, Visuality* (Stanford, CA: Stanford University Press, 1996), 64.
46. This point about fetal atemporality is indebted to Lauren Berlant's work in *The Queen of America Goes to Washington City: Essays on Sex and Citizenship* (Durham, NC: Duke University Press, 1997), on which I expand in my chapter on Hawthorne.
47. Michel Foucault, *The Birth of the Clinic: An Archaeology of Medical Perception*, trans. A. M. Sheridan Smith (New York: Vintage Books, 1994), xvii.

48. Newman, *Fetal Positions*, 67, 64.
49. Morris Mattson, *The American Vegetable Practice: Or a New and Improved Guide to Health, Designed for the Use of Families*, vol. 1 (Boston, MA: Daniel L. Hale, 1841), 629.
50. Mrs. Benjamin Thurlow, "Advice to Midwives," in *The New England Botanic, Medical, and Surgical Journal*, vol. 3, ed. Calvin Newton (Worcester, MA: Calvin Newton, MD, 1849), 235–38, 237.
51. Dana Nelson, *National Manhood: Capitalist Citizenship and the Imagined Fraternity of White Men* (Durham, NC: Duke University Press, 1998), 161.
52. Thomas Jefferson quoted in Caitlin Rosenthal, *Accounting for Slavery: Masters and Management* (Cambridge, MA: Harvard University Press, 2018), 155.
53. Leslie Regan, *When Abortion Was a Crime: Women, Medicine, and Law in the United States, 1867–1973* (Berkeley: University of California Press, 1997), 11.
54. Nathan Allan, "Increase of Population in Massachusetts," *Boston Medical and Surgical Journal* 75, no. 23 (January 3, 1867): 453–58, 458.
55. I am here also indebted to historian Rickie Solinger for her research on the role of race in abortion's criminalization; Rickie Solinger, *Pregnancy and Power: A Short History of Reproductive Politics in America* (New York: New York University Press, 2007). She discusses an earlier form of white supremacy, the one generated by slavery and the investment in Black women's enslaved offspring. In addition, this point that enslaved women equaled capital to the slave economy of the antebellum United States is made most clearly by Constance Sublette and Ned Sublette in *The American Slave Coast: A History of the Slave-Breeding Industry* (Chicago, IL: Chicago Review Press, 2015). These are points to which I return in later chapters.
56. Jennifer Morgan, "*Partus sequitur ventrem*: Law, Race, and Reproduction in Colonial Slavery," *Small Axe; A Caribbean Journal of Criticism* 22, no. 1 (March 2018): 1–17, 6.
57. Saidiya Hartman, "The Belly of the World: A Note on Black Women's Labor," *Souls* 18, no. 1 (January–March 2016): 163–77, 169.
58. Diane Klein, "Emancipation Unlocke'd: Partus Sequitur Ventrem, Self-Ownership, and No 'Middle State' in Maria vs. Surbaugh," *University of Maryland Law Journal of Race, Religion, Gender and Class* 20, no. 1 (2020): 73–111, 80.
59. Morgan, "*Partus sequitur ventrem*," 14.
60. Londa Schiebinger, "Agnotology and Exotic Abortifacients: The Cultural Production of Ignorance in the Eighteenth Century Atlantic World," *Proceedings of the American Philosophical Society* 149, no. 3 (September 2005): 316–43.
61. Dr. Collins, *Practical Rules for the Management and Medical Treatment of Negro Slaves in the Sugar Colonies* (London: J. Barfield, for Vernor and Hood, 1803), 156.
62. *Anti-Slavery Reporter*, vol. 5–6, ed. Zachary Macaulay (London: London Society for the Mitigation and Abolition of Slavery in the British Dominion, 1833), 11.
63. *American Slavery as It Is: Testimony of a Thousand Witnesses* (New York: The American Anti-Slavery Society, 1839), 110.
64. *American Slavery as It Is*, 182.
65. Deirdre Cooper Owens, *Medical Bondage: Race, Gender, and the Origins of American Gynecology* (Athens: University of Georgia Press, 2017), 8, 60.
66. Marie Jenkins Schwartz, *Birthing a Slave: Motherhood and Medicine in the Antebellum South* (Cambridge, MA: Harvard University Press, 2006).
67. As reported by O. C. Gibbs, MD, "Monthly Summary of Medical Journalism—Abortion," *American Medical Monthly and New York Review* (July 1860): 309–310,

309. J. H. Morgan's full article, "An Essay on the Causes of the Production of Abortion among Our Negro Population," appears in the *Nashville Journal of Medicine and Surgery*, no. 19 (August 1860): 122–23.
68. Gibbs, "Monthly Summary," 310.
69. Edgar Allan Poe, "The Mystery of Marie Rogêt," in *Poetry, Tales, and Selected Essays*, ed. Patrick Quinn and G. R. Thompson (New York: The Library of America, 1996), 506–54, 526.
70. Rev. Richard Shepherd, *Discourses on a Future Existence, Tending to Establish the Doctrine of a Recognition of Each Other* (London: A. Hancock, 1826), 9.
71. Giorgio Agamben, *Homo Sacer: Sovereign Power and Bare Life*, trans. Daniel Heller-Roazen (Stanford, CA: Stanford University Press, 1998), 143. Penelope Deutscher takes definitions from *Homo Sacer* into her conceptualization of the fetus' sovereignty, a subject I touched on in chapter 1.

Part I: Detection, Confession, Termination

1. Loisa Nygaard's "Winning the Game: Inductive Reasoning in Poe's 'Murders in the Rue Morgue'" explores the tradition of scholarship in which Dupin's intelligence is either revered or subject to suspicion; *Studies in Romanticism* 33, no. 2 (1994): 223–54.
2. See Samuel Edwards's *The Vidocq Dossier: The Story of the World's First Detective* (Boston, MA: Houghton Mifflin, 1977) for details about Vidocq's crime-solving methods, including studying fingerprints and handwriting.
3. Edgar Allan Poe, "The Murders in the Rue Morgue," *Poetry, Tales, and Selected Essays*, ed. Patrick Quinn and G. R. Thompson (New York: The Library of America, 1996), 397–431, 412, 397.
4. Edgar Allan Poe to Phillip P. Cooke—, August 9, 1846 (LTR-240), https://www.eapoe.org/works/letters/p4608090.htm.

Chapter One: Stargazing on the Rue Morgue

1. Edgar Allan Poe, "The Murders in the Rue Morgue," in *Poetry, Tales, and Selected Essays*, ed. Patrick Quinn and G. R. Thompson (New York: The Library of America, 1996), 417.
2. Poe, "Rue Morgue," 431, 418, 400. All italics are Poe's, unless otherwise stated.
3. Poe, "Rue Morgue," 421, 398.
4. Poe, "Rue Morgue," 399, 398.
5. Poe, "Rue Morgue," 399.
6. See the chapter "On Procuring Miscarriage by Drugs" (293–94) in Alex Burnett, MD, *The Medical Adviser, and Guide to Health and Long Life*, vol. 1 (London: Knight and Lacey Publishers, 1824.). Savin was a known abortifacient; Poe alludes to it when his narrator says he and Dupin worship the Sabine goddess.
7. Poe, "Rue Morgue," 399.
8. Poe, "Rue Morgue," 403–4, 404.
9. W. J. Watts, "Ovid, the Law and Roman Society on Abortion," *Acta Classica* 16 (1973): 89–101, 98–99.
10. John Tresch, "'Matter No More': Edgar Allan Poe and the Paradoxes of Materialism," *Critical Inquiry* 42, no. 4 (2016): 865–98, 888, 896.
11. Matthew Taylor, *Universes without Us: Posthuman Cosmologies in American Literature* (Minneapolis: University of Minnesota Press, 2013), 41.

12. Poe, "Rue Morgue," 403, 405, 398, 428, 401.
13. Poe, "Rue Morgue," 424.
14. Poe scholars concur that the scenes describing the captivity and whipping of the orangutan move the viciousness of slavery into view too. It is a "zoological recontextualization," Christopher Peterson asserts, in which the disavowed connection between humans and other animals surfaces at the origins of the detective genre; "The Aping Apes of Poe and Wright: Race, Animality, and Mimicry in 'The Murders in the Rue Morgue' and *Native Son*," *New Literary History* 41, no. 1 (2010): 151-71, 155.
15. Poe, "Rue Morgue," 405, 407.
16. Wooster Beach, *An Improved System of Midwifery* (New York: Baker and Scribner, 1851), 138, 42.
17. Helen Lefkowitz Horowitz reproduces this ad from the March 2, 1842, edition of the *New York Herald* in full in her *Attitudes toward Sex in Antebellum America: A Brief History with Documents* (Boston, MA: Bedford/St. Martin's, 2006), 22.
18. Robert H. Black and Andrea L. Bonnicksen, ed. *Medicine Unbound: The Human Body and the Limits of Medical Intervention* (New York: Columbia University Press, 1994).
19. Penelope Deutscher, "The Inversion of Exceptionality: Foucault, Agamben, and 'Reproductive Rights,'" *South Atlantic Quarterly* 107, no. 1 (2008): 55-70, 67, 66, 66, 67, 59.
20. Poe, "Rue Morgue," 407.
21. Poe, "Rue Morgue," 407, 400, 407.
22. Poe, "Rue Morgue," 400, 400, 401, 424, 414.
23. Poe, "Rue Morgue," 410, 423, 415, 420-24.
24. Tresch, "Matter No More," 877.
25. Poe, "Rue Morgue," 431, 431.
26. Both this excerpt and the next two come from Marvin Olasky's *The Press and Abortion, 1838-1988* (Hillsdale, NJ: Lawrence Erlbaum, 1988), 6.
27. Poe, "Rue Morgue," 404, 405, 412, 412, 412.
28. Poe, "Rue Morgue," 408, 414, 404.
29. As Nicole Livengood argues about Dixon's editorials, they "appealed to white, middle-class men uncertain of their gender roles and class status in Jacksonian-era New York" and affirmed their sense of influence and authority; Nicole C. Livengood, "'Thus Did Restell Seal This Unfortunate Lady's Lips with a Lie': George Washington Dixon's *Polyanthos* and the Seductive Abortion Narrative," *American Journalism* 33, no. 3 (2016): 289-316, 289.
30. Poe, "Rue Morgue," 417.
31. For example, "The known MSS of the officer" in "The Mystery of Marie Rogêt" (551); Dupin's recognizable manuscript in "The "Purloined Letter."
32. Poe, "Rue Morgue," 431.
33. Poe, "Rue Morgue," 424.
34. Shawn Rosenheim senses there is another story to the one Dupin tells, wondering why it is that he "reverses Cuvier's claims" about the docility of orangutans into the complete opposite and then cuts the tale short with an "extreme brevity [of] denoument"; Shawn Rosenheim, "Detective Fiction, Psychoanalysis, and the Analytic Sublime," in *The American Face of Edgar Allan Poe*, ed. Shawn Rosenheim and Stephen Rachman (Baltimore, MD: Johns Hopkins University Press, 1995), 153-76, 161, 172.
35. Poe, "Rue Morgue," 431.

36. Poe, "Rue Morgue," 411, 415.
37. Eric Homberger, *Scenes from the Life of a City: Corruption and Conscience in Old New York* (New Haven, CT: Yale University Press, 1996), 101–12.
38. "Madame Restell, and Some of Her Dupes," in *The New York Medical and Surgical Reporter*, ed. Clarkson T. Collins, MD (New York: Piercy & Reed, 1846), 158–65, 164. See Marvin Olasky, *Press and Abortion*, 10, for quotations from newspapers printed in 1845 and 1846.
39. "Criminal Abortions," *Boston Medical and Surgical Journal*, 30, no. 15 (May 15, 1844), 302.
40. This untitled article appears in the *National Police Gazette* 1, no. 25 (February 28, 1846): 220.
41. Abortionists such as Madame Restell not only worked out of their residences but also sent their remedies by mail. As a result, they obtained the return addresses and often the names of the women who wrote to them. This mail-order business threatened the male order or patriarchal investment in paternity's mattering, in pregnancy's meaningfulness.
42. Poe, "Rue Morgue," 405.
43. John Carlos Rowe's "chapter "Edgar Allan Poe's Imperial Fantasy and the American Frontier" discusses the orangutan as racially inflected—a "fantasy regarding civilized women" caught in a "fantasy of slave insurrection"; *Literary Culture and U.S. Imperialism: From the Revolution to World War II* (Oxford: Oxford University Press, 2000), 99.
44. Poe, "Rue Morgue," 400.
45. Poe, "Rue Morgue," 410, 411.
46. William Sanger, *The History of Prostitution: Its Extent, Causes, and Effects throughout the World* (New York: Harper & Brothers, 1858). Working with public-health statistics of New York City in the decade before 1858, Sanger notes the "brutal tyranny" of husbands who beat their wives, the numbers of sex workers beaten to death "by ruffians," and the thousands of impoverished, raped women forced into prostitution; Sanger, *History of Prostitution*, 476, 486. "The whole force of the world's opinion has been directed," he wrote, "[at] the poor wronged sufferer" (647).
47. Poe, "Rue Morgue," 405.
48. Gillian Brown, "The Poetics of Extinction," in *The American Face of Edgar Allan Poe*, ed. Shawn Rosenheim and Stephen Rachman (Baltimore, MD: Johns Hopkins University Press, 1995), 330–44, 334.
49. Sam Jordison, "Murders in the Rue Morgue: There'd Have Been No Sherlock Holmes without Detective Dupin," *Guardian*, October 16, 2013, https://www.theguardian.com/books/2013/oct/16/tales-mystery-imagination-edgar-allan-poe.
50. *Mystery and Detective Fiction: An Exhibit*, The British Library, Spring 2013. I visited this exhibit and took notes from the posters.
51. Poe, "Rue Morgue," 427.
52. Theodric Romeyn Beck, *Elements of Medical Jurisprudence*, 2nd ed. (Albany, NY: John Anderson, 1825), 174. Beck is quoting Dr. Thomas Percival on abortion (140).
53. Beck, *Elements*, 2ff, 142, 152.
54. Edwin Hale, *The Great Crime of the Nineteenth Century: Why Is It Committed? Who Are the Criminals? How Shall They Be Detected? How Shall They Be Punished?* (Chicago, IL: C. S. Halsey, 1867), 4, 5, 28, 6, 21.

55. Jo Turner et al., *A Companion to the History of Crime and Criminal Justice* (Bristol, UK: Polity Press, 2017). Tracing the criminalization of fortune-telling by state legislatures in the nineteenth century, Jo Turner and Paul Taylor et al. assert that it was not only classified as a form of fraud but also associated with a criminal underworld that consisted of abortionists. Their research demonstrates that the courts aimed to stop fortune-tellers from selling nostrums and from providing reproductive advice themselves, as well as to prevent them from acting "as intermediaries between women and abortionists" (Turner et al., *Companion*, 93). For Turner et al., it is crucial to see how whiteness and paternalism played into the legislation—how fortune-tellers were racialized and how women (their primary clientele) were described as vulnerable to misinformation.

56. James Mohr, *Abortion in America: The Origins and Evolution of National Policy, 1800–1900* (Oxford: Oxford University Press, 1978), 53–54.

57. Charles Roback, *The Mysteries of Astrology, and the Wonders of Magic: Including a History of the Rise and Progress of Astrology, and the Various Branches of Necromancy: Together with Valuable Directions and Suggestions Relative to the Casting of Nativities, and Predictions by Geomancy, Chiromancy, Physiognomy, &c. Also, Highly Interesting Narratives, Anecdotes, &c. Illustrative of the Marvels of Witchcraft, Spiritual Phenomena, and the Results of Supernatural Influence* (London: Sampson Low, Son, 1854), xi, xii.

58. Roback, *Mysteries of Astrology*, 133, 88, 24.

59. Charles Leland, *Aradia: Or, The Gospel of the Witches* (London: D. Nutt, 1899), 93–95.

60. Horace, *Epistles* 1:16 Loeb Classical Edition, trans. H. Rushton Fairclough (Cambridge: Harvard University Press, 1926).

61. In the well-known *A General Dictionary, Historical and Critical*, vol. 8, edited by John Peter Bernard, Thomas Birch, and John Lockman (London: G. Strahan, 1739), entries on Horace and Ovid occur alongside the "secrets of midwives" who devised "remedies to prevent conception," and descriptions of invocations of Laverna are paired with references to abortion (for help to "kill the child in the womb") and to the prayer by Laverna's followers ("let all believe me good") (186). Ovid, as the editors of the dictionary note, mentions women "concealing their faults" by means of abortion.

62. Barry Stephenson, *Ritual: A Very Short Introduction* (Oxford: Oxford University Press, 2015), 5, 19, 47.

63. Poe, Rue Morgue," 410.

64. Poe, "Rue Morgue," 410, 410.

65. Another mistake of the narrator's, Dupin does not read his mind so much as his body language, his tripping, muttering, attentiveness to certain things. Dupin simply puts those movements together and pronounces it as access to the narrator's thinking.

66. Poe, "Rue Morgue," 421.

67. Poe, "Rue Morgue," 431.

68. Poe, "Rue Morgue," 405, 422, 422.

69. Poe, "Rue Morgue," 398, 399.

70. Poe, "Rue Morgue," 397.

71. Eliza Richards makes a similar point about Poe himself, arguing that the "cross-gendered identification" Poe could make in his tales took him beyond the "rational inquiry" of male-directed reading. That is, the epigraph points in two different directions: the first, toward Poe and the possibility of seeing from the women's point of view or

from within their world, whether or not one is a cis-gendered woman; the second, toward the mode of Dupin's entry into that world, disguised as a woman, acting out of a cunning and conservative misogyny; *Gender and the Poetics of Reception in Poe's Circle* (Cambridge: Cambridge University Press, 2004), 54.
72. Poe, "Rue Morgue," 409, 406, 430, 407.
73. Poe, "Rue Morgue," 425, 399.
74. Poe, "Rue Morgue," 406.
75. Poe, "Rue Morgue," 401. The allusion is ostensibly to the night or to a lunar goddess, but it includes a reference to counterfeiters, and they come under Laverna's protection.
76. Between the eighteenth and early twentieth centuries, free and enslaved Black women labored or found work as washer-women. The image of the Black washer-woman was as well-known as that of the shoe-shiner in the racialized and racist iconography of American laborers. See, for instance, Teresa Amott and Julie Matthaei, *Race, Gender, and Work* (Boston, MA: South End Press, 1996), 150.
77. Barbara Johnson, "Apostrophe, Animation, and Abortion," *Diacritics* 16, no. 1 (1986): 34.
78. Poe, "Rue Morgue," 423, 431.

Chapter Two: Averse from Swerving in "The Mystery of Marie Rogêt"
1. Theodric Romeyn Beck, *Elements of Medical Jurisprudence*, 2nd ed. (Albany, NY: John Anderson, 1825), 156.
2. Edgar Allan Poe, "The Mystery of Marie Rogêt," in *Poetry, Tales, and Selected Essays*, ed. Patrick Quinn and G. R. Thompson (New York: The Library of America, 1996), 506–54, 538.
3. Poe, "Marie Rogêt," 540, 538.
4. Poe, "Marie Rogêt," 532.
5. Edgar Allan Poe, "The Murders in the Rue Morgue," in *Poetry, Tales, and Selected Essays*, ed. Patrick Quinn and G. R. Thompson (New York: The Library of America, 1996), 401.
6. Poe, "Marie Rogêt," 550.
7. Poe, "Marie Rogêt," 538, 548.
8. Poe's narrator repeats the imperative to pay attention that he slides into "The Murders in the Rue Morgue" by setting up Dupin's feigned attention to the Prefect's description of Marie's murder and then returning to the necessity of paying attention in the last paragraph of the tale. Poe directs us to the kind of reading that is active and careful as a way of escaping the kind of misogynistic manipulation Dupin enacts on us.
9. Poe, "Marie Rogêt," 509, 534, 542, 540, 537, 553.
10. Zoë Sofia, "Exterminating Fetuses: Abortion, Disarmament, and the Sexo-Semiotics of Extraterrestrialism," *Diacritics* 14, no. 2 (Summer 1984): 47–59, 55, 54, 57.
11. Poe, "Marie Rogêt," 537, 539.
12. Poe, "Marie Rogêt," 508. See Elizabeth Fee's careful introduction to "Public Health, Past and Present: A Shared Social Vision," in *A History of Public Health: Revised Expanded Edition*, by George Rosen (Baltimore, MD: Johns Hopkins University Press, 1993), xiii-lii.
13. Fee, "Public Health," xxii.
14. Horatio Storer's *On Criminal Abortion in America* (Philadelphia, PA: J. B. Lippincott, 1860) and Edwin Hale's *Systematic Treatise on Abortion* (Chicago, IL: C. S.

Halsey, 1866), for example, provide overviews of the 1840s and 1850s in the language of probability.
15. Poe, "Marie Rogêt," 508, 543, 550.
16. Giorgio Agamben, *Potentialities: Collected Essays in Philosophy*, trans. Daniel Heller-Roazen (Stanford, CA: Stanford University Press, 1999), 245, 261, 262.
17. Poe, "Marie Rogêt," 510.
18. Poe, "Marie Rogêt," 549, 411, 510, 527, 518, 506.
19. Poe, "Marie Rogêt," 527, 522, 550.
20. Poe, "Marie Rogêt," 544, 550, 552, 539.
21. Poe, "Rue Morgue," 405.
22. Poe, "Marie Rogêt," 547, 542, 508.
23. J. H. Kellogg, *Ladies Guide to Health and Disease* (Des Moines, IA: W. D. Condit, 1884), 364.
24. Poe, "Marie Rogêt," 506.
25. Poe, "Marie Rogêt," 554.
26. Poe, "Marie Rogêt," 553.
27. Thank you to Caitlin McIntyre for this reading of the line as man's invention of god and nature and not god's creation of nature.
28. Amy Gilman Srebnick, *The Mysterious Death of Mary Rogers: Sex and Culture in Nineteenth-Century New York* (New York: Oxford University Press, 1995), 35.
29. Poe, "Marie Rogêt," 518, 540, 528.
30. See Pseudo Anti-Marcus in *Notes on the Population Question* (London: J. Watson, 1841) on the "arts" of contraception (18) and other "artificial checks" to population growth (16).
31. Drucilla Cornell, *The Imaginary Domain: Abortion, Pornography and Sexual Harrassment* (London: Routledge, 1995), 50, 50.
32. Lorraine Rothman quoted in Cornell, *Imaginary Domain*, 50.
33. Poe, "Marie Rogêt," 531.
34. Poe, "Marie Rogêt," 512.
35. Poe, "Marie Rogêt," 520.
36. Elizabeth Miller, "'At a Distance from the Scene of the Atrocity': Death and Detachment in Poe's 'The Mystery of Marie Rogêt,'" in *Representations of Death in Nineteenth-Century US Writing and Culture*, ed. Lucy Frank (Aldershot, UK: Ashgate, 2007), 173–88, 174.
37. Poe, "Marie Rogêt," 516, 514, 517.
38. Poe, "Marie Rogêt," 516, 511, 509.
39. Poe, "Marie Rogêt," 533.
40. Susan Klepp explains that this phrase was a codeword for "abortion" (*Revolutionary Conceptions: Women, Fertility, and Family Limitations in America, 1760–1820* [Chapel Hill: North Carolina University Press, 2017], 100); see also Marvin Olasky on "the desired result" as a common expression in abortion advertising (*The Press and Abortion, 1838–1988* [Hillsdale, NJ: Lawrence Erlbaum, 1988], 17).
41. Laura Saltz, "(Horrible to Relate!) Recovering the Body of Marie Rogêt," in *The American Face of Edgar Allan Poe*, ed. Shawn Rosenheim and Stephen Rachman (Baltimore, MD: Johns Hopkins University Press, 1995), 237–70, 262.
42. Miller, "At a Distance," 173.
43. In *The Beautiful Cigar Girl*, Daniel Stashower tracks down all the connections between Poe's story and the news reports about Mary Rogers, noting that Dupin asks us "to

Notes to Pages 71–80

take a great deal on faith" (234); *The Beautiful Cigar Girl: Mary Rogers, Edgar Allan Poe, and the Invention of Murder* (New York: Dutton, 2006). Although Stashower does not name Dupin as Marie Rogêt's killer, he sees Dupin as a figure of secrecy and lies. He also meticulously pairs factual forensic data with the exaggerations and distortions of Dupin's claims about the activity surrounding dead bodies.

44. John Loudon, *An Encyclopedia of Gardening; Comprising the Theory and Practice of Horticulture, Floriculture, Aboriculture, and Landscape-Gardening* (London: Longman, Hurst, Rees, Orme, and Brown, 1822), 771.
45. Merlin Sheldrake, *Entangled Life: How Fungi Make Our Worlds, Change Our Minds, and Shape Our Futures* (New York: Random House, 2020), 5, 216.
46. Anna Lowenhaupt Tsing, *The Mushroom at the End of the World: On the Possibility of Life in Capitalist Ruins* (Princeton, NJ: Princeton University Press, 2015), vii.
47. Poe, "Marie Rogêt," 552, 552, 552.
48. Poe, "Marie Rogêt," 551, 536.
49. Edgar Allan Poe quoted in Saltz, "(Horrible to Relate!)," 261; Poe's italics. My chapter here on "The Mystery of Marie Rogêt" is indebted to Saltz's brilliant essay on the tale, taking it as the groundwork for developing my argument on Dupin's guilt and the trilogy as the narrator's extended confession.
50. Poe, "Marie Rogêt," 509, 548, 525.
51. Poe, "Marie Rogêt," 554, 514, 527.

Chapter Three: An Unusual Gaping in the Joints

1. William A. Alcott, *The Young Man's Guide,* 16th ed. (Boston, MA: T. R. Marvin, 1846), 313, 334, 311, 314.
2. Ronald Walters, *Primers for Prudery: Sexual Advice to Victorian Americans* (Baltimore, MD: Johns Hopkins University Press, 2000).
3. Janet Farrell Brodie, *Contraception and Abortion in 19th-Century America* (Ithaca, NY: Cornell University Press, 1994), 184.
4. *Sunday Daily News,* July 21, 1839. For more on this particular editorial, see the section titled "Backward from the Death of Madame Restell" in the introduction to this volume.
5. Helen Lefkowitz Horowitz, *Attitudes toward Sex in Antebellum America: A Brief History with Documents* (Boston, MA: Bedford/St. Martin's, 2006), 284.
6. Pseudo-Aristotle, *Aristotle's Masterpiece, Completed* (New York: Company of Flying Stationery, 1817), v.
7. Edgar Allan Poe, "Purloined Letter," in *Poetry, Tales, and Selected Essays,* ed. Patrick Quinn and G. R. Thompson (New York: The Library of America, 1996), 680–98, 687.
8. Poe, "Purloined Letter," 681.
9. Jacques Lacan, "Seminar on 'The Purloined Letter,'" trans. Jeffrey Mehlman, in *The Purloined Poe: Lacan, Derrida, and Psychoanalytic Reading,* ed. John P. Muller and William J. Richardson (Baltimore, MD: Johns Hopkins University Press, 1988), 28–54, 34.
10. Poe, "Purloined Letter," 698.
11. Poe, "Purloined Letter," 686, 682.
12. Poe, "Purloined Letter," 682, 690.
13. Poe, "Purloined Letter," 682, 680.
14. Poe, "Purloined Letter," 680, 695.
15. Poe, "Purloined Letter," 697, 684–86.
16. See, for instance, Anti-Marcus, *Notes on the Population Question* (London: J. Watson,

1841). Here, he or she discusses different types of contraceptives and notes that condoms are often called "French Letters" (22).
17. Barbara Johnson, "The Frame of Reference: Poe, Lacan, Derrida," in *The Purloined Poe: Lacan, Derrida, and Psychoanalytic Reading*, ed. John P. Muller and William J. Richardson (Baltimore, MD: Johns Hopkins University Press, 1988), 213–51, 231, 248.
18. Lacan, "Seminar," 45.
19. Poe, "Purloined Letter," 690.
20. Lacan, "Seminar," 42, 40, 33.
21. Jacques Derrida, *The Post Card: From Socrates to Freud and Beyond*, trans. Alan Bass (Chicago, IL: University of Chicago Press, 1987), 444, 423.
22. Derrida, *Post Card*, 472–73, 478–79, 424, 436, 480–81, 438.
23. Johnson, "Frame of Reference," 236, 236.
24. Johnson, "Frame of Reference," 216, 214.
25. Poe, "Purloined Letter," 694.
26. Poe, "Purloined Letter," 683, 683, 687.
27. Poe, "Purloined Letter," 691.
28. Poe, "Purloined Letter," 682.
29. Johnson, "Frame of Reference," 214.
30. Poe, "Purloined Letter," 682.
31. Poe, "Purloined Letter," 684.
32. John Muller and William Richardson, "Lacan's Seminar on 'The Purloined Letter': Notes to the Text," in Muller and Richardson, *Purloined Poe*, 83–98, 95.
33. Poe, "Purloined Letter," 695, 695, 695–96.
34. Colin Dayan, "Poe, Persons, and Property," in *Romancing the Shadow: Poe and Race*, ed. J. Gerald Kennedy and Liliane Weissberg (Oxford: Oxford University Press, 2001), 106–26, 119.
35. Poe, "Purloined Letter," 688.
36. Thomas Burgeland, *Physiological Observations on Mental Susceptibility* (London: W. Day, 1837), 35.
37. Hester Pendleton, *The Parent's Guide for the Transmission of Desired Qualities to Offspring* (New York: Fowlers and Wells, 1848), 1.
38. Poe, "Purloined Letter," 695.
39. James Ricci, *One Hundred Years of Gynaecology, 1800–1900* (Philadelphia, PA: Blakiston, 1945), 5, 25.
40. Poe, "Purloined Letter," 685–86.
41. Poe, "Purloined Letter," 684.
42. Poe, "Purloined Letter," 697.
43. Poe, "Purloined Letter," 693.
44. Thomas Jefferson, letter to Francis C. Gray, March 4, 1815, Founders Online, https://founders.archives.gov/documents/Jefferson/03-08-02-0245.
45. Jefferson to Gray.
46. Poe, "Purloined Letter," 691, 691.

Part II: Nation, Plantation, Annihilation

1. Margaret Fuller, *Papers on Literature and Art*, vols. 1 and 2 (New York: Wiley and Putnam, 1846), 124.
2. While the word "abortion" could pertain more generally to something misshapen or badly made, it is arises in the context of metaphors of birth; when Hawthorne uses it

in his novels, he draws out the word's medical and legal denotations for a terminated pregnancy.
3. J. Gerald Kennedy, *Strange Nation: Literary Nationalism and Cultural Conflict in the Age of Poe* (Oxford: Oxford University Press, 2016), 9.
4. Willie James Jennings, *The Christian Imagination: Theology and the Origins of Race* (New Haven, CT: Yale University Press, 2010), 25, 37, 230. In this brilliant study, Jennings explores the production of race in the conquest of the Americas, specifically in relation to kidnapping and displacement. Christianity, Jennings demonstrates, contorted itself in the era of conquest and reconfigured whiteness in proximity to God's plans.
5. In "How the Soil Remembers Plantation Slavery" Raina Martens and Bill Robertson discuss nineteenth-century tobacco production in terms of a haunting presence, arguing that the history of brutal exploitation reveals itself in the large tracts of still-exhausted soil. Referred to as the "vampire crop" in the 1840s, because it rapidly depleted the soil in which it was grown, tobacco and its production became synonymous with the ruthless extraction of labor and land. Martens and Robertson write, "It takes a thousand years to regenerate 3 centimeters of topsoil. At a Maryland correctional facility in Jessup, 30 miles from Sandy Spring, women are still shackled during childbirth. These violences are not unrelated." The entwined worlds of plantation labor and forced reproduction remain readable in the spaces and lives that mark slavery not as a past event but—in Fred Moten's words—as a "durational field." Raina Martens and Bill Robertson, "How the Soil Remembers Plantation Slavery, *Edge Effects*, March 29, 2019, https://edgeeffects.net/soil-memory-plantationocene/.
6. For this quotation and the context in which it circulated, see Albert Post's *Popular Freethought in America, 1825–1850* (London: Octagon Press, 1974), 145.

Chapter Four: Passwords and Countersigns
1. Nathaniel Hawthorne, *The Scarlet Letter* (1850), ed. Millicent Bell (New York: The Library of America, 1983), 115–345, 259, 277.
2. Hawthorne, *Scarlet Letter*, 140.
3. Caitlin Rosenthal, *Accounting for Slavery: Masters and Management* (Cambridge, MA: Harvard University Press, 2018), 79.
4. Hawthorne, *Scarlet Letter*, 297. Hawthorne scholars such as Teresa Goddu, Jay Grossman, and Leland Person have carefully explored the novel's representation of slavery, illuminating the frameworks of motherhood and personhood on which it draws. I return to their work later in this chapter.
5. Hawthorne, *Scarlet Letter*, 231, 332, 231, 232.
6. Hawthorne, *Scarlet Letter*, 214, 215.
7. Hawthorne, *Scarlet Letter*, 232, 308.
8. Hawthorne, *Scarlet Letter*, 133, 135, 133.
9. Hawthorne, *Scarlet Letter*, 134. "The beasts of the field," the narrator notes in "The Custom House," do not die into a "hereafter" but die altogether, into nonentities. The terminology aligns with that surrounding slavery and the notion of Black humanity's animal status inside the violent justifications for it.
10. Hawthorne, *Scarlet Letter*, 200.
11. Hawthorne, *Scarlet Letter*, 303, 323, 131.
12. Rickie Solinger, *Pregnancy and Power: A Short History of Reproductive Politics in America* (New York: New York University Press, 2007), 29, 30.

13. Liam Hogan, "The 'Forced Breeding' Myth in the 'Irish Slaves' Meme," *Medium* (October 23, 2015), https://limerick1914.medium.com)/the-racist-myth-within-a-racist-myth-8eac2c890e92.
14. John Winthrop, "City upon a Hill" speech, 1630, Gilder Lehrman Institute of American History, https://www.gilderlehrman.org/sites/default/files/inline-pdfs/Winthrop's %20City%20upon%20a%20Hill.pdf.
15. Hawthorne, *Scarlet Letter*, 343, 340.
16. Arthur Cleveland Coxe, "The Writings of Hawthorne," in *The Scarlet Letter and Other Writings*, ed. Leland Person (New York: Norton, 2005), 259.
17. Arthur Cleveland Coxe, in a letter to physician Andrew Nehinger, quoted in Janet Farrell Brodie, *Contraception and Abortion in 19th-Century America* (Ithaca, NY: Cornell University Press, 1994), 154.
18. Coxe, "Writings," 262. The reference is to the 1848 Seneca Falls Convention devoted to the subject of women's rights.
19. Coxe, "Writings," 256, 258, 262, 259.
20. Hawthorne, *Scarlet Letter*, 186, 158, 128, 126, 158.
21. Hawthorne, *Scarlet Letter*, 290.
22. Hawthorne, *Scarlet Letter*, 330.
23. Hawthorne, *Scarlet Letter*, 330, 195, 260.
24. Hawthorne, *Scarlet Letter*, 261, 202, 277, 145.
25. Arthur Riss, *Race, Slavery, and Liberalism in Nineteenth-Century American Literature* (Cambridge: Cambridge University Press, 2006), 121.
26. Laura Doyle, "'A' for Atlantic: The Colonizing Force of Hawthorne's *The Scarlet Letter*," *American Literature* 79, no. 2 (2007): 243–73, 244.
27. Franny Nudelman, "'Emblem and Product of Sin': The Poisoned Child in *The Scarlet Letter* and Domestic Advice Literature," *Yale Journal of Criticism* 10, no. 1 (1997): 193–213, 194.
28. "Index," *National Police Gazette* 1, no. 52 (September 5, 1846), 433.
29. My contention echoes Alison Easton's, in which she asserts that "there was no way Hawthorne could have been unaffected" by the issues affecting women's lives; Alison Easton, "Hawthorne and the Question of Women," in *The Cambridge Companion to Nathaniel Hawthorne*, ed. Richard H. Millington (Cambridge: Cambridge University Press, 2004), 79–98, 81. "Women were not insulated from the public realm," she explains, "nor were men detached from the domestic" (81). As I will show, unwanted pregnancies concerned men too, given their interconnection with the subjects of pleasure and nonreproductive sex in antebellum America.
30. Robert Martin, "Hester Prynne, *C'est Moi*: Nathaniel Hawthorne and the Anxieties of Gender," in Person, *The Scarlet Letter and Other Writings*, 512–22, 518, 521.
31. Hawthorne, *Scarlet Letter*, 146.
32. Hawthorne, *Scarlet Letter*, 344, 146.
33. Brodie, *Contraception and Abortion*, x.
34. James Mohr, *Abortion in America: The Origins and Evolution of National Policy, 1800–1900* (Oxford: Oxford University Press, 1978), 50, 47.
35. Brodie, *Contraception and Abortion*, 6.
36. "Criminal Abortions," 302.
37. A Physician of New York, *Madame Restell: An Account of Her Life and Horrible Practices* (New York: Charles V. Smith, 1847), 13, 12.

Notes to Pages 109–113

38. Helen Lefkowitz Horowitz, *Rereading Sex: Battles over Sexual Knowledge and Suppression in Nineteenth-Century America* (New York: Alfred A. Knopf, 2002), 194, 97.
39. Hawthorne, *Scarlet Letter*, 277.
40. Mohr, *Abortion in America*, 6.
41. Their efforts to establish themselves as the sole legitimate caretakers of prospective mothers did not go uncontested, however, and a petition circulated by New England irregulars in 1828 to protest the new restrictions placed on their operations had, by 1840, gathered thirty thousand signatures in support of the right of patients to "choose one's own fate" (Mohr, *Abortion in America*, 39). I am drawn to this particular historical detail because *The Scarlet Letter* repeatedly raises the issues of choice and fate, in addition to its portrait of Mistress Hibbins, who seeks signatories for her "Book" of dissenting allegiances.
42. Orson Squire Fowler, *Maternity; or, the Bearing and Nursing of Children*, 2nd ed. (New York: Fowlers and Wells, 1849), 188.
43. Willard Philipps and Samuel Baker Walcott (commissioners), "Causing Abortion: Concealing the Death of an Infant," *Report of the Penal Code of Massachusetts: Prepared under a Resolve of the Legislature, Passed on the 10th of February, 1837* (Boston, MA: Dutton and Wentworth, State Printers, 1844), chapter 13.
44. David Greven, "Masculinist Theory and Romantic Authorship, and *The Scarlet Letter*," *Textual Practice* 7, no. 1 (1993): 971–87, 978. Or, in Leland Person's words, "Hawthorne shows more sympathy and ironic understanding of the politics of motherhood than his nineteenth- and twentieth-century detractors have allowed"; Leland Person, "The Dark Labyrinth of the Mind: Hawthorne, Hester, and the Ironies of Racial Mothering," *Studies in American Fiction*, no. 1 (2001): 33–38, 36.
45. Hawthorne, *Scarlet Letter*, 286, 260, 260.
46. Hawthorne, *Scarlet Letter*, 260, 265.
47. Theodric Romeyn Beck, *Elements of Medical Jurisprudence*, 2nd ed. (Albany, NY: John Anderson, 1825), 140.
48. Thomas Radford, "A Few Practical Observations on Abortion, &c.," *Provincial Medical and Surgical Journal* 9, no. 38 (September 17, 1845): 577–78, 577.
49. "Criminal Abortions," 302.
50. Charles Knowlton, *Elements of Modern Materialism* (Adams, MA: A. Oakey, 1829), 63.
51. Charles Knowlton, *Fruits of Philosophy, or the Private Companion of Adult People*, 2nd ed. (Philadelphia, PA: F. P. Rogers, 1839), 74. *Fruits of Philosophy* was considered a scandalous and obscene book that encouraged infidelity, and it landed Knowlton in jail for three months. Like *The Scarlet Letter*, it also sold widely, with 1.5 million copies sold internationally.
52. Knowlton, *Fruits of Philosophy*, 74, 21.
53. Charles Knowlton quoted in Brodie, *Contraception and Abortion*, 155.
54. A. M. Mauriceau, *The Married Woman's Private Medical Companion* (New York: Liberty Street, 1847), 129–30.
55. A. M. Mauriceau was the nom de plume of Charles Lohman, husband to Madame Restell (Caroline Lohman). As the laws against abortion progressed throughout the 1830s and 1840s, Restell found herself increasingly targeted in the press; through editorials and published transcripts of her trials, she came to represent the category of "the female abortionist" writ large. A scapegoat burdened with the weight of existential

and political disquiet, she was cast as a contaminating force within New England's borders. Perceived as a particular type, "the abortionist" traded in the concealment of women's mistakes and allowed them to slip undetected back into their lives. Pairing this female scapegoat with Hester's characterization makes for a compelling way of seeing *The Scarlet Letter*'s burdened protagonist.

56. Hawthorne, *Scarlet Letter*, 341, 344.
57. Nathaniel Hawthorne quoted in Mohr, *Abortion in America*, 148.
58. Hawthorne, *Scarlet Letter*, 187.
59. These are subtitles of books containing abortion remedies in the 1840s, quoted in John Riddle's *Eve's Herbs: A History of Contraception and Abortion in the West* (Cambridge: Cambridge University Press, 2004), 232.
60. Hawthorne, *Scarlet Letter*, 126, 126.
61. Gillian Brown, "Hawthorne, Inheritance, and Women's Property," *Studies in the Novel* 23, no. 1 (1991): 107–18.
62. Hawthorne, *Scarlet Letter*, 138, 319. Sacvan Bercovitch, in *The Office of The Scarlet Letter*, most famously declares that Hester "rejoins the community [by] compromising for principle" ([York: Routledge, 2017], 30).
63. Hawthorne, *Scarlet Letter*, 146.
64. Quoted in A. Cheree Carlson, *The Crimes of Womanhood: Defining Femininity in a Court of Law* (Urbana-Champaign: University of Illinois Press, 2009), 118.
65. A Physician of New York, *Madame Restell*, 17, 19.
66. Quoted in Clifford Browder, *The Wickedest Woman in New York: Madame Restell, the Abortionist* (Hamden, CT: Archon, 1988), 44. Theodric Beck publicized abortion as a married woman's crime in his *Elements of Medical Jurisprudence*, which was multiply republished throughout the antebellum period. What I wish to point out here is the strong cultural connection between abortion and adultery and how it might merge in Hester's characterization.
67. A Physician of New York, *Madame Restell*, 19, 13.
68. Quoted in Carlson, *Crimes of Womanhood*, 111.
69. Carlson, *Crimes of Womanhood*, 111.
70. Hawthorne, *Scarlet Letter*, 192, 260.
71. Hawthorne, *Scarlet Letter*, 197, 200, 233, 145.
72. Lauren Berlant, *The Anatomy of National Fantasy: Hawthorne, Utopic, and Everyday Life* (Chicago, IL: University of Chicago Press, 1991), 34.
73. Hawthorne, *Scarlet Letter*, 151, 156, 200, 197.
74. Berlant, *Anatomy of National Fantasy*, 20.
75. Hawthorne, *Scarlet Letter*, 123.
76. Hawthorne, *Scarlet Letter*, 155, 211.
77. By the turn of the eighteenth century, two camps were broadly established, one insisting on the embryo's epigenesis, the other on its preformation. For the former, the embryo developed out of material particles that layered into tissue; for the latter, the embryo followed from a performed pattern and, in the case of the human embryo, developed with a soul into God's image. Clara Pinto-Correia's *The Ovary of Eve: Egg and Sperm and Preformation* documents the extent to which the history of the preformation-epigenesis argument interconnects with "some of the most important intellectual subjects in science, religion and general culture," their doctrines fundamental to the understanding of origins, of "defining our place in the universe"; Clara Pinto-Correia,

The Ovary of Eve: Egg and Sperm and Preformation (Chicago, IL: University of Chicago Press, 1997), xvi.
78. Hawthorne, *Scarlet Letter*, 259, 134.
79. Hawthorne, *Scarlet Letter*, 332, 332, 150.
80. Hawthorne, *Scarlet Letter*, 224, 229.
81. Hawthorne, *Scarlet Letter*, 332, 292, 304.
82. Hawthorne, *Scarlet Letter*, 174, 163, 164, 163.
83. Hawthorne, *Scarlet Letter*, 145, 292.
84. Hawthorne, *Scarlet Letter*, 252, 226, 252, 251, 163, 176, 175.
85. Hawthorne, *Scarlet Letter*, 261, 267, 288.
86. Brook Thomas, "Love and Politics, Sympathy and Justice in *The Scarlet Letter*," in Millington, *Cambridge Companion to Nathaniel Hawthorne*, 162–85, 163.
87. Hawthorne, *Scarlet Letter*, 252.
88. Hawthorne, *Scarlet Letter*, 268, 332. Even the reader is placed before diverging lines of interpretation, particularly near the conclusion of the novel, when Dimmesdale either confesses his paternity or not, and when Pearl herself becomes a mother, or not. "The reader may choose among these theories," the narrator notes about the final scaffold scene. "We have thrown all the light we could acquire on the portent" (340).
89. Berlant, *Anatomy of National Fantasy*, 58.
90. Hawthorne's narrator feels his imagination "quicken" (as a fetus does in the second trimester), and the cloth he stares at "assum[es]" its shape, as if coming into being (*Scarlet Letter*, 145).
91. Hawthorne, *Scarlet Letter*, 156. Dimmesdale's "unfinished" sermon, the writing within the writing of the novel, is described as "gush[ing] out upon the page" in such a bloody way that it almost overshadows the "inky pen" on the table beside it (310).
92. "Report on Criminal Abortion," *The Transactions of the American Medical Association*, vol. 12 (Philadelphia, PA: Collins, 1859): 75–78, 76.
93. Alfred Valpeau and William Harrison, *A Elementary Treatise on Midwifery; or, Principles of Tokology and Embryology* (Philadelphia, PA: Grigg & Elliott, 1838), 42.
94. Hawthorne, *Scarlet Letter*, 181, 252.
95. Riss, *Race*, 7. The representation of Pearl, the dark-haired, black-eyed, and "wild infant," underscores the issue of race in the novel (Hawthorne, *Scarlet Letter*, 339). Teresa Goddu also links Pearl to the Caribbean and to the schooner *Pearl*, "a ship that attempted to free seventy-six fugitive slaves from Washington, DC, in 1848, only to be recaptured (fittingly enough) by the steamboat *Salem*"; Teresa Goddu, "Letters Turned to Gold: Hawthorne, Authorship, and Slavery," *Studies in American Fiction* 29, no. 1 (2001): 49–76, 65.
96. Hawthorne, *Scarlet Letter*, 128.
97. Gillian Brown, "Hawthorne's American History," in Millington, *Cambridge Companion to Nathaniel Hawthorne*, 121–42, 122.
98. Hawthorne, *Scarlet Letter*, 160 161, 123.
99. Berlant, *Anatomy of National Fantasy*, 6.
100. Hawthorne, *Scarlet Letter*, 194. Hawthorne scholars, such as Teresa Goddu, Jay Grossman, and Lee Person, have carefully explored the novel's sense of antebellum

race relations, each arguing that it is profoundly attentive to discourses of slavery, miscegenation, and blackness.
101. Hawthorne, *Scarlet Letter*, 131.
102. Doyle, "'A' for Atlantic," 244, 255, 265.
103. Hawthorne, *Scarlet Letter*, 131.
104. Philipps and Walcott, "Causing Abortion," chapter 13.
105. John Palfrey, Secretary of the Commonwealth, *Fourth Annual Report to the Legislature Relating to the Registry and Returns of Births, Marriages, and Deaths in Massachusetts, for the Year Ending April 30, 1845* (Boston, MA: Dutton and Wentworth, 1845), 58, 83.
106. Wooster Beach, *An Improved System of Midwifery* (New York: Baker and Scribner, 1851), 80.
107. Hawthorne, *Scarlet Letter*, 345.
108. Hawthorne's source for the cryptic line is Andrew Marvell's poem "The Unfortunate Lover" (1649), which describes a ship splitting on a rock, birthing the dead beloved in "a Caesarean section."
109. Hawthorne, *Scarlet Letter*, 139, 153.

Chapter Five: Alleged Necromancies within a System

1. Nathaniel Hawthorne, *The House of the Seven Gables* (1851), ed. Millicent Bell (New York: The Library of America, 1983), 347–627, 461, 461.
2. Nathaniel Hawthorne, *The Scarlet Letter* (1850), ed. Millicent Bell (New York: The Library of America, 1983), 128.
3. Hawthorne, *House of the Seven Gables*, 585. Hawthorne's narrator frames Jaffrey inside the origins of the image of Uncle Sam as a meat-packer in the War of 1812, turning him into the substance of what US violence required to work: meat shipped to soldiers.
4. John O'Sullivan, "Annexation," *United States Magazine and Democratic Review* 17, no. 85 (July/August 1845): 5. O'Sullivan, editor of the *Democratic Review*, penned the term that became a slogan of Anglo-American westward expansion and Indian removal legislation. "The fulfillment of our manifest destiny to overspread the continent," O'Sullivan declared, "[was] allotted by Providence for the free development of our yearly multiplying millions." It was carried into the twentieth century as the ideological justification for one land grab after another. Manifest Destiny was, as Donald Scott reminds us, "a racial doctrine of white supremacy," the phrase propelling "white American expropriation of Indian lands"; Donald M. Scott, "The Religious Origins of Manifest Destiny," *Divining America*, TeacherServe, National Humanities Center, http://nationalhumanitiescenter.org/tserve/nineteen/nkeyinfo/mandestiny.htm.
5. Hawthorne, *House of the Seven Gables*, 353.
6. Colonial Maryland's 1664 *Act Concerning Negroes and Other Slaves* stipulates: "Be it further enacted by the authority, advise, and consent aforesaid, that whatsoever freeborn woman shall marry any slave from and after the last day of this present Assembly shall serve the master of such slave during the life of her husband. And that all the issue of such freeborn women so married shall be slaves as their fathers were"; quoted in Hogan, "Forced Breeding."
7. Hawthorne, *House of the Seven Gables*, 461.
8. Hawthorne, *House of the Seven Gables*, 352, 556, 592, 352.

9. Hawthorne, *House of the Seven Gables*, 437, 397, 612, 555.
10. Lauren Berlant, *The Queen of America Goes to Washington City: Essays on Sex and Citizenship* (Durham, NC: Duke University Press, 1997), 6, 87.
11. Hawthorne, *House of the Seven Gables*, 396.
12. Hawthorne, *House of the Seven Gables*, 352, 562, 372, 352.
13. For the "act declaring the Negro, Mulatto, and Indian slaves within this dominion, to be real estate" in Virginia, see the "Original Documents" collection for "Slavery and the Making of America," *PBS*, Thirteen, https://www.thirteen.org/wnet/slavery/experience/legal/docs1.html. It is important to note that Hawthorne directly links the Pyncheon wealth with a Virginia plantation.
14. Hawthorne, *House of the Seven Gables*, 374, 457, 374.
15. Hawthorne, *House of the Seven Gables*, 374, 414, 359, 366, 365.
16. Hawthorne, *House of the Seven Gables*, 355, 366.
17. Saidiya Hartman, "The Belly of the World: A Note on Black Women's Labor," *Souls* 18, no. 1 (January–March 2016): 166–73, 166.
18. Hawthorne, *House of the Seven Gables*, 399.
19. Herman Melville's famously pronounced about *The House of the Seven Gables*: "And perhaps, after all, there is *no* secret. We incline to think that the Problem of the Universe is like the Freemason's mighty secret, so terrible to all children. It turns out, at last, to consist in a triangle, a mallet, and an apron,—nothing more! ... There is the grand truth about Nathaniel Hawthorne. He says No! in thunder; but the Devil himself cannot make him say *yes*." Melville's letter to Hawthorne, dated April 1851, in *Hawthorne and Melville: Writing a Relationship*, ed. Jana Argersinger and Leland Person Athens, GA: University of Georgia Press, 2008), 39.

    The notion of perspective arises in "The Arched Window" chapter when the narrator discusses different a vantage point on the "broad mass of existence," to "behold it, not in its atoms, but in its aggregate" (Hawthorne, *House of the Seven Gables*, 494).
20. Marie Jenkins Schwartz, *Birthing a Slave: Motherhood and Medicine in the Antebellum South* (Cambridge, MA: Harvard University Press, 2006), 13, 14.
21. Constance Sublette and Ned Sublette, *The American Slave Coast: A History of the Slave-Breeding Industry* (Chicago, IL: Chicago Review Press, 2015), 45.
22. Referring to such difficult phrases as "slave breeding" and "slave owning," the Sublettes note that they use them only to illuminate the language of the antebellum business. Contemporary terms (such as "enslaved person") make moral sense but do not always work to convey the legal terminology for the traffic in enslaved people—the buying and selling of slaves. "We hope the reader will cut us some slack," the say (Sublette and Sublette, *American Slave Coast*, 19).
23. Sublette and Sublette, *American Slave Coast*, 31, 34.
24. Hawthorne, *House of the Seven Gables*, 587, 618, 554, 447.
25. Hawthorne, *House of the Seven Gables*, 359.
26. Liese Perrin, "Resisting Reproduction: Reconsidering Slave Contraception in the Old South," *Journal of American Studies* 35, no. 2 (2001): 255–74, 259. See also Richard H. Steckel, "Women, Work, and Health under Plantation Slavery in the United States," in *More Than Chattel: Black Women and Slavery in the Americas*, ed. David Barry Gaspar and Darlene Clark Hine (Bloomington: Indiana University Press, 1996).
27. Perrin, "Resisting Reproduction," 256, 260, 270.

28. Angela Davis, "Racism, Birth Control, and Reproductive Rights," in *The Reproductive Rights Reader: Law, Medicine, and the Construction of Motherhood*, ed. Nancy Ehrenreich (New York: New York University Press, 2008), 86–93, 87.
29. James Ricci, *The Development of Gynecological Surgery and Instruments: A Comprehensive Review of the Evolution of Surgery and Surgical Instruments for the Treatment of Female Diseases from the Hippocratic Age to the Antiseptic Period* (Philadelphia, PA: Blakiston, 1949), 277.
30. Schwartz, *Birthing a Slave*, 1.
31. James Ricci, *One Hundred Years of Gynaecology, 1800–1900* (Philadelphia, PA: Blakiston, 1945), vii. See also *A System of Gynaecology by American Authors*, edited by physician Matthew Mann in 1886 (Philadelphia, PA: Lea Brothers), who accounts for the "negresses" (unnamed) on whom many of the first ovariotomies were performed in early nineteenth-century America. For while Marion Sims might have been one of the first surgeons to successfully stitch up enslaved young women—their vaginal and rectal passageways torn by childbirth—he was not the only plantation physician at work in the antebellum South. Laura Briggs's "The Race of Hysteria: 'Overcivilization' and the 'Savage' Woman in Late Nineteenth-Century Obstetrics and Gynecology" provides an excellent overview of the racialized and racist frameworks of ob-gyn in the nineteenth-century United States (*American Quarterly* 52, no. 2 [June 2000]: 246–73).
32. E. M. Pendleton, "Comparative Fecundity of the Caucasian and African Races," *Charleston Medical Journal and Review* 6 (1851): 351–56, 351, 354, 356.
33. Untitled article, *The Medical Times: A Journal of English and Foreign Medicine, and Miscellany of Medical Affairs* 12, no. 289 (April 5, 1845): 43–44.
34. Pendleton, "Comparative Fecundity," 356.
35. Barbara Bush-Slimani, "Hard Labour: Women, Childbirth and Resistance in British Caribbean Slave Societies," *History Workshop Journal* 36, no. 1 (Autumn 1993): 83–99, 96, 96.
36. Hawthorne, *House of the Seven Gables*, 358. This space turns women into mothers, making them a sort of reproductive technology, in line with the representation of daguerreotypes. For Paul Gilmore, the daguerreotypes in *The House of the Seven Gables* capture the its "racial unconscious," given their role as images of the "progressive white nation," a political visualization that occurred in tandem with Louis Agassiz's daguerreotypes of enslaved men and women; Paul Gilmore, *The Genuine Article: Race, Mass Culture, and American Literary Manhood* (Durham, NC: Duke University Press, 2001), 146. Following Gilmore, the daguerreotypes arise in the novel's sexual unconscious, too, pointing to anxieties surrounding reproduction: of images and bodies and their circulation in the marketplace. According to Megan Williams, Hawthorne represents the daguerreotype as an object of memorialization, connecting the past, present, and future in *The House of the Seven Gables*, in the same way (as I argue) he represents patriarchal reproduction; Megan Williams, *Through the Negative: The Photographic Image and the Written Word in Nineteenth-Century American Literature* (New York: Routledge 2003). For Allan Trachtenburg, a daguerreotype "comes to life . . . in a specific triangulation of view, image, and light"; Allan Trachtenburg, "Seeing and Believing: Hawthorne's Reflections on the Daguerrotype in *The House of the Seven Gables*," *American Literary History* 9, no. 3 (Autumn 1997): 460–81, 462). As such, it exposes the contingency of seeing, he notes, as well as of being. Hawthorne thus

explores the ways in which the material of conceiving (the way that a daguerreotypist directs the angle of the sun's penetration; the way a storyteller pretends omniscience) reproduces reality as it is seen.

37. Hawthorne, *House of the Seven Gables*, 358, 361.
38. Hawthorne, *House of the Seven Gables*, 480, 480, 538, 530, 530.
39. Hawthorne, *House of the Seven Gables*, 516, 522.
40. Hawthorne, *House of the Seven Gables*, 530, 467, 473, 545, 590.
41. William Alcott, *The Physiology of Marriage* (Boston, MA: John P. Jewett, 1856), 179. For Dallas Baker, "reading queerly" takes place at the points where lucidity and opacity interact, attending to a sense of recognition rather than revelation. "Writing and Reading Queerly: Foucault's Aesthetics of Existence and Queer Self-Making," *Journal of Writing and Writing Courses* 31 (2015): 2. As Christopher Castiglia maintains that the novel invites such forms of reading, allowing for deviations from heterosexuality to open up other forms of reinvention; Christopher Castiglia, "The Marvelous Queer Interiors of the House of the Seven Gables," in *The Cambridge Companion to Nathaniel Hawthorne*, ed. Richard H. Millington (Cambridge: Cambridge University Press, 2004), 186–206.
42. Hawthorne, *House of the Seven Gables*, 352, 352.
43. Hawthorne, *House of the Seven Gables*, 360.
44. The first Pyncheon, of course, bequeaths this appetite to Jaffrey, who devours "turtle, salmon, tautog, woodcock, boiled turkey, Southdown mutton, pig, roast-beef" (a twice-repeated list)—in rumors that "his Creator made him a great animal, but that the dinner-hour made him a great beast"; Hawthorne, *House of the Seven Gables*, 588, 586. His name's immortality can be secured only in relation to this capital-C Creator and its justified consuming.
45. Hawthorne, *House of the Seven Gables*, 381.
46. Here, I borrow Derrida's nomenclature in *The Beast and the Sovereign*, particularly in the section where he defines his conceptualization of the sovereign as implicitly male and the beast implicitly female. Jacques Derrida, *The Beast and the Sovereign*, vol. 1, trans. Geoffry Bennington (Chicago, IL: Chicago University Press, 2010), 97.
47. Hawthorne, *House of the Seven Gables*, 356.
48. Cotton Mather's pamphlet "The Negro Christianized: An Essay to Excite and Assist that Good Work, the Instruction of Negro-Servants in Christianity" (Boston, MA: 1706) clearly captures the debates in New England regarding the possession of souls by Africans and the question of baptism as conferring manumission. Cotton Mather's pamphlet "The Negro Christianized: An Essay to Excite and Assist that Good Work, the Instruction of Negro-Servants in Christianity" (Boston, MA: 1706) clearly captures the debates in New England regarding the possession of souls by Africans and the question of baptism as conferring manumission. Mather's *The Wonders of the Invisible World* (Boston, MA: 1693) sets the witchcraft crisis in Salem in direct correspondence with the "Devil's Territory" surrounding New England.
49. Hawthorne, *House of the Seven Gables*, 367.
50. Hawthorne, *House of the Seven Gables*, 484, 494. As Shawn Michelle Smith puts it, the Pyncheon genealogy "carefully avoids the unnamed branches of interracial family lines engendered by rape during slavery," which remain present in the "swarthy" whiteness of the descendants; Shawn Michelle Smith, *American Archives: Gender, Race, and Class in Visual Culture* (Princeton, NJ: Princeton University Press, 1999), 141. David

Anthony also argues that blackness and Black humanity emerge in the repressed forms of cultural knowledge and uncanny appearances throughout *The House of the Seven Gables;* David Anthony, "Class, Culture, and the Trouble with White Skin in Hawthorne's *The House of the Seven Gables,*" *Yale Journal of Criticism* 12, no. 2 (1999): 249–68.
51. Hawthorne, *House of the Seven Gables,* 506, 360. The Genesis-evolution debates were underway in Hawthorne's time, giving rise to Darwin's appearance within them. For instance, an 1841 edition of the popular *Eclectic Review* (vol. 1, no. 8) outlines the trends in natural history, arguing on behalf of humankind's biblical genealogy and against the philosophers of the day who assert that "our progenitor was an ape"; Review of W. Cooke Taylor's *The Natural History of Society in the Barbarous and Civilized State: An Essay towards Discovering the Origin and Couse of Human Improvement, The Eclectic Review* (London: Jackson & Walford, 1841), 137–38, 152, 137.
52. Hawthorne, *House of the Seven Gables,* 525.
53. Hawthorne, *House of the Seven Gables,* 375, 507.
54. Edgar Allan Poe, "The Fall of the House of Usher," in *Poetry, Tales, and Selected Essays,* ed. Patrick Quinn and G. R. Thompson (New York: The Library of America, 1996), 317–36, 319; Hawthorne, *House of the Seven Gables,* 398.
55. Hawthorne, *House of the Seven Gables,* 375, 403, 558.
56. Hawthorne, *House of the Seven Gables,* 544, 437, 413.
57. A. Samuel Kimball, "Contraceiving the Truth in *The Scarlet Letter,*" in *Nathaniel Hawthorne: La function éthique de l'oeuvre (Narrative and the Ethical),* ed. Annick Duperray and Adrian Harding (Paris: Publibook, 2006), 139–53, 143, 150.
58. Quoting Louis Althusser; Kimball, "Contraceiving the Truth," 139.
59. Hawthorne, *House of the Seven Gables,* 511, 510–11, 612.
60. Hawthorne, *House of the Seven Gables,* 352.
61. Hawthorne, *House of the Seven Gables,* 490. The physiology of suspended animation fascinated early nineteenth-century scientists, as a range of physicians explored how to resuscitate near-drowning victims and worked to understand the effects of momentary obstetrical asphyxiations in the birth canal.
62. Robert S. Levine, "Genealogical Fictions: Race in *The House of the Seven Gables* and *Pierre,*" in *Hawthorne and Melville: Writing a Relationship,* ed. Jana Argersinger and Leland Person (Athens: University of Georgia Press, 2008), 227–47, 232.
63. Hawthorne, *House of the Seven Gables,* 409, 382, 365, 442, 352.
64. William Scheick, "The Author's Corpse and the Humean Problem of Personal Identity in Hawthorne's *The House of the Seven Gables,*" *Studies in the Novel* 24, no. 4 (1992): 131–53, 145, 144.
65. Hawthorne, *House of the Seven Gables,* 615.
66. For example, Hawthorne, *House of the Seven Gables,* 427, 497.
67. Hawthorne, *House of the Seven Gables,* 396.
68. Hawthorne, *House of the Seven Gables,* 589.
69. Hawthorne, *House of the Seven Gables,* 589. David Anthony also focuses on this scene, arguing that it forces "elitist American culture" to face itself as "diluted," and the whiteness on which it stands a failure and illusion (Anthony, "Class," 263–64).
70. Hawthorne, *House of the Seven Gables,* 588.
71. Hawthorne, *House of the Seven Gables,* 536, 588, 430.
72. Hawthorne, *House of the Seven Gables,* 413, 580, 581, 562.

73. Hawthorne, *House of the Seven Gables*, 370, 454, 370.
74. Hawthorne, *House of the Seven Gables*, 370, 370.
75. According to Chris Castiglia, Hawthorne's novel creates moments for queerness to flourish (Castiglia, "Marvelous Queer Interiors," 197). Castiglia wishes not to pin down "queerness in sexual identity" but rather to propose that no identity is a natural state from which queerness deviates. I underscore the queer old bachelor as nonreproductive of patrilineal identity and lineage, in the same way as abortion operates as a renunciation of one's so-called natural purposes. Nonprocreative arrangements, queer or otherwise, allow for what Castiglia calls the "alternative collective life" imagined in *The House of the Seven Gables* (Castiglia, "The Marvelous Queer Interiors," 200).
76. Lee Edelman, "The Future Is Kid Stuff: Queer Theory, Disidentification, and the Death Drive," *Narrative* 6, no. 1 (1998): 18–30, 26.
77. Hawthorne, *House of the Seven Gables*, 373.
78. Hawthorne, *House of the Seven Gables*, 579.
79. Jane Bennett, *Vibrant Matter: A Political Ecology of Things* (Durham, NC: Duke University Press, 2010).
80. Hawthorne, *House of the Seven Gables*, 485, 471, 590.
81. Wooster Beach, *An Improved System of Midwifery* (New York: Baker and Scribner, 1851), 62, 28.
82. Hawthorne, *House of the Seven Gables*, 483.
83. Hawthorne, *House of the Seven Gables*, 482–83. Phoebe's characterization, with her "knack" for unpaid labor, friendship with the chickens, and curly black hair, call up the history of her maternal line, the "mother's blood" that Hepzibah identifies in her. While Hawthorne's narrator avers that his work is an American Romance ("infring[ing] upon nobody's private rights, appropriating [only] castles in the air"), he composes the exact opposite, making tangible the deeds through which Black humanity comes to be capital, and Indigenous peoples nothing but the land purged from witchcraft (Hawthorne, *House of the Seven Gables*, 418, 357).

Chapter Six: *The Blithedale Romance* and Abortion's Conditional Perfect

1. Laurent Berlant, "Fantasies of Utopia in *The Blithedale Romance*," *American Literary History* 1, no. 1 (Spring 1989): 30–62, 50.
2. Berlant, "Fantasies," 49.
3. Lauren Berlant, *The Queen of America Goes to Washington City: Essays on Sex and Citizenship* (Durham, NC: Duke University Press, 1997), 23, 100.
4. It is as if Berlant's early scholarly dedication to Hawthorne's novels remains in her unconscious, engendering her thinking about the role of "fetality" (her word, echoing "fatality," I think) in the ideal of providential history still present in American patriotism.
5. John Stevens, *Man-Midwifery Exposed, Or the Danger and Immorality of Employing Men in Midwifery Proved; and the Remedy for the Evil Fraud* (London: William Horsell, 1849), 11, 22, 50, 51.
6. Frank Nicholls, "The Petition of the Unborn Babes to the Censors of the Royal College of Physicians of London" (London: M. Cooper, 1751), 6.
7. Stevens, *Man-Midwifery Exposed*, 52.
8. Nathaniel Hawthorne, *The Blithedale Romance* (1852), ed. Millicent Bell (New York: The Library of America, 1983), 629–848, 847–48.
9. Hawthorne, *Blithedale Romance*, 746.

10. Tony Tanner, *The American Mystery: American Literature from Emerson to DeLillo* (Cambridge: Cambridge University Press, 2000).
11. Hawthorne, *Blithedale Romance*, 756.
12. Hawthorne, *Blithedale Romance*, 648, 847, 847, 736.
13. Tanner, *American Mystery*, 24.
14. Hawthorne, *Blithedale Romance*, 660, 667.
15. Hawthorne, *Blithedale Romance*, 846, 845, 846.
16. Hawthorne, *Blithedale Romance*, 795, 721, 803, 653.
17. Berlant, "Fantasies," 43, 42.
18. Hawthorne, *Blithedale Romance*, 708.
19. Hawthorne, *Blithedale Romance*, 736, 848.
20. Hawthorne, *Blithedale Romance*, 735.
21. Lee Edelman, *No Future: Queer Theory and the Death Drive* (Durham, NC: Duke University Press, 2004), 21–22.
22. Hawthorne, *Blithedale Romance*, 721, 695.
23. Hawthorne, *Blithedale Romance*, 633, 746, 633, 633.
24. Hawthorne, *Blithedale Romance*, 791.
25. Hawthorne, *Blithedale Romance*, 779, 691.
26. Hawthorne, *Blithedale Romance*, 769.
27. Hawthorne, *Blithedale Romance*, 748.
28. Hawthorne, *Blithedale Romance*, 750.
29. See, for example, Hawthorne, *Blithedale Romance*, 715, for Coverdale's portrait of Westervelt as "a wizened little elf, gray and decrepit, with nothing genuine about him."
30. Hawthorne, *Blithedale Romance*, 755.
31. Hawthorne, *Blithedale Romance*, 646, 799, 800, 826, 847.
32. Hawthorne, *Blithedale Romance*, 633, 783, 661, 795, 740, 779, 695, 824.
33. Hawthorne, *Blithedale Romance*, 721, 772, 692, 791, 801.
34. Hawthorne, *Blithedale Romance*, 841.
35. Hawthorne, *Blithedale Romance*, 837.
36. Hawthorne, *Blithedale Romance*, 645, 669.
37. Barbara Stafford, *Body Criticism: Imagining the Unseen in Enlightenment Art and Medicine* (Cambridge, MA: MIT Press, 1993), 247, 254, 249, 248. These are "the abortive creatures" of feminist reform, according to Hollingsworth—and why Zenobia seems to come so close to Eve, as artistic creation.
38. Karl Ernst von Baer, *Über Entwickelungsgeschichte der Tiere: Beobachtung und Reflexion* [On the development of animals] (Stuttgart, Ger.: Bei den Gebrüdern Bornträger, 1828).
39. Adrian Desmond, *The Politics of Evolution: Morphology, Medicine, and Reform in Radical London* (Chicago, IL: University of Chicago Press, 1989), 329, 288.
40. Hawthorne, *Blithedale Romance*, 758.
41. Hawthorne, *Blithedale Romance*, 804–5, 804.
42. Hawthorne, *Blithedale Romance*, 669. As James Mohr notes, the rising numbers of abortions in New England in the 1840s was blamed on advocates of women's rights, those "domestic subversives" who threatened to undermine society as a whole (*Abortion in America: The Origins and Evolution of National Policy, 1800–1900* [Oxford: Oxford University Press, 1978], 106).
43. Hawthorne, *Blithedale Romance*, 805.

44. Hawthorne, *Blithedale Romance*, 762, 814, 755.
45. Berlant, *Queen of America*, 98–99.
46. Hawthorne, *Blithedale Romance*, 746, 648, 746.
47. David Greven, "In a Pig's Eye: Masculinity, Mastery, and the Returned Gaze of *The Blithedale Romance*," *Studies in American Fiction* 34, no. 2 (Autumn 2006): 131–59, 132.
48. Hawthorne, *Blithedale Romance*, 747, 686.
49. Jordan Stein, "*The Blithedale Romance*'s Queer Style," *ESQ: A Journal of the American Renaissance* 55, no. 3 (2009): 211–36, 219.
50. Hawthorne, *Blithedale Romance*, 791.
51. Hawthorne, *Blithedale Romance*, 645, 671. When Coverdale catches her in a grammatical slip (as "an auditor—auditress, I mean"), he raises the possibility that she too is a categorical confusion ("neither man nor woman," as Hollingsworth puts it), having potentially inherited her father's "innate . . . ignominy" along with his money (Hawthorne, *Blithedale Romance*, 740, 791, 792).
52. Hawthorne, *Blithedale Romance*, 837, 835.
53. Hawthorne, *Blithedale Romance*, 669, 754, 739, 785.
54. Hawthorne, *Blithedale Romance*, 671, 685.
55. See Gale Temple, "'Affrighted at the Eager Enjoyment': Hawthorne, Nymphomania, and Medical Manhood," *Textual Practice* 28, no. 3 (2014): 405–25, 415. Temple's essay is an excellent study of capitalism in *The Blithedale Romance* as an addictive substance or bad drug, analogous to "the more explicitly useless and artificial pleasure offered by drugs and alcohol" (412). He discusses Foucault's explorations of the regulatory practices unfolding in the nineteenth century, pairing this regulation with definitions of alcoholism.
56. Richard H. Millington, "American Anxiousness: Selfhood and Culture in Hawthorne's *The Blithedale Romance*," *New England Quarterly* 63, no. 4 (December 1990): 558–83, 558, 559, 564, 564.
57. Hawthorne, *Blithedale Romance*, 770; Nathaniel Hawthorne, *The House of the Seven Gables* (1851), ed. Millicent Bell (New York: The Library of America, 1983), 442.
58. Hawthorne, *Blithedale Romance*, 740.
59. Hawthorne, *Blithedale Romance*, 791, 746, 687.
60. Hawthorne, *Blithedale Romance*, 718.
61. Hawthorne, *Blithedale Romance*, 719, 722.
62. Hawthorne, *Blithedale Romance*, 747.
63. Hawthorne, *Blithedale Romance*, 822, 824, 671, 805.
64. Thomas Strychacz, "Coverdale and Women: Feverish Fantasies in *The Blithedale Romance*," *Transcendental Quarterly* 62 (1986) 29–46, 32, 40, 41.
65. Hawthorne, *Blithedale Romance*, 836–38.
66. Hawthorne, *Blithedale Romance*, 735, 746.
67. Hawthorne, *Blithedale Romance*, 681, 816. Coverdale also voyeuristically watches a small family through the window at the hotel. It flickers into view before he turns his attention to watch the young man in the other room.
68. Hawthorne, *Blithedale Romance*, 633, 633, 689.
69. Gillian Brown, *Domestic Individualism: Imagining Self in Nineteenth-Century America* (Berkeley: University of California Press, 1992), 128, 131, 131, 131.
70. John Harmon McElroy and Edward L. McDonald, "The Coverdale Romance," *Studies in the Novel* 14, no. 1 (1982): 1–16, 12–13.

71. Beverly Hume, "Restructuring the Case against Hawthorne's Coverdale," *Nineteenth-Century Fiction* 40, no. 4 (1986): 387–99, 393, 399, 393.
72. Theodric Romeyn Beck, *Elements of Medical Jurisprudence*, 2nd ed. (Albany, NY: John Anderson, 1825), 186.
73. Hawthorne, *Blithedale Romance*, 750.
74. Joel Pfister, *The Production of Personal Life: Class, Gender, and the Physical in Hawthorne's Fiction* (Stanford, CA: Stanford University Press, 1991), 88.
75. Hawthorne, *Blithedale Romance*, 845.
76. Hawthorne, *Blithedale Romance*, 845, 847.
77. Coverdale uses variations on the word "concealment" ("conceal," "concealed") throughout the novel (seven times), as well as "abortive" (three times); while the meaning of the latter word is perhaps only a little more self-evident, the former invokes a long legal and public connection with hidden, clandestine pregnancies and suspicious infant deaths. Hawthorne's nineteenth-century audience would have known that the word "concealment"—accompanied by rumors of a missing or dead newborn—denoted a serious crime; in fact, until 1807, concealment itself could be used as the sole proof of murder, even in the absence of any other evidence.
78. John O'Sullivan, "The Great Nation of Futurity," *United States Magazine and Democratic Review* 6, no. 23 (November 1939): 428–29. Hawthorne knew O'Sullivan and published in his paper, one reason why his antiutopianism works in the darkness of his ambiguous prose. "His friend Nathaniel Hawthorne," writes Anders Stephanson, "considered him bizarre, not to say a little crazy"; Anders Stephanson, *Manifest Destiny: American Expansionism and the Empire of Right* (New York: Hill and Wang, 1995), xi. Poe also thought of him in the same way.
79. Hawthorne, *Blithedale Romance*, 683.
80. Hawthorne, *Blithedale Romance*, 841, 842, 845.
81. Hawthorne, *Blithedale Romance*, 841–42.

Conclusion

1. Nathaniel Hawthorne, *The House of the Seven Gables* (1851), ed. Millicent Bell (New York: The Library of America, 1983), 347–627, 596.
2. John Dryden, *The Aeneid*, ed. Charles Eliot (New York: Collier and Son, 1909), book 6, 212–21.
3. Hawthorne, *House of the Seven Gables*, 596–97.
4. Laverna's role in the polytheistic worlds of the Etruscans and Romans, as the goddess who oversaw unwanted pregnancies, shifted at some point to include protecting men in the commission of petty theft and counterfeit; the practice of disburdening someone of a pregnancy and that of relieving someone of a bag of coins came to reflect one another. Horace's account of Laverna's laughter and resourcefulness frames both abortion and pilfering as minor offenses—as a lightening of a load, easily recuperated by the one divested of it.
5. Edgar Allan Poe, *Poe: Essays and Reviews*, ed. G. R. Thompson (New York: The Library of America 1984), 588.
6. John O'Sullivan, "The Great Nation of Futurity," *United States Magazine and Democratic Review* 6, no. 23 (November 1939): 427.
7. James Mohr, *Abortion in America: The Origins and Evolution of National Policy, 1800–1900* (Oxford: Oxford University Press, 1978), 130.

Index

abortifacient, xvi, 3, 8, 17, 35, 47, 56, 80, 89, 107, 109, 114, 134–36, 147, 179, 188n6
Agamben, Giorgio, 22, 36, 61–62
American Medical Association, 11, 61, 103, 122
antiabortion, 3, 10, 12, 15, 26, 36, 61, 110, 152, 179. *See also* life: pro-life
atheism, xi, 32, 34, 118, 140, 161. *See also* materialism

Beach, Wooster, 10, 35, 125, 148
Beck, Theodric Romeyn, 21, 45–46, 57, 109, 112, 172–73
Berlant, Lauren, 116, 122, 124, 129, 150–51, 154, 163, 206n4
birth rate, 7–8, 14–17, 43, 46, 100, 108, 110, 135. *See also* population
breed, 6, 14, 15, 17, 97, 101, 102, 124, 126, 128, 132, 136, 139, 146, 159, 202n22. *See also* reproduction: forced
Brodie, Janet Farrell, 8, 76, 108, 184n13

concealment, as a crime, 45, 49, 57, 65, 85, 111, 120, 133, 209n77
conception. *See* soul
contraception, xvi, 1, 76, 108, 165, 193n30. *See also* abortifacient
Cornell, Drucilla, 67

Derrida, Jacques, 78, 80, 81–83, 88, 140, 204n46
Deutscher, Penelope, 36, 188n71
Duden, Barbara, 13–14

Edelman, Lee, 147, 155–56
embryo, 9–13, 21, 29, 46, 59, 81, 112, 116, 117, 135, 148, 158, 160, 161, 186n39, 199–200n77
embryology. *See* embryo
eternity 13, 19, 32, 63, 95, 102, 165
existential, 7, 19, 34, 43, 50, 72, 102, 110, 112, 116–17, 146, 162, 198–99n55

expansionism, 95, 100, 127, 144, 176. *See also* Manifest Destiny

fetus, 8, 10–13, 21, 29, 31, 35–37, 45, 47–48, 50, 51, 54, 65, 81–82, 85, 87, 109, 110, 112, 118, 129, 145, 148, 150, 159, 185n16, 186n34, 188n71, 200n90
forceps, 9, 18, 33, 74, 151–52
forensics, 50, 57, 174. *See also* Beck, Theodric Romeyn
fortune-tellers, 29, 31, 43, 46–48, 54, 179, 191n55
Foucault, Michel, 36, 75, 89, 208n55
Fuller, Margaret, xi, 96
fungus, 57, 71–73, 140–42, 144, 147

genealogy/genealogical, 6, 21, 35, 96, 72, 78, 100, 104, 124, 158, 170–71
gestation, xiv, 6, 36, 46, 71, 78, 81, 97, 99, 104, 105, 109, 123, 131, 158, 170, 176, 186n34
gynecology, 4, 8–9, 17, 74, 81, 88, 90, 118, 134–35

Hale, Edwin, 46, 88, 110
Hartman, Saidiya, 15, 131
Hawthorne, Nathaniel: "The Artist of the Beautiful," 6; "The Birth-Mark," xvi, 5–6; personal life, xi–xiii, xiv; "Rappaccini's Daughter," 5–6
Hodge, Hugh, 12

immigrants/immigration, xvi, 14, 12, 24, 32, 43, 60, 66, 68, 72, 140, 154. *See also* population
Indigenous peoples, 8, 15–18, 60, 97, 100, 133, 140, 144, 150–55, 171, 206n83
infanticide, x, 9, 13, 57, 83, 103, 109, 136, 159, 165, 172, 173, 183n5

Jefferson, Thomas, 14, 16, 91, 187n52, 195n44
Johnson, Barbara, 12, 54, 78, 80, 83–84, 86

211

Index

Klepp, Susan, 7–8, 190n40
Knowlton, Charles, 108, 112–13, 198n51

Lacan, Jacques, 78, 80–83, 86
Laverna, 31, 41, 46–50, 54, 56, 179, 180, 191n61, 192n75, 209n4
life: at conception, 18, 109–10, 112, 148, 167, 170; pro-life, 24, 60, 69, 72, 155–56, 167; as a substantive, 7, 12–14, 20–23, 30, 36, 50–51, 61, 63, 67, 72, 82, 103, 111–12, 118, 122–23, 141, 147, 157, 176, 180
Lohman, Ann. *See* Restell, Madame
Luker, Kristin, 10–11, 118, 186n39

Manifest Destiny, 7, 127, 147, 157, 181, 201n4, 209n78. *See also* expansionism
materialism, 19, 32–34, 97, 117, 147, 153, 159, 161–62, 169, 176
maternal, 15, 16, 35, 69, 81, 86, 90, 100, 117, 122, 151, 157, 159, 162, 167, 206n83
maternity, xi, xii, xiv, 7, 15–16, 23, 97, 110, 119, 131, 147, 159, 176
Mauriceau, A. M., 112, 184n5
midwifery, 2, 10, 13, 18, 29, 34–35, 74, 76, 122, 125, 134, 148, 151
miscarriage, xvi, 6, 17, 76, 100, 107, 111, 122, 134, 137, 172, 181
modernity 13, 22, 32, 61, 66, 97, 162
Mohr, James, 7–9, 46, 110, 181
Morgan, Jennifer, 15–16
murder: abortion as, 12–13, 18, 21, 36, 42–43, 45–47, 59, 106, 111, 125, 172; of Mary Rogers, 70–71

nation, 10, 14–15, 21–23, 43, 46, 60, 91, 95–96, 102, 104, 116–21, 123–25, 129, 151, 152, 154–57, 162–63, 170, 175, 181; nationalism, 6, 7, 43, 66, 96–97, 104, 123, 126, 144
National Police Gazette, 42, 106, 107–8
Native American peoples. *See* Indigenous peoples
nature, as a substantive, 64, 66–67, 72, 121, 133, 156, 158, 161–63, 166–67, 175–77

Nichols, Mary Gove, x–xi
nothingness, 19, 20, 61, 93, 120, 138, 140, 142, 144, 162, 166

obstetrics, 8, 12, 17, 74, 134, 151, 152

partus sequitur ventrem, 15–17, 88, 91, 100, 132. *See also* reproduction: forced
patriarchy, xiv, 7, 19, 21, 24, 41, 60, 66, 67, 81, 82, 97, 116, 136, 145
Pendleton, E. M., 135–36
personhood, x, 12, 14, 15, 36, 54, 103, 123, 157, 176, 190n4
plantation, 6, 14, 16–18, 97, 99, 100, 127, 131, 133–36, 139, 171, 175–76, 185n16, 196n5, 202n13
Poe, Edgar Allan: "The Fall of the House of Usher," 87, 141–42, 146; personal life, xiii–xiv, xvi; "William Wilson," xii, xiv, 87
population, 12, 14, 23, 24, 46, 60, 72, 75, 103, 129, 134, 138, 193n213
potential, 14, 15, 22, 36, 50, 61–62, 66, 79, 82, 84, 87, 104, 106, 110, 117, 120, 122, 133, 135, 151, 166, 177, 180
print, x, xv, 2, 6, 7, 8, 10, 12, 21, 38, 53, 54, 69, 75–77, 85, 109–10, 117, 138, 151–52, 181, 184n13
probability, 22, 52, 60–62, 174, 193n14. *See also* statistics
prostitution, 2, 3, 4, 24, 61, 115, 155, 177, 190n46

queer, xiv, 14, 138, 146–47, 156, 163–64, 204n41, 206n75. *See also* reproduction: nonreproductive

rape, xii, xiii, 30, 40, 45, 57, 62, 68, 72, 91, 128, 132–33, 160, 170, 172, 180, 183n2, 190n46, 204n50. *See also* reproduction: forced
reproduction, x, xiv, xvi, 5–7, 15, 19, 70, 71, 73, 78, 95, 96, 103, 104, 131, 136–38, 143, 148–51, 156, 158, 161, 163, 171, 203n36; forced, xv, 14–17, 133, 135, 136, 196n5 (*see also* rape);

nonreproductive, xiv, 43, 96, 107, 123, 128, 164, 197n29, 206n75 (*see also* queer)
Restell, Madame, ix, 1–6, 27, 35, 39, 42, 56, 69, 71, 76, 88, 106–7, 109, 114, 115, 190n41
Ricci, James, 8, 9, 11, 88, 135

Sanger, William, 7, 190n46
Schwartz, Marie Jenkins, 17, 18, 132, 135
sex work. *See* prostitution
Sims, Marion, 18, 203n3
slavery, xvii, 6, 10, 14–19, 54, 60, 68, 69, 86, 88, 91, 95, 97, 99–103, 123–27, 130–41, 146, 149, 153–57, 180–81, 187n55, 189n14, 196n5, 200n95, 201–2n100, 202n13
Solinger, Rickie, 102–3, 187n55
soul, 7, 9, 19, 31–35, 41, 46, 64, 65, 72, 83, 96, 97, 101, 102, 112, 117, 118, 139, 140, 142, 148, 152, 157–58, 160–63, 165, 167, 169, 175, 199–200n77
statistics, 14, 46, 60, 68, 134, 136, 190n46
stillbirth, 12, 14, 17, 46, 61, 64, 125, 137, 152, 183n5
Storer, Horatio, 12, 15

unborn, x, xvi, 13–14, 16, 26, 42, 60, 105, 143, 151–52, 155–56, 167, 172, 175

Vidocq, E. F., 24–26, 39
vital statistics. *See* statistics

whiteness, 6, 16, 19, 22, 68, 87, 96–97, 101, 124, 128, 130, 140, 141, 155, 176, 191n55, 204n50, 205n69
white supremacy, xvi, xvii, 14, 15–17, 19, 60, 82, 88, 96, 99, 101, 127, 139, 141, 145, 153, 154, 187n55, 201n4
Wright, Frances, xi, 97

DANA MEDORO is professor of American literature at the University of Manitoba, which is located in Winnipeg, Manitoba, and on Treaty 1 territory.